My beutiful Sam
We will meet Again
Someday.
2006

ONE WORLD | ONE VISION

THE PHOTOGRAPHS OF ART WOLFE

FRYE ART MUSEUM

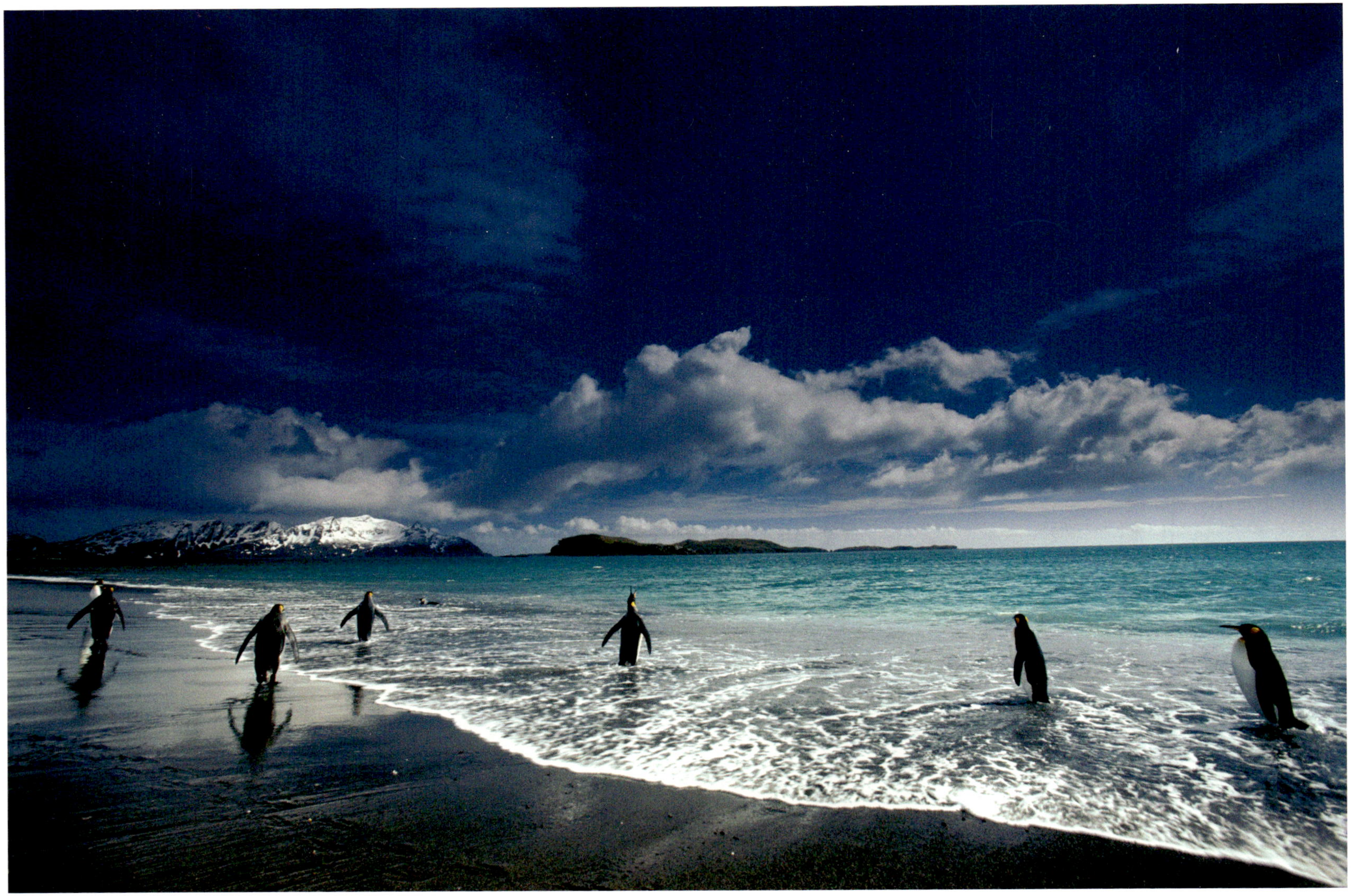

King Penguins in the Surf, 1993, South Georgia Island
Antarctica

CONTENTS

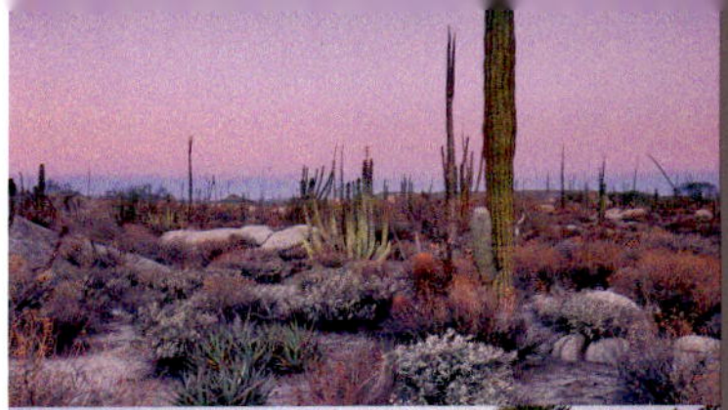

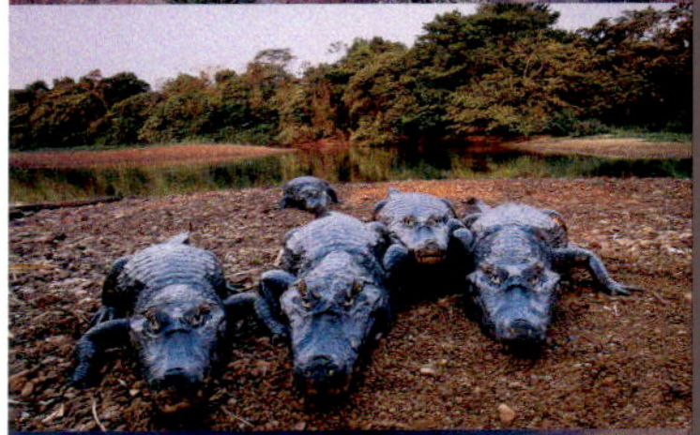

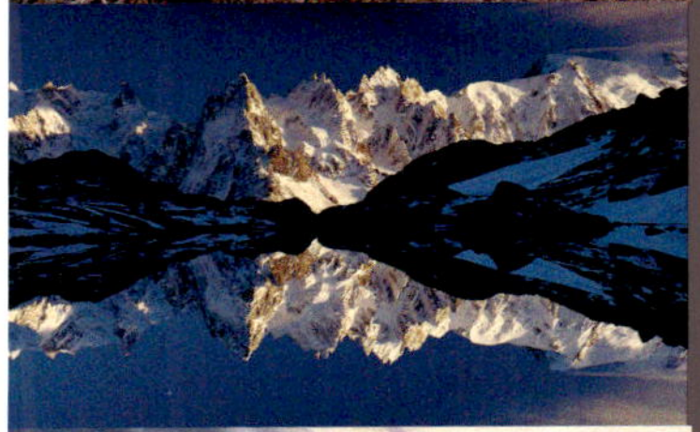

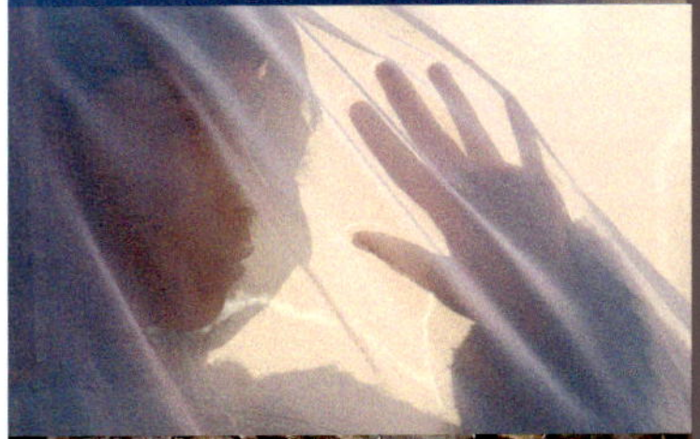

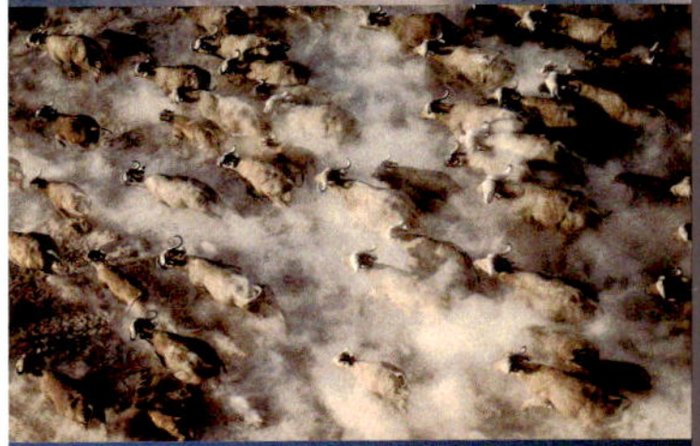

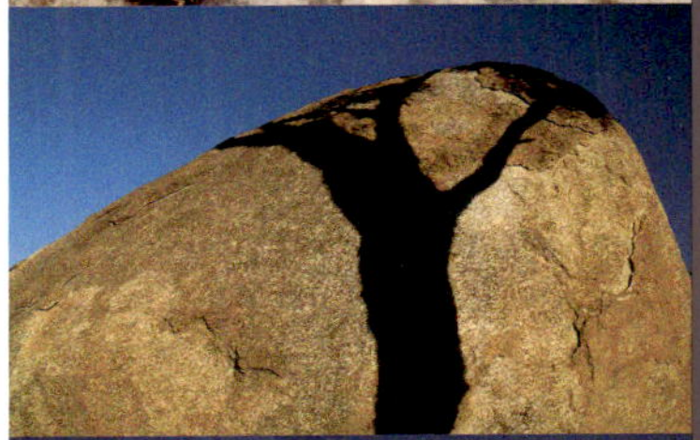

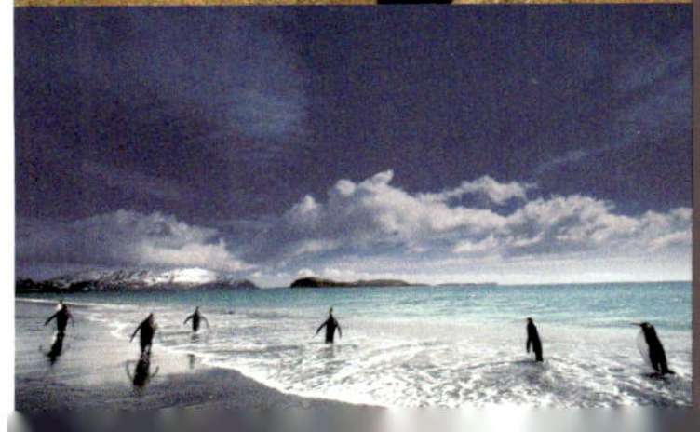

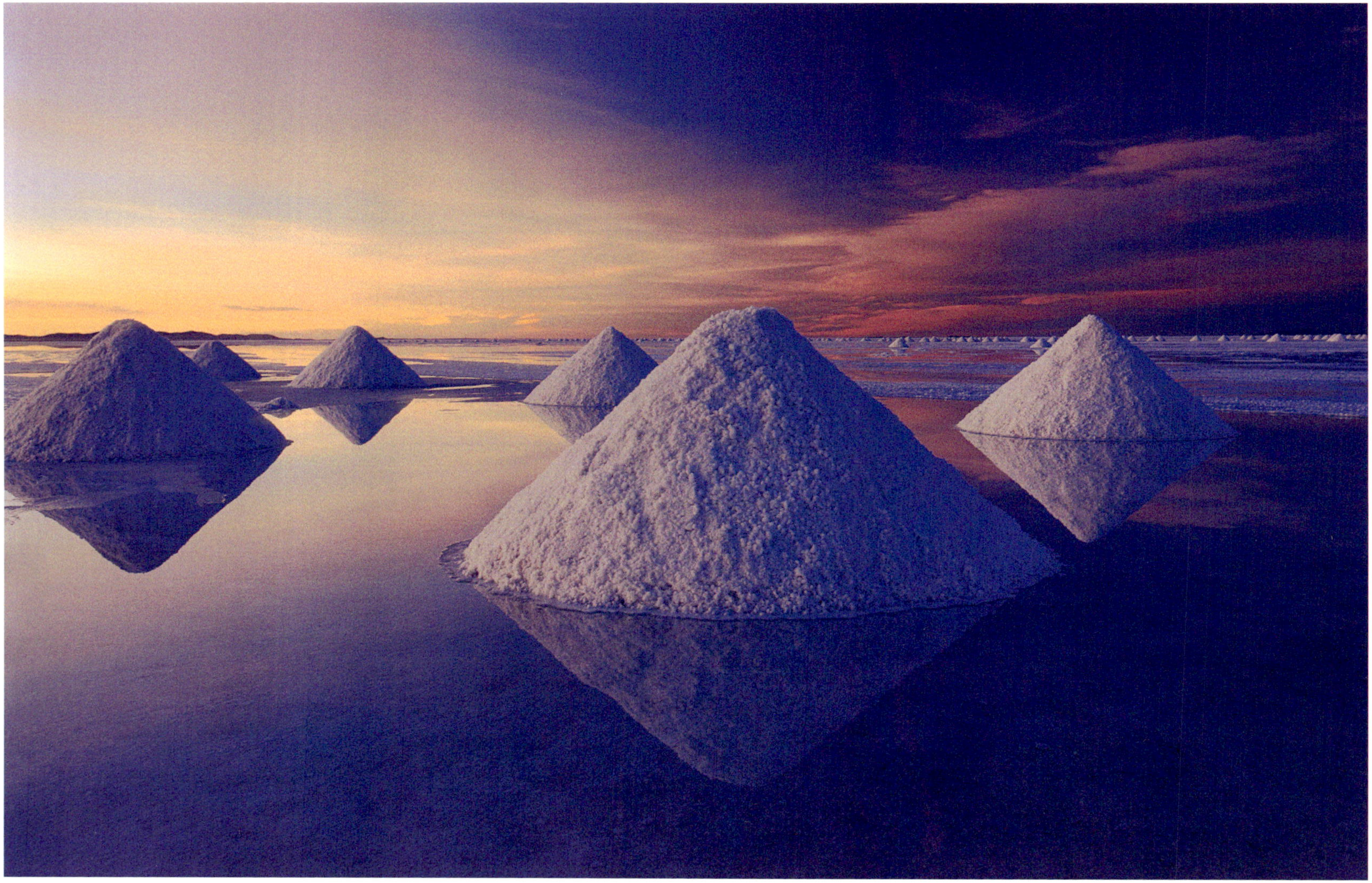

Salar de Uyuni, 2002, Altiplano, Bolivia
South America

ACKNOWLEDGMENTS

It is with great pleasure that the Frye Art Museum, a long-time supporter of Art Wolfe, presents *One World, One Vision*. In 1981, early in Wolfe's career, the museum exhibited his watercolors alongside his photographs. In 1983, the Frye featured a comprehensive exhibition of his photographs. This current retrospective continues our appreciation for this artist, and reveals the aesthetic and geographical breadth of his rich body of work. Wolfe has gone to the farthest reaches of the seven continents to capture images of the vanishing wildlife, landscapes, and indigenous cultures of our planet. Through book publications, video and television productions, and lecture tours, he further educates viewers about environmental issues. This exhibition is particularly significant now, as the world faces new global ecological challenges. We hope this project provides a worthy example of how art can affect life.

The *One World, One Vision* exhibition and catalogue could not have been realized without the talents, cooperation, and generosity of many people. Foremost, we would like to express our gratitude to the artist. Art Wolfe not only took the photographs but assisted in many substantive ways throughout the planning and implementation stages of this project.

Our thanks also go to Lewis Blackwell for his essay, Getty Images, Inc. for its support, and Larsen-Juhl, Seattle, for framing materials and supplies.

We appreciate the support and able assistance of Art Wolfe's staff: for research and fact checking, Deirdre Skillman; color profiling and pre-press, Christine Marie Larsen and Julie Sotomura; photographic printing and framing, Riko Colin Chock; and especially Christine Eckhoff, Craig Scheak, and Kate Campbell for coordinating with the Frye staff.

We are indebted to David Andersen, museum exhibition designer; Charla Reid, museum graphic designer, who created this handsome exhibition catalogue; and Carole Levinthal, copy editor. MaryAnn Barron, director of community relations, Steven Broocks, director of education, Mark Eddington, assistant preparator, Roxanne Hadfield, executive assistant to the director, Donna Kovalenko, collections manager, and Heather Reed, museum educator, were other staff members who helped transform the ideas for this project into vital public experiences.

Richard V. West
Director Emeritus
Frye Art Museum

Debra J. Byrne
Director for Curatorial Affairs and Exhibitions
Frye Art Museum

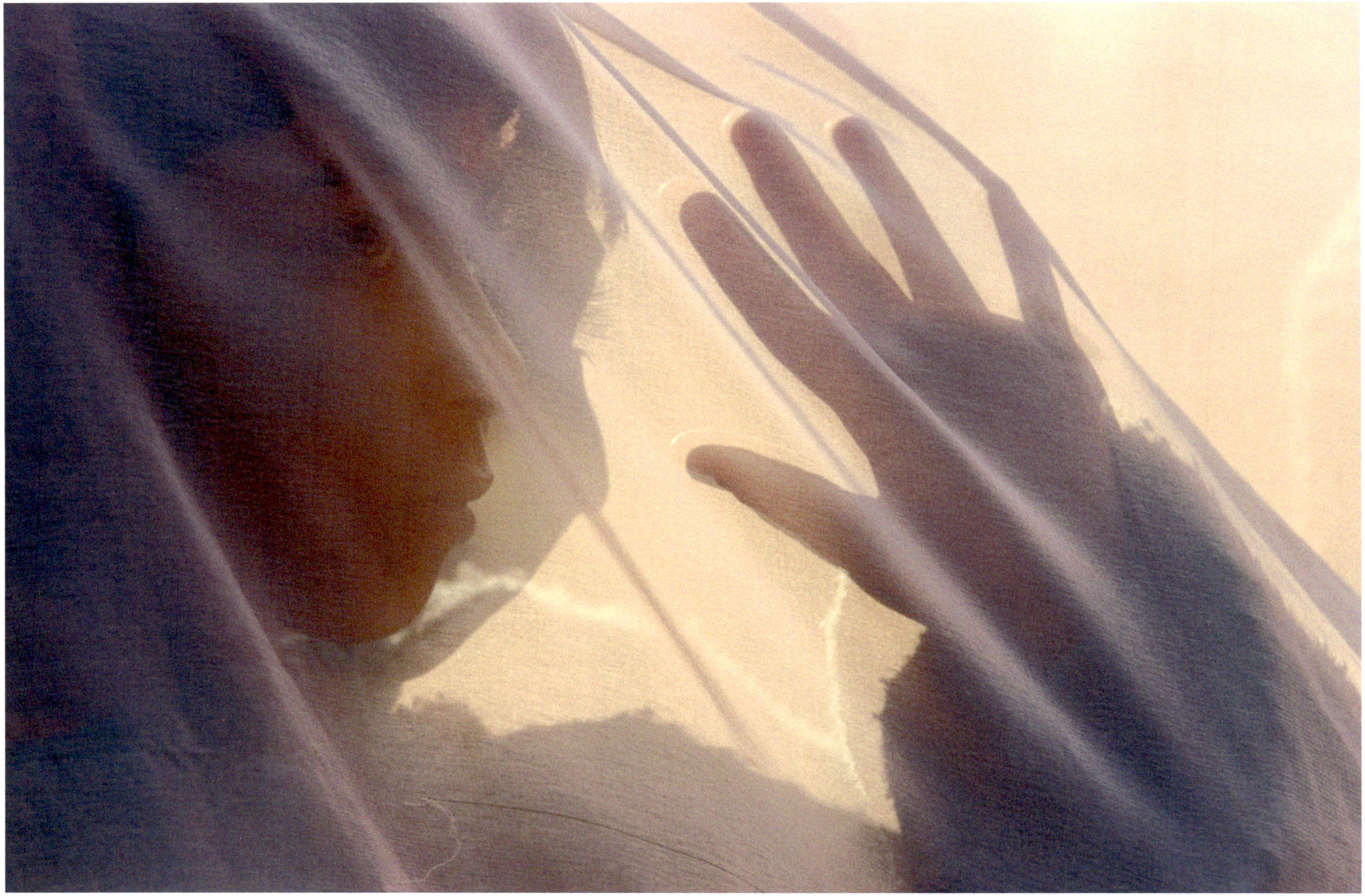

Girl Obscured by Sari, 2001, Varanasi, Uttar Pradesh, India
Asia

ROMANCING THE EARTH

ESSAY BY LEWIS BLACKWELL

Art Wolfe has a good name—Art + Wolfe. Blessed with a double entendre, it sets up our expectations. He is an *ARTist*, whose work focuses on our environment. He is a photographer who loves collective work and good company but is always off on a lone trek out in the wild. So he is *WOLFlike*, with a communal and solitary intelligence. If this sounds a little forced and more than a little romantic, that is as well, because he is the ultimate Romantic.

Art Wolfe is part of a great tradition of remarkable image makers and is immensely skilled at the photographic craft. More than just a technical wizard, he is something of a pioneer in how to get the picture that really matters, the shot that goes beyond our previous visions of certain locations, animals, or human groups. He is even somewhat of a groundbreaker in the contentious field of image manipulation, readily accepting the new technology's potential to add to the old magic of photographic science. And then there is what he actually does when he heads off with a large bag of cameras and lenses, hundreds of rolls of film, airline tickets, maps, and dreams.

We can take these elements to assemble and deconstruct our knowledge about Art Wolfe's photographs. We can look at the parts to understand what lies behind the illusion—one possible version of events that connect him with us. At which point we realize that while there might be an Art Wolfe who lives in West Seattle and travels the world, it is through his images that we come to know him. They are and will be his record. Instead of focusing on the equipment and processes, let us look at the content.

The content is what we see and know even without perusing the catalogue essay or the label on the gallery wall. Stripped back to the reflected or projected light alone, we can still read these user-friendly pictures.

The meaning is what we find in the images; their reflections are a mirror of our interests and passions. The power of these photographs, seen and used around the world, is a force that draws strength from our collective concerns. So, what are these matters? What we view in Wolfe's photography is about the living world—and its enemies.

Whether it is a photograph of landscape, wildlife, or people, at the center of Wolfe's work is the environment, which he interrogates and reveres with a religious intensity. This can seem strangely old-fashioned, but the issues prompting environmental concern never go away. They multiply. The need to care about flora, fauna, and all natural things around us has never been greater. The particular causes turn on the politics of the day. Life and the resources on which it depends are always in tension.

As we view this changing and dynamic world, we can look forward to a new range of soul-searching about the physical health of our planet and its life forms. Given these conditions, we expect that the extraordinary photographs of our natural world, its inhabitants, and its spirit will continue to be highly prized. Perhaps this is why Wolfe's star has never shone more brightly or broadly than now. With many years of professional photographic experience to his credit, and numerous books and features dedicated to his imagery, Wolfe's finest work is now emerging. He persists in his artistic pursuit, one that is taken with long and careful tread, bringing him in closer contact with the meaningful center of his subject. The scenes of landscapes, animals, people, and events are at once transparent, communicative, and appealing. Yet, they have another agenda, a hidden power, perhaps even a subversive intent.

You wouldn't necessarily recognize it immediately in the beautifully framed prints hanging on the gallery walls or the fine reproductions that appear in art books and magazines, but these images are also political documents. They wear their political intent lightly, but they are all the more powerful for doing so. Wolfe's photographs are subtle manifestos to treasure the environment, which is almost always under threat. Our initial exposure to the images makes us feel an engagement with the planet; they remind us to contemplate our dependencies and interactions. And when we care, we are potential recruits for the cause. That's the plan. "I don't want people to look at the art and move on," says Wolfe. "We help lift activists and their organizations, give them representation through association with some of the work in books, direct people to them, and even provide a blueprint for activism."

An outstanding example of this aspect of Wolfe's work was apparent in the *The Living Wild* project. More than three years of planning and shooting around the globe resulted in a large-format book, published in 2001, celebrating endangered animals in environments everywhere. Through the sheer seductive beauty of large color images that show fragile natural balances, the viewer is introduced to the harder arguments carried in the accompanying essays. Wolfe underscored the importance of this project with a worldwide lecture tour. In this respect, you can place Wolfe in the vein of iconic American photographers and artists, such as Carleton Watkins and Ansel Adams, who also raised awareness of the environment through images that triggered action. Wolfe is at work in this distinguished tradition.

There is, however, a big difference between Wolfe and his cultural ancestors. His stage is the entire world. Although he has crisscrossed the United States and recorded much of its life and landscapes, there is no uniquely American agenda to Wolfe's work. Environmental concerns are a global issue today, and what is in one person's backyard quickly affects others. Nobody owns the bald eagle or the rainforests when viewed from the environmentalist perspective. The emotions surrounding this collective responsibility are communicated through Wolfe's photography.

For example, he presents the unique spiritual path of an Indian holy man as well as the birth of a tiger for all of us to see and consider. This openness to interconnectedness drives many of Wolfe's projects, past and future.

Historically, the battleground of environmental image making has been divided into two camps: those photographers who love and praise the wonders of nature, and those who lament, groan, and prophesy doom based on the continual erosion of natural states. Wolfe is clearly in the first camp. He represents those aspects of the world that are threatened, but rather than featuring the threat, he reveals that which we treasure. His quest is for the spirit of the place and its occupants.

He does not so much document as take what he sees as the key elements to tell the story. If it is the innocent, fearless curiosity of a seal pup on the beach of the Atlantic island of South Georgia, he is happy to bring that across with an anthropomorphic intensity. He can be as sentimental as Norman Rockwell in the arrangement of forms, coloration, and composition. He can also be a hard-line modernist in stripping away components to focus on the core message. At his best, Wolfe combines a tough underlying message with the techniques of mass communication to deliver highly charged, powerful, and accessible images. It is this generosity and breadth of aesthetic vision that makes the work difficult to categorize, but more significant for all that.

In contrast, noted art photographers such as Richard Misrach and Edward Burtynsky belong to the camp that shows environmental threat and the threatened in one. They reveal how nature is transformed by the impact of humans, depicting strange or terrifying new beauty and ugliness. In the darkness of such work, they adopt an artistic position that is outside the popular mainstream of imagery—there is a clear comment in their choice. By staying with the more romantic and sentimental views, Wolfe may be somewhat more complex and difficult to appreciate. It is possible to mistake the depiction of beauty as being facile rather than fragile, derivative rather than unique. We need to reclaim the wonder that is captured within Wolfe's finest images. He is open about the optimism of his approach:

> I shoot a diverse range of subjects. I mix it up—people, landscapes, wildlife. This already makes me seem a little too loose in some specialist's eyes. People also talk of "eco-porn" when they see the seductive image…but beauty is my focus, and beauty in nature is misunderstood and even misrepresented. My response is that some people can shoot the more negative stuff, but my spirit runs high with something different. I am a pretty "up" person spiritually; I am guided in my spirit to shoot like this. I create an environment that I love to live in. I seek images that are uplifting. I know other people don't necessarily do that. But what I can contribute is uplifting for the spirit. Positive energy gets results faster than negative. I rally people to my environmental cause by interesting them in the value. I believe it is better to be open, to give.

Wolfe's work is firmly in the tradition of Ansel Adams in terms of the environment having a heroic quality. Adams once remarked, "Photography is a way of showing how you feel about a place." Wolfe clearly and consistently puts forward a respectful sense of place and a sense of spiritual awe for the subjects he shoots. In this, he moves away from being an environmental agitator (albeit that is a powerful subtext). Instead, as part of a long tradition in art history, he engages the viewer at a deeper and more complex level.

His photographs find a rich reading when placed in relation to late eighteenth- and nineteenth-century European Romanticism. Like Wolfe, the Romantics displayed an interest in nature worship, primitivism, and vanished or exotic cultures, as well as philosophic idealism.

Their expressions celebrated the cultivation of emotion. Such practices were the hallmarks of Romantic poets and writers such as Jean Jacques Rousseau in France; Friedrich von Schiller and Johann Wolfgang von Goethe in Germany; and William Wordsworth, Samuel Taylor Coleridge, John Keats, and Lord Byron in England. The visual artists Théodore Géricault, Eugène Delacroix, and J. M. W. Turner typified a Romanticism of tempestuous landscapes (which also featured wild animals in the paintings of Géricault and Delacroix) and of enormous energy, rendering the struggle of the human and animal spirit, heroic or tragic, against the forces of nature. Wolfe's imagery can be seen to demonstrate all of these interests and visual characteristics.

It is, perhaps, worthwhile to dwell on this link, which is not one that comes directly out of Wolfe's fine-art studies. Nor does it simply come out of an association with the tradition of American landscape and wildlife photographers and artists. It is a conclusion waiting to be drawn. To truly understand Wolfe's accomplishments, an international vision is required.

So let us get back to that Romantic past. The nineteenth-century English poets Keats and Wordsworth and painter John Constable are associated with a private and personal strain of Romanticism that is perhaps closest to Wolfe's focus. Theirs was a vision that cultivated an intimate perspective, a lyrical and introspective spirit, and a feeling for an emotional truth of observed experience. Consider this passage from Wordsworth's *Prelude*: "For I would walk alone under the quiet stars…listening to notes that are the ghostly language of the ancient earth, or make their dim abode in distant winds." Or this sentiment in a sonnet by Keats: "When I behold, upon the night's starr'd face, Huge cloudy symbols of a high romance…" We find in these creative expressions a conception of humanity's relationship with nature. Nothing more or less is being embarked upon in the Wolfe oeuvre, in which we find an open celebration of beauty, a sensitivity to revealing subtle order, a deliberate seeking out of the wondrous. The relationship is one where we—humanity—are invited to view an emotionally charged record of nature.

Coleridge writes about the existence of a "religious meaning" in the forms of nature, and Wolfe's pictures reach towards this intensity of expression. They go beyond mere photographic documents by means of the artist's selection and shaping of those moments that reflect nature at its most awe-inspiring, beautiful, spiritual, mysterious, or fragile. In both style and content, Wolfe's photographs are in keeping with the wider Romantic tradition.

We find similarities between Wolfe's motivations and those of his predecessors. The Romantics were reacting strongly against the eighteenth-century Rationalists' conception of nature as empty of moral or spiritual meaning, except as it embodied abstract laws and patterns that reflected a rational God. In contrast, Wordsworthian nature was alive in itself and was also a medium that conveyed fundamental spiritual truths that inspired creativity. Many changes have occurred since then. Perhaps we have replaced the battle of the "Rationalists versus the Romantics" with the "Industrialists versus the Environmentalists." The Industrialist looks to the logic of business and political reality. The Environmentalist resists and adds a dash of "belief" in the cause, in Gaia, in a one-world balance, in the spiritual power of nature.

The Romantic view of nature is fundamentally a way of projecting certain human values into the universe. For the Romantics, nature was a living organic structure that took more than reason to understand. Imagination and a moral sense were equally important in the perception of nature. "To me this world is all One continued vision of Fancy and Imagination," wrote William Blake, one of the most visionary and campaigning of Romantics. It is a line that strikes a strong chord with the tonality of Wolfe's photographs. Wolfe uses reason and imagination in his development of the scenes. He often introduces an anthropomorphic element into wildlife and sees structure in landscapes. He composes his photographs to suggest a deep order, an independent spirit, and a collective soul in his subject matter.

Indeed, Wolfe's subject matter is closely related to that of the Romantic painters. Marine scenes, especially shipwrecks and the threatening moods of the sea, were important themes during the Romantic movement. For example, the sea has a particularly strong meaning in Turner's *Slave Ship* (1840) and Géricault's *Raft of the Medusa* (1819). These works had their source in historical events as well as in the concept of the sublime. In a similar vein, Wolfe exhibits an acute aesthetic sensibility for weaving contemporary issues into traditional motifs. Like the Romantic painters, his photographic compositions are reinforced by colors and tones that are carefully deployed to augment the mood.

The exoticism of distant places such as Africa or the Near East was frequently a Romantic theme, as was the depiction of animals to convey the wild and primitive emotions of man. In carrying forward this tradition, Wolfe's depictions of natural scenes and creatures also impinge on the emotions and produce strong psychological responses. Like the Romantics, Wolfe uses nature to reflect emotional states and natural subjects to symbolize an escape from the confines of urban, civilized existence.

Wolfe's work, like that of many landscape and wildlife photographers, has a hidden debt to the achievements of German Romanticism, most particularly to the work of noted painter Caspar David Friedrich. His paintings, often based on literary narratives, were infused with an eerie, melancholy light. The importance of light to reflect moods is also a crucial element in Wolfe's photographic images. Light cannot be separated from the circumstances of color, which is sometimes considered the "soul" of Romantic painting for its sensuality and expressive potential. Color is also at the heart of Wolfe's imagery. No cool abstractions of black and white for him, or even the restraint of color printing shown by other fine-art photographers. Instead, Wolfe embraces the heightened color of contemporary film stock to achieve emotional trigger points.

We are supposed to be considering the images, so why is it valid to investigate Wolfe's quest? We do not impute meaning to an image solely on the basis of what we know about the artist or about the circumstances under which it was created, but we can't entirely avoid the man and background information either. Like the Romantic artists, Wolfe cherishes his independence, originality, and freedom from rules: he takes an unfettered, liberated pleasure in traversing our world. His passion is made manifest in the images that call attention to the sublime of our own age. His is not a selfish passion. Wolfe has remarked, "As you get older, your sense of place in your extended community becomes more profound. As I've made a living from my interest in the natural world, so I feel a growing need to put more of my energy back for the benefit of the environment."

In order to be part of an effective dialogue with the community, Wolfe's photographs are meticulously designed communication tools, not vanity pieces for his personal aggrandizement. The images are researched, planned, executed, reviewed, and ruthlessly edited. Production processes bring the resulting expression close for the vision and experience of the viewer.

Such rigor and control have landed Wolfe in hot water with certain parts of the nature photography lobby. His early adoption of digital technology was criticized, especially when he openly manipulated images, drawing attention to such features as patterns in nature, notably in his *Migrations* book. Pioneers often provoke criticism; now his first experiments are taken as part and parcel of legitimate photographic creativity. Wolfe is scrupulous in making clear which photographs are manipulated.

In his editorial book work and fine-art images the line is very precisely drawn. Today, photography is understood and accepted as an instrument for painting with light, a way of selecting and defining a moment. Photography is no longer seen as a guaranteed tool for the documenting of "truth." It is perhaps a response to a shifting public perception of the medium that has encouraged Wolfe to position and enrich his images in our editorially enhanced environment.

For all that new technology allows, there are few more committed seekers of the real experience than Wolfe. He relishes going to the ends of the earth to seek a shot, and if he doesn't get it, he will look forward to going back again. The majority of his year is spent on the road (or, more correctly, off the orthodox road). He withstands discomfort, and he searches beneath the surface detritus to find the beauty in many situations. I joined him once for a trip in India, a country that fascinates us both. The journey took us from the Khumb Mela festival (the largest gathering of people on Earth that takes place every twelve years as the planets align) down to the city of Benares. We followed the *naga sadhus*, the naked holy men of Hinduism. At some point during our adventure, I lost Wolfe in a crowd of hundreds of chanting sadhus, proceeding in a highly traditional and disorderly fashion down a narrow main street to the banks of the Ganges. The possibility of taking an effective shot seemed remote. Wolfe, the incurable Romantic, found a way to transfer the spirit and emotion that was in the air and swirling in the dust, into his images. He expressed the same passion that carries forward his work in this publication, and attending exhibition: "I want to capture the imagination with a photograph. I try to dazzle my audience. Extreme beauty, places that are unseen. That's what I do. I try to do it a little better each time I go out."

Lewis Blackwell is senior vice-president of creative direction at Getty Images, the world's leading imagery company, which is headquartered in Seattle. Lewis has published many books, including the best-selling design book The End Of Print *and the recently published* Soon: The Future Culture of Brands. *When not traveling the world for Getty Images, and occasionally with Art Wolfe, he is working on a book about the use of photography today.*

BIOGRAPHY

Over the course of Art Wolfe's career, he has worked in hundreds of locations around the world. He spends nearly nine months each year traveling, and shoots more than 2,000 rolls of film annually. His unique aesthetic vision and passionate advocacy for environmental concerns affirm his dedication to his work.

The son of commercial artists in Seattle, Wolfe graduated from the University of Washington in 1975, with bachelor degrees in fine arts and art education. His background in watercolor has influenced his mastery of color, composition, perspective, and pattern. Wolfe is also an ardent activist for ecological issues and strives to educate the public through his imagery. Three years after graduating, Wolfe's first book, *Indian Baskets of the Northwest Coast,* was published. Over the ensuing years, that book has been joined by fifty-one others, including foreign editions. *Edge of the Earth/Corner of the Sky* is the artist's most recent book project. Magazines all over the world publish his images and portfolios. Wolfe has also ventured into the world of television production with *On Location with Art Wolfe, Techniques of the Masters*, and *American Photo's Safari.* His latest instructional video, *The Living Wild,* documents his work in several global locations. By employing both artistic and journalistic skills, Wolfe presents his subjects, enlightens his viewers, and delights his audiences.

Wolfe's talent has been widely acknowledged. In 1998, he was named Outstanding Nature Photographer of the Year by the North American Nature Photography Association. In the same year, the National Audubon Society recognized the artist's efforts in support of the National Wildlife Refuge System with its first-ever Rachel Carson Award. In April 2000, he was awarded a coveted Alfred Eisenstaedt Magazine Photography Award. He is a member of Explorers of Light, Canon's elite list of renowned photographers, and the Fujifilm Talent Team. Art Wolfe's studio is located in downtown Seattle, and his work can also be seen on the internet at ArtWolfe.com. In addition, his photographs are on display at his galleries in the REI flagship stores in Seattle and Denver.

One World, One Vision reveals the aesthetic and geographical breadth of Art Wolfe's successful career. This is in keeping with the Frye Art Museum's mission to celebrate excellence in representational art forms.

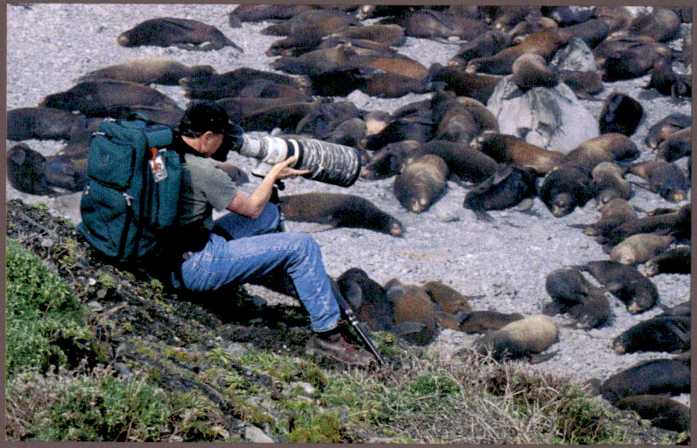

NORTH AMERICA

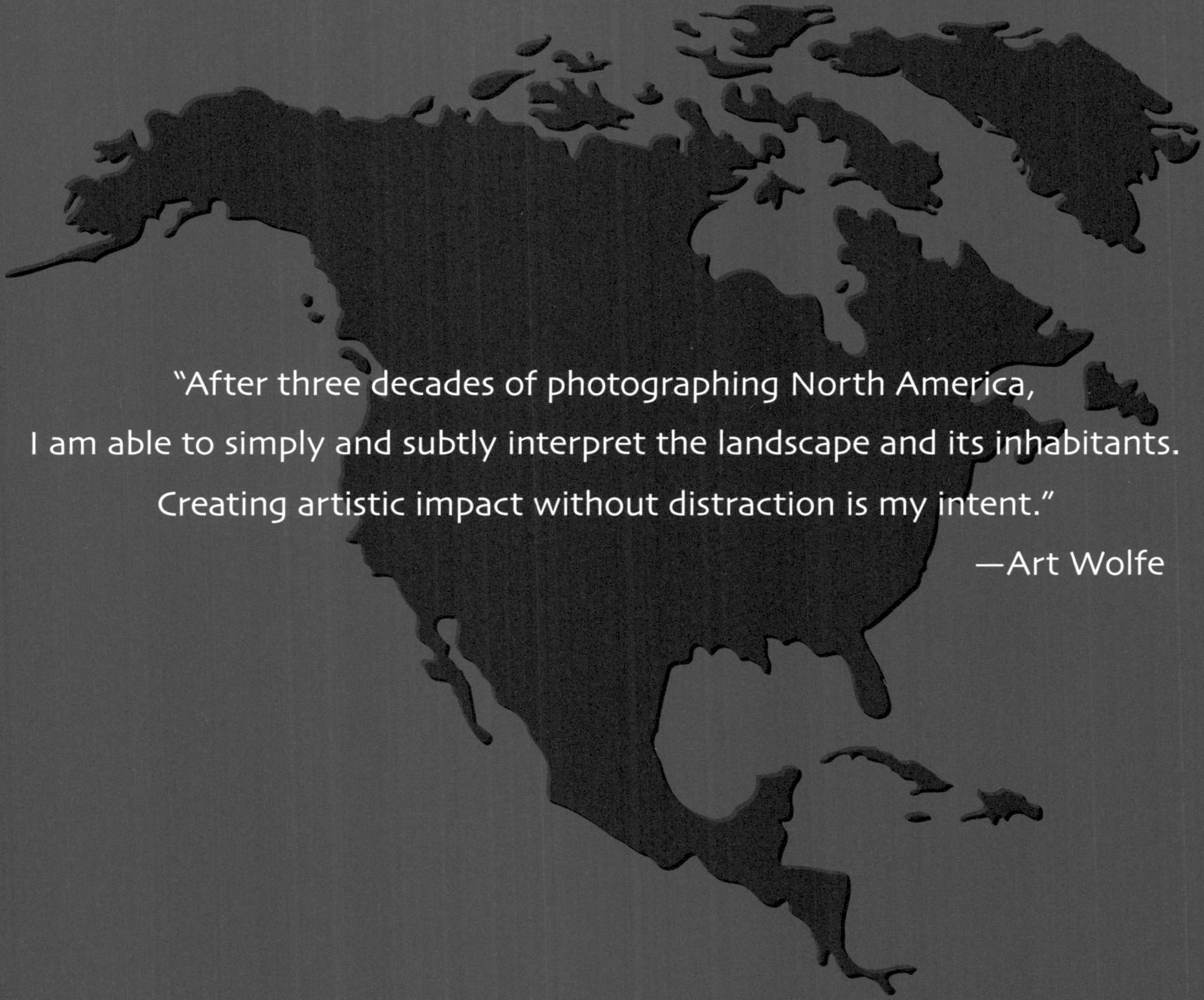

"After three decades of photographing North America,
I am able to simply and subtly interpret the landscape and its inhabitants.
Creating artistic impact without distraction is my intent."

—Art Wolfe

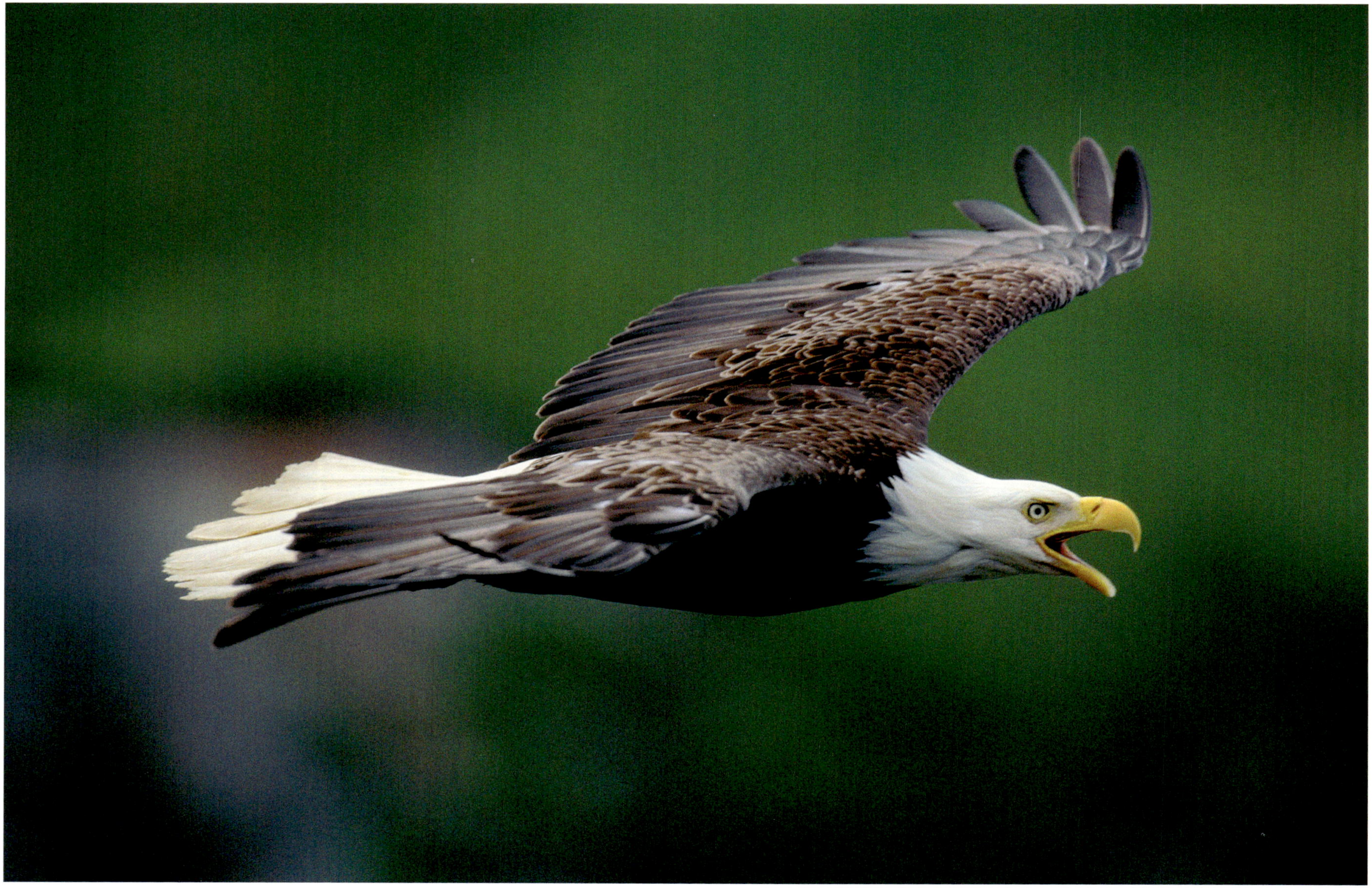

Bald Eagle in Flight, 1995, Unalaska Island, Alaska, United States

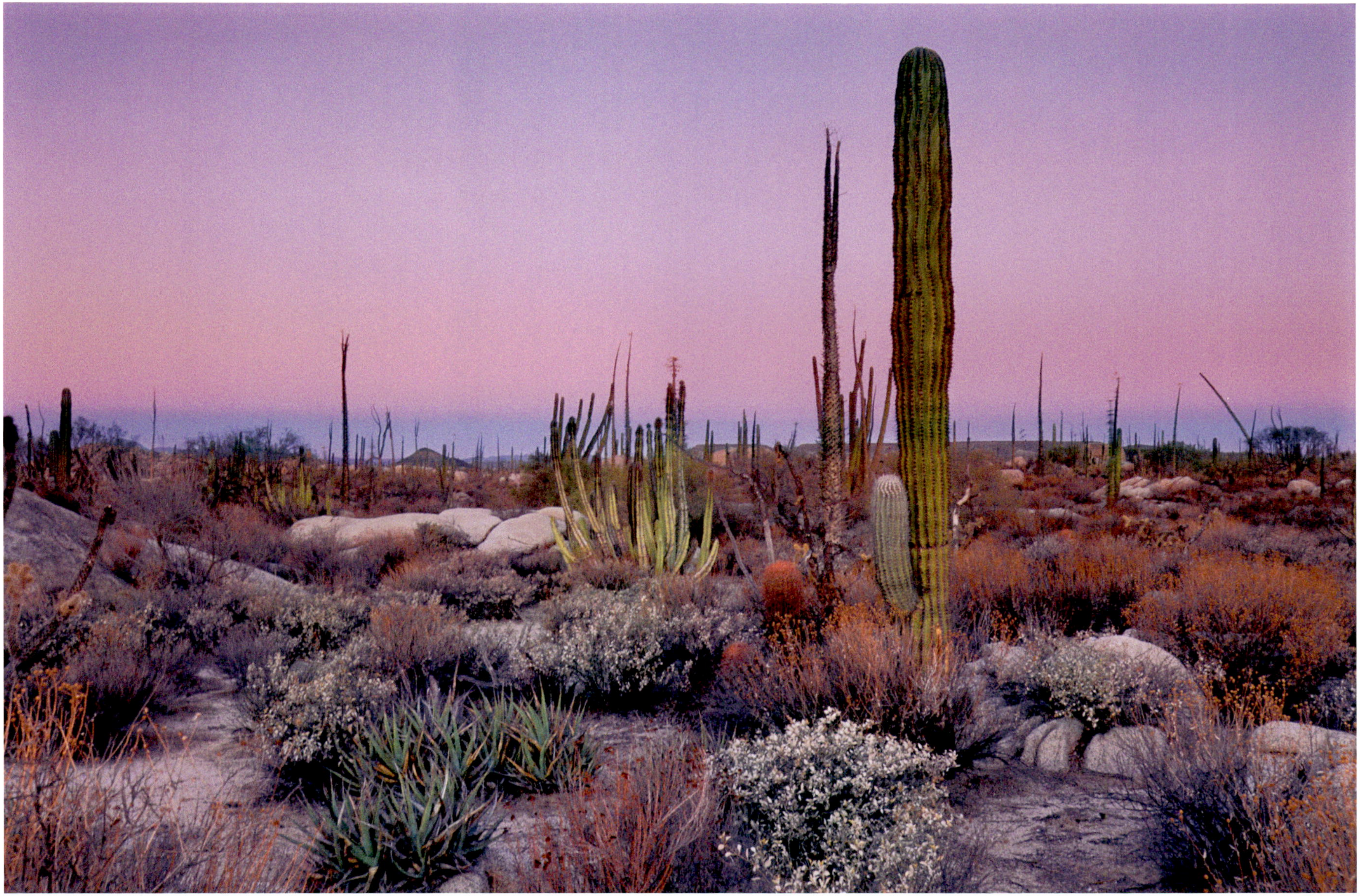

Cataviña Desert at Dawn, 1996, Baja California, Mexico

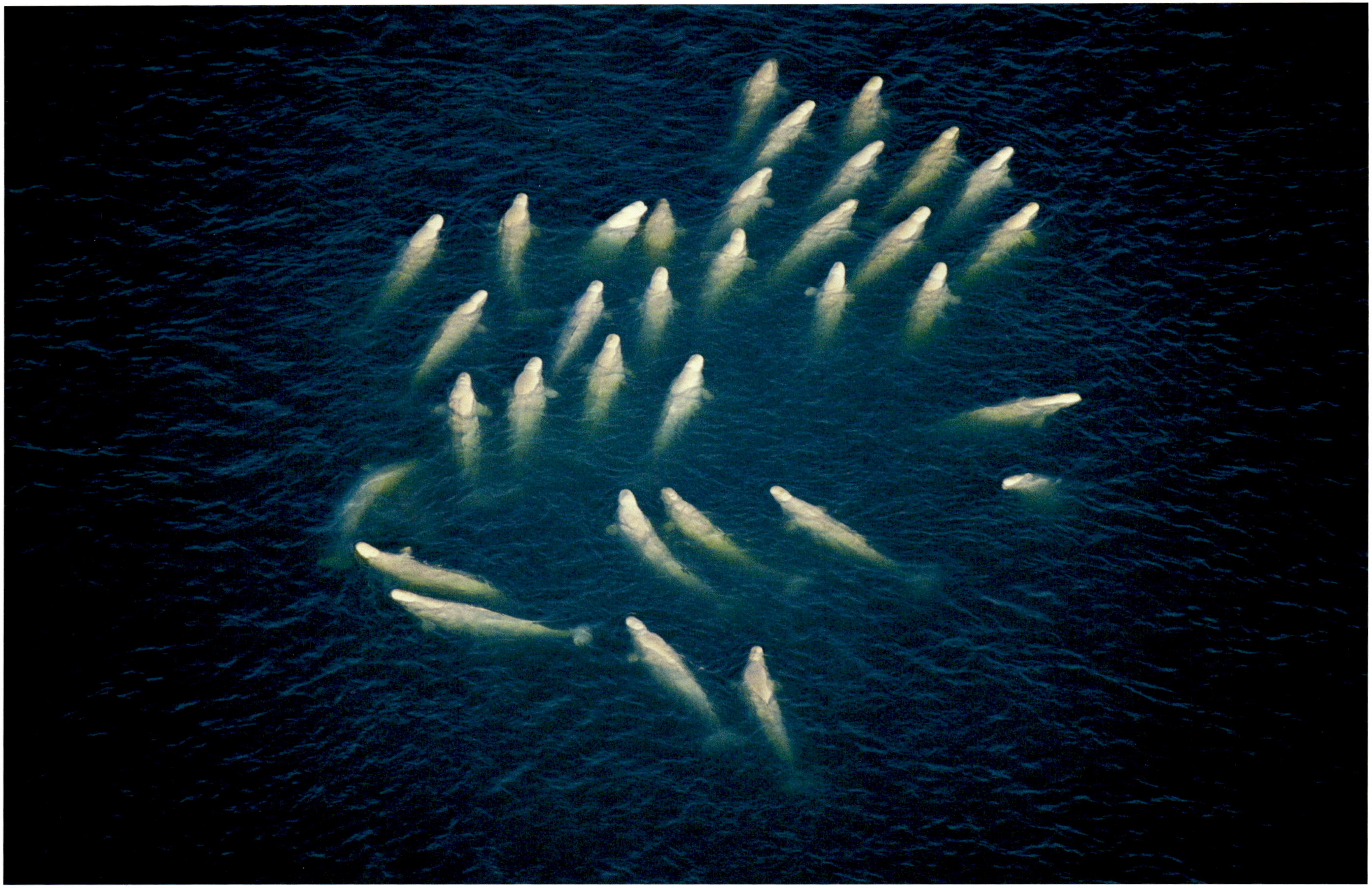

Beluga Whales, 1992, Somerset Island, Nunavut, Canada

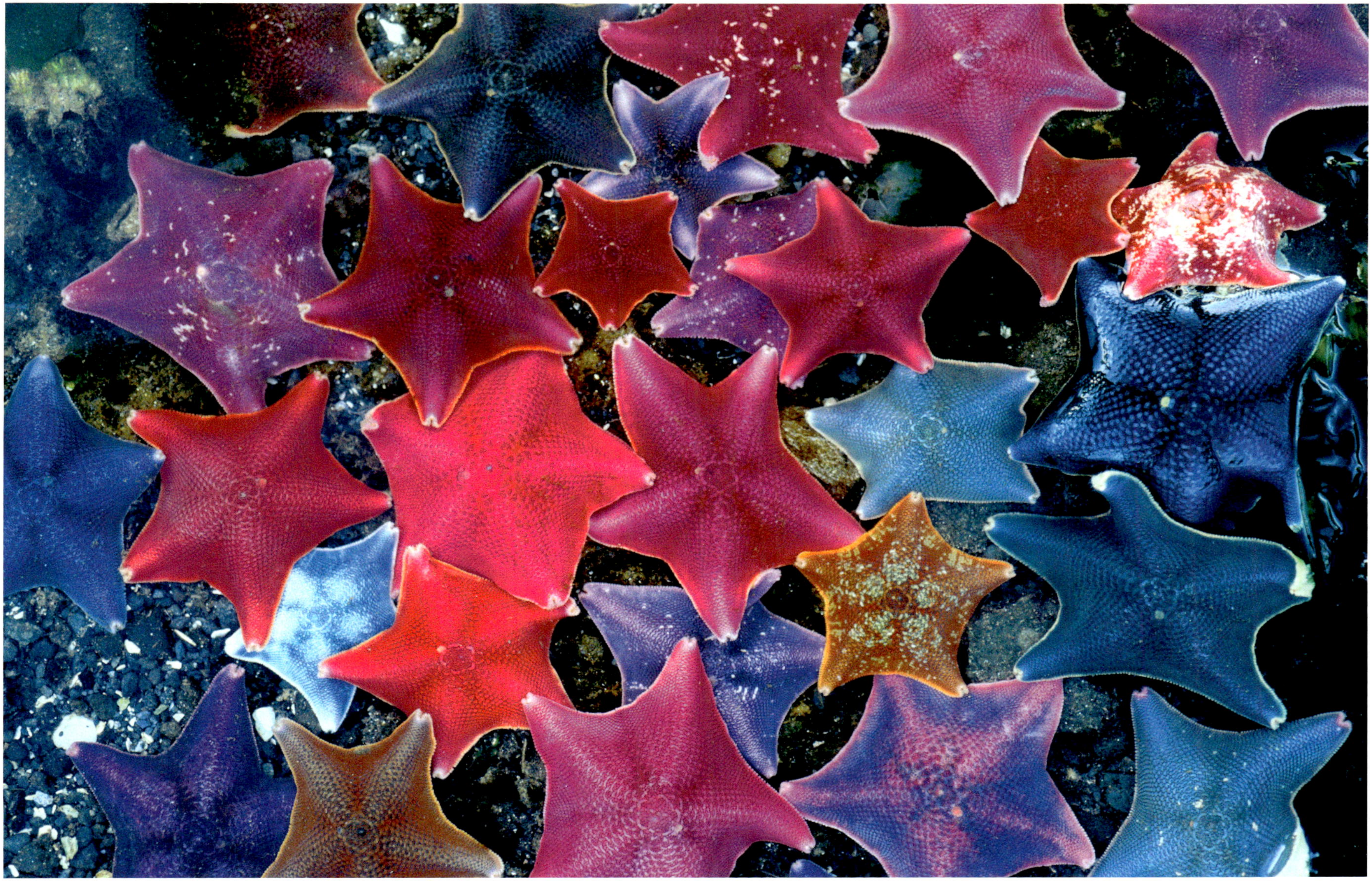

Batstars, 1990, Queen Charlotte Islands, British Columbia, Canada

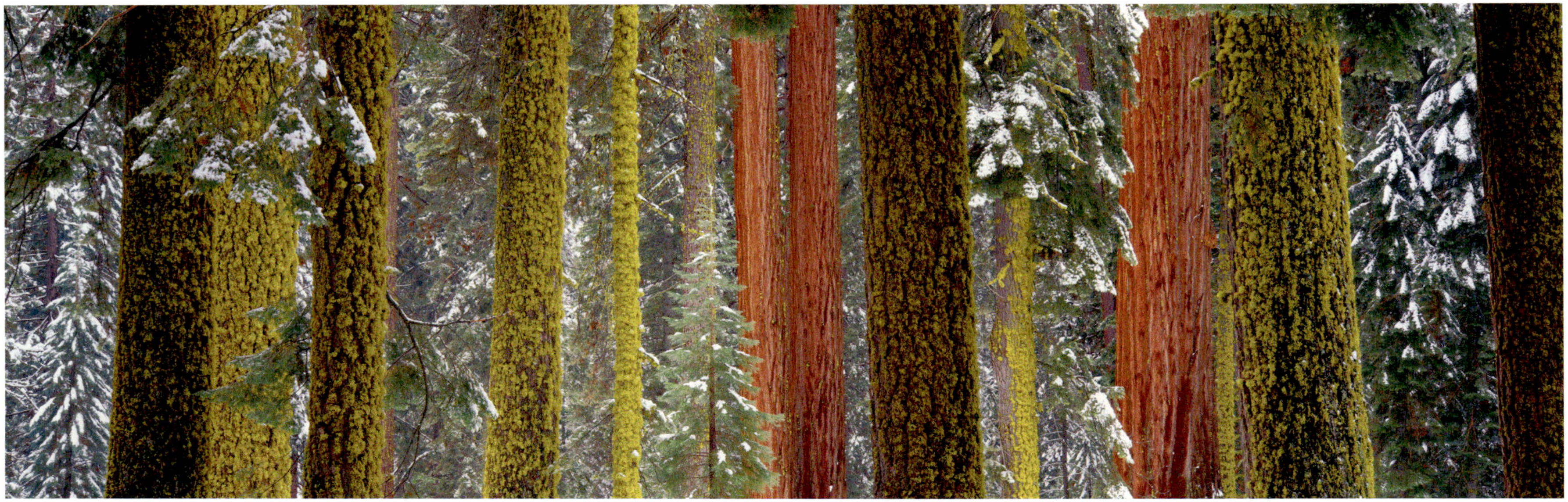

Giant Sequoia, 1997, Sequoia National Park, California, United States

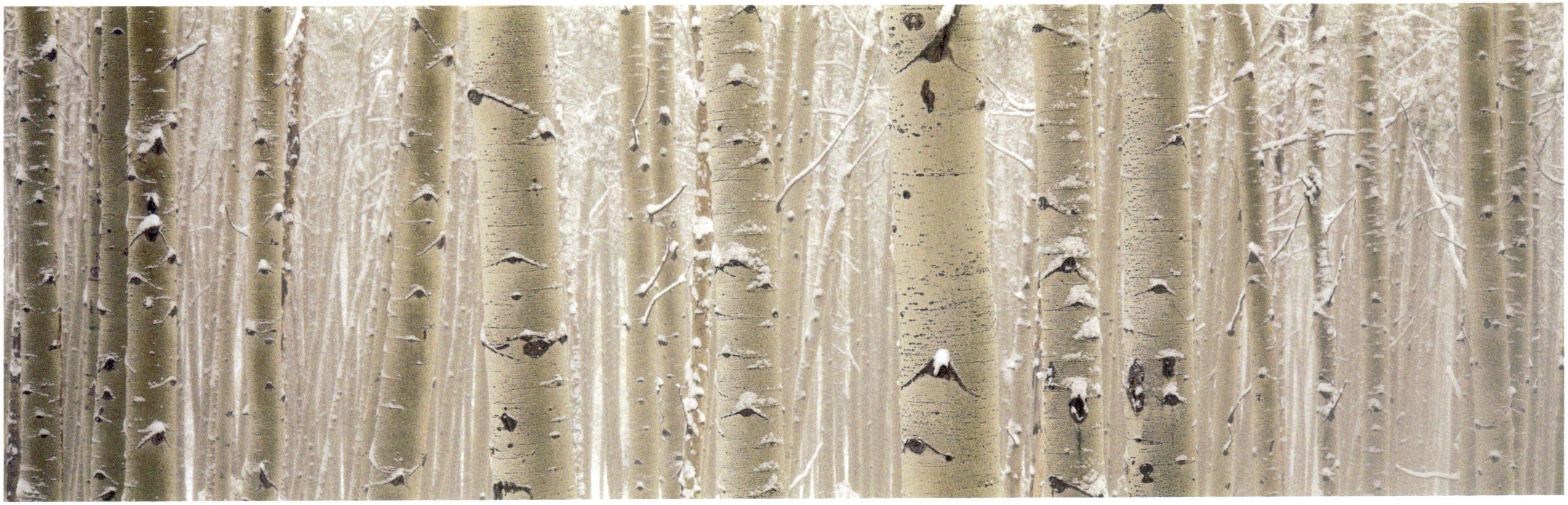

Aspens in Snow, 1998, Uncompahgre National Forest, Colorado, United States

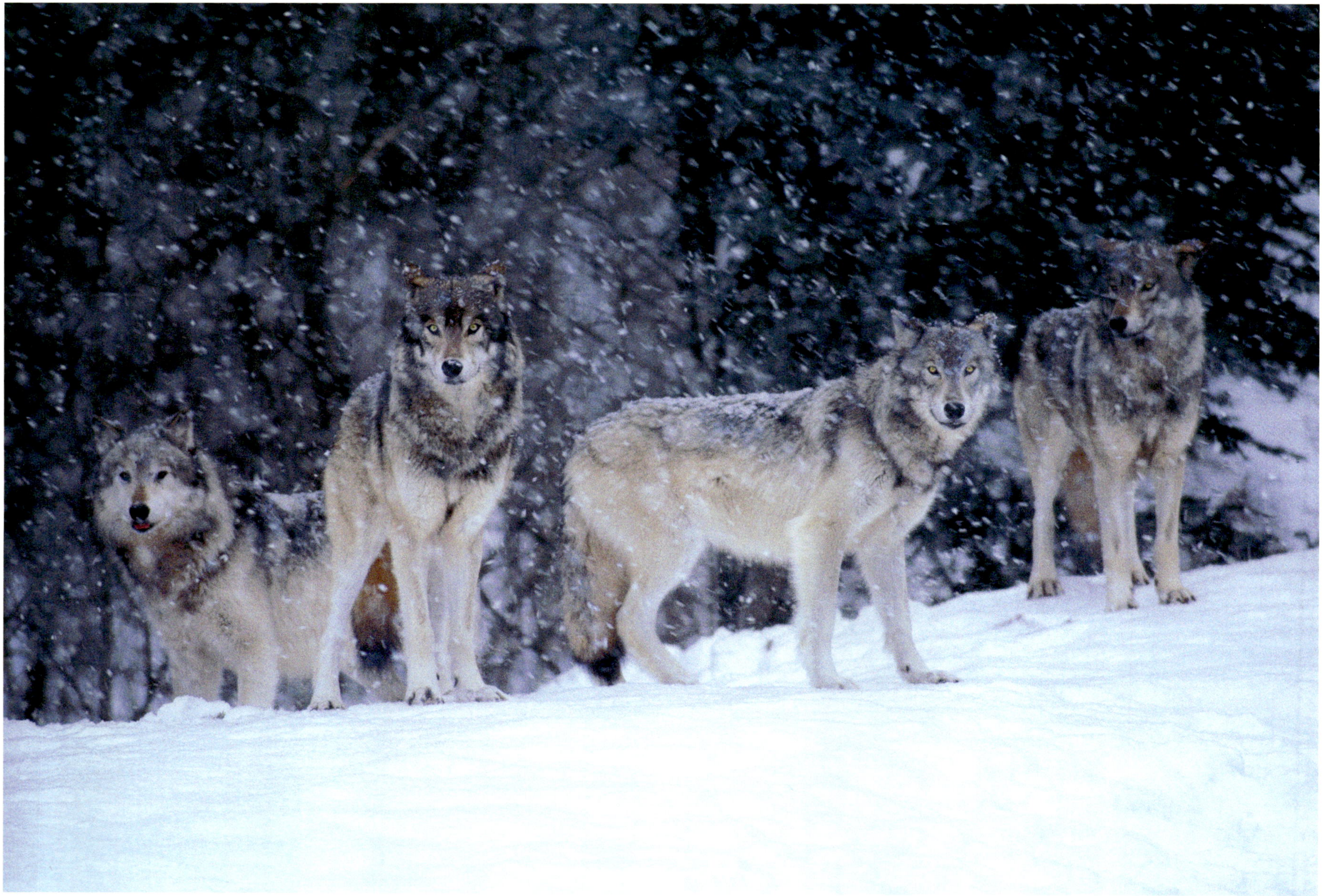

Grey Wolves, 1993, Northern Canada

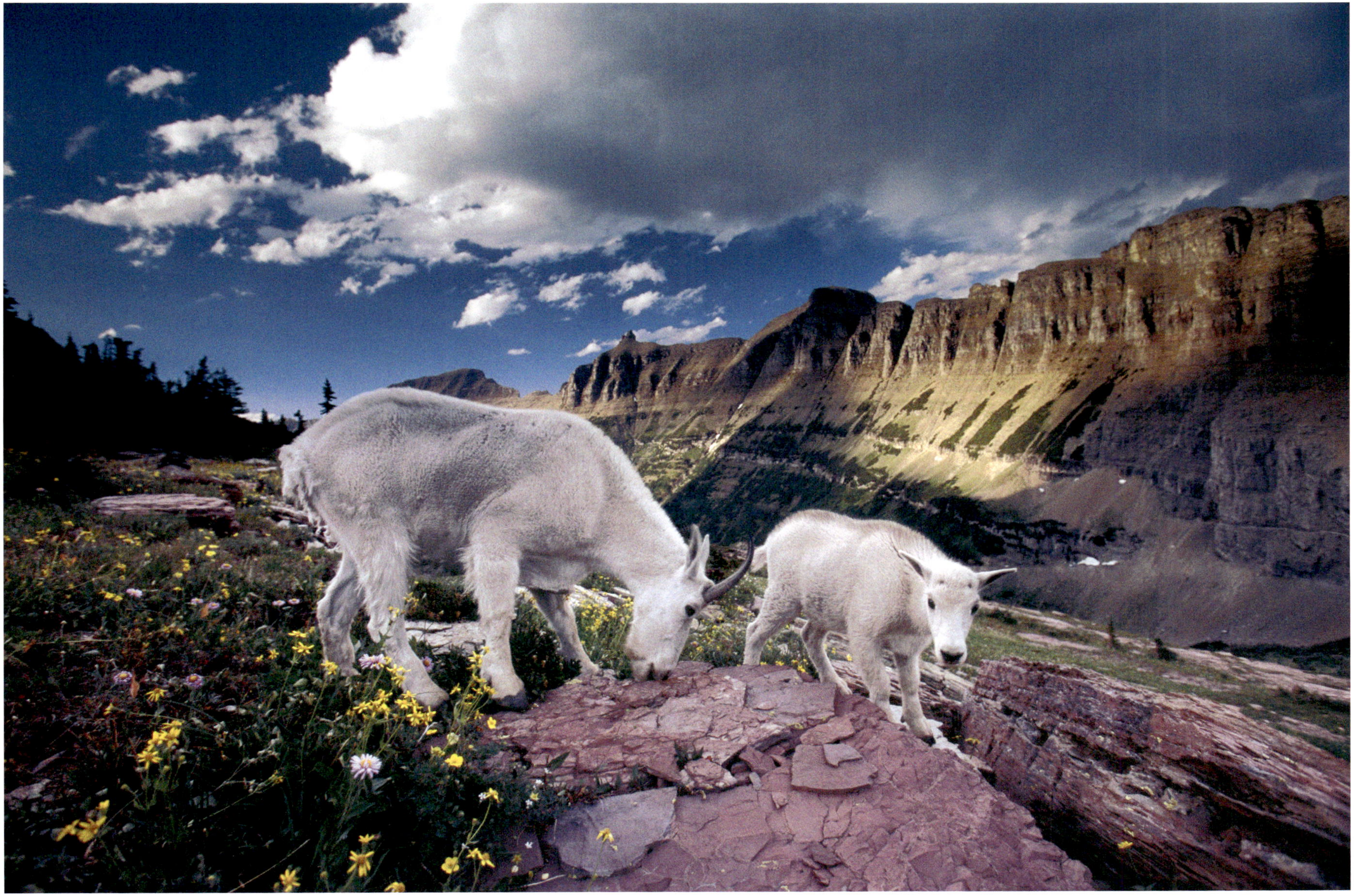

Mountain Goats, 2000, Glacier National Park, Montana, United States

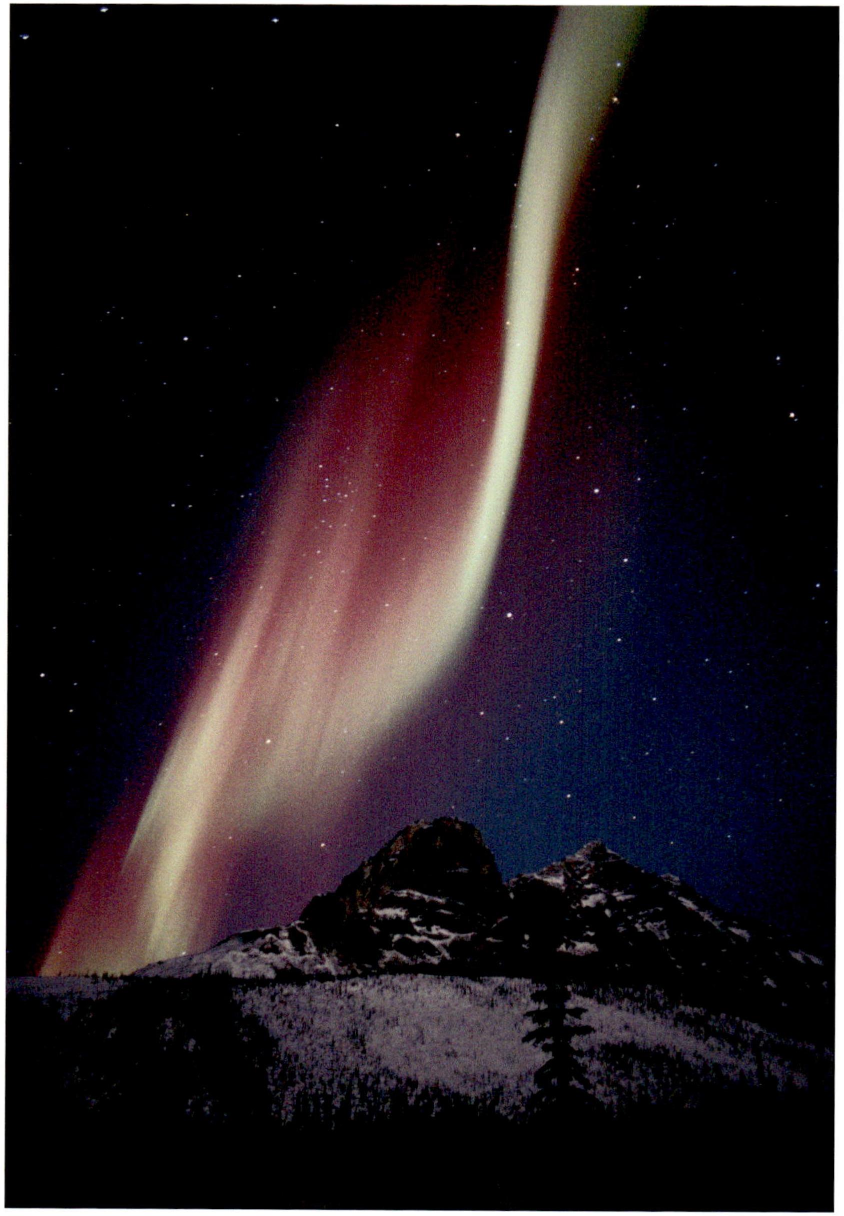

Aurora Borealis, 2002, Brooks Range, Alaska, United States

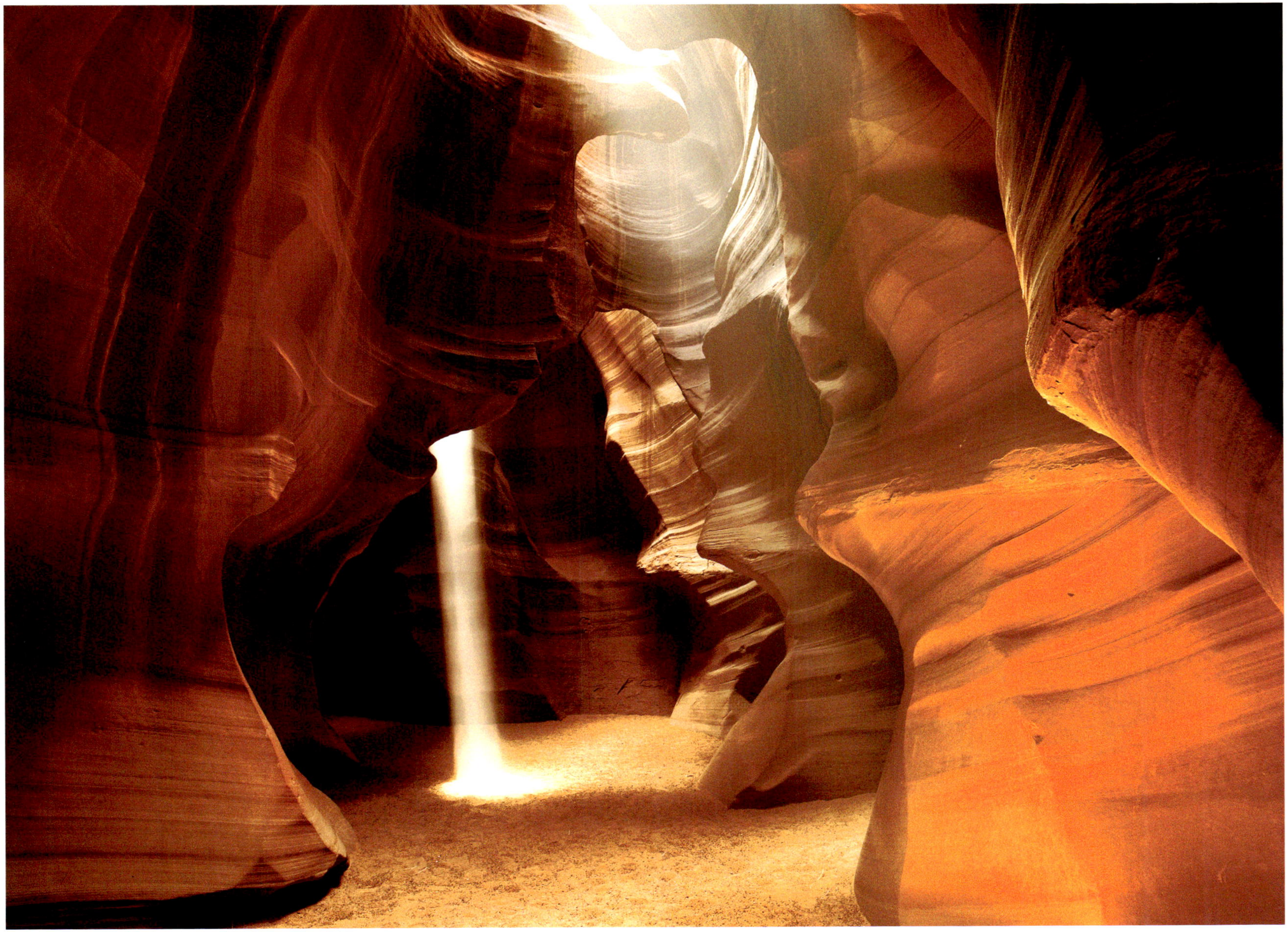

Antelope Canyon, 2002, Page, Arizona, United States

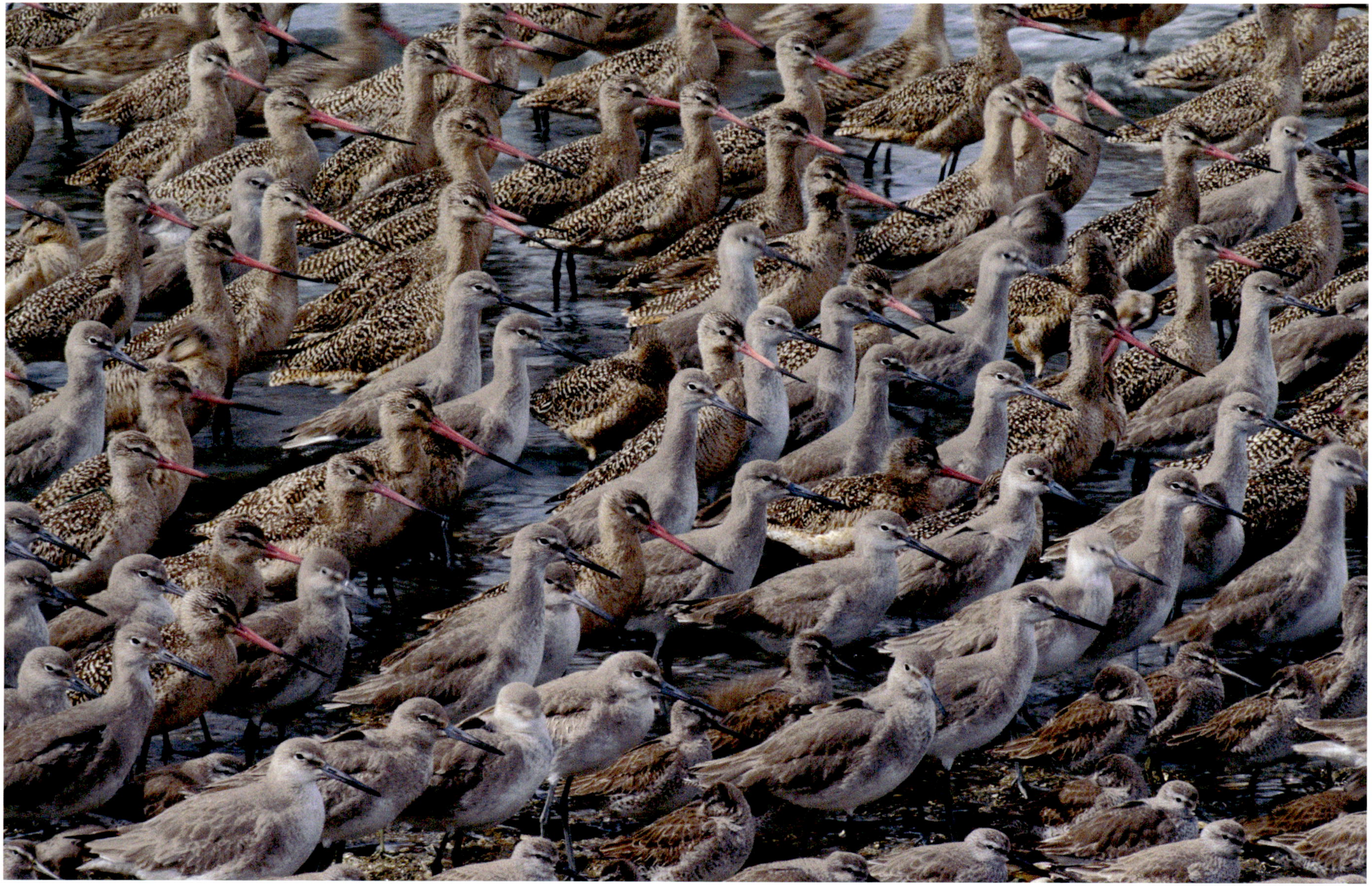

Marbled Godwits, Willets, and Short-billed Dowitchers, 1999, Laguna San Ignacio, Baja California, Mexico

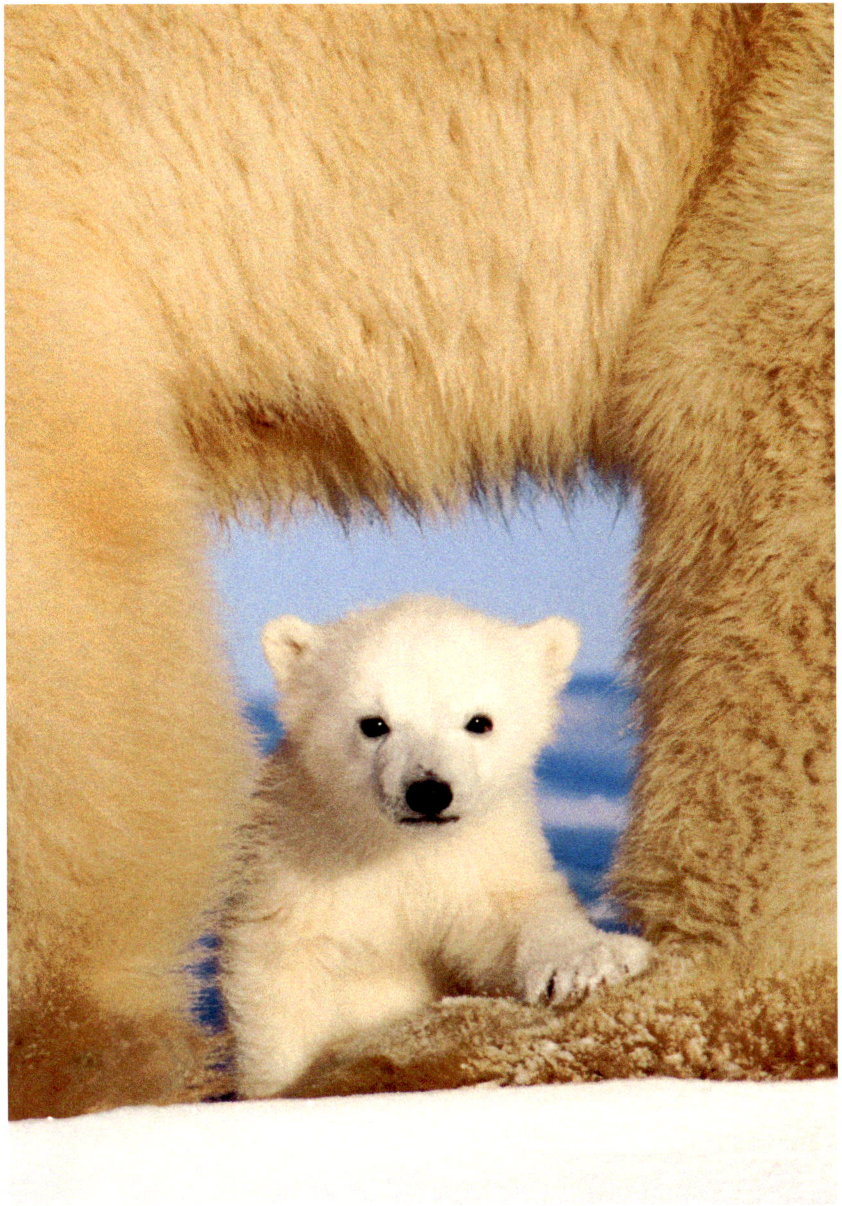

Polar Bear Cub, 2000, Churchill, Manitoba, Canada

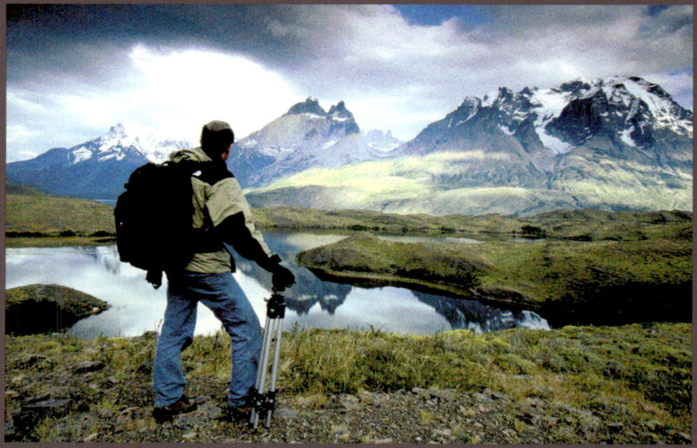

SOUTH AMERICA

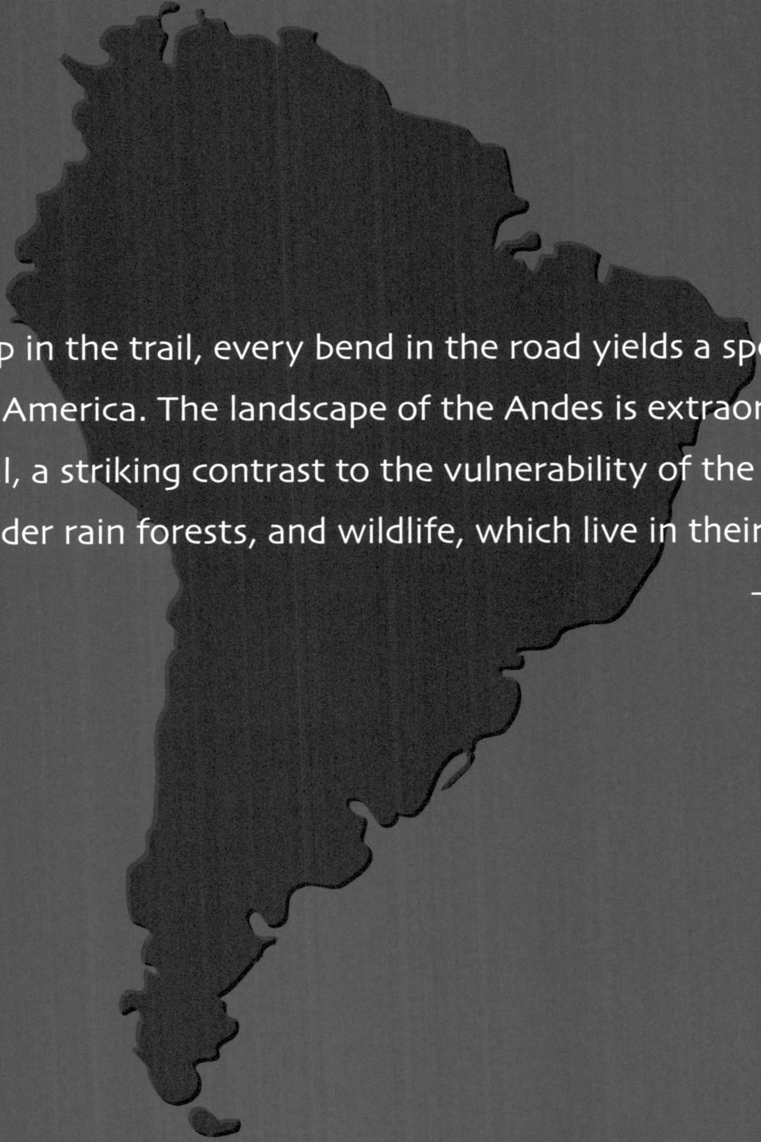

"Every step in the trail, every bend in the road yields a spectacular sight in South America. The landscape of the Andes is extraordinarily bold and powerful, a striking contrast to the vulnerability of the indigenous cultures, tender rain forests, and wildlife, which live in their shadows."

—Art Wolfe

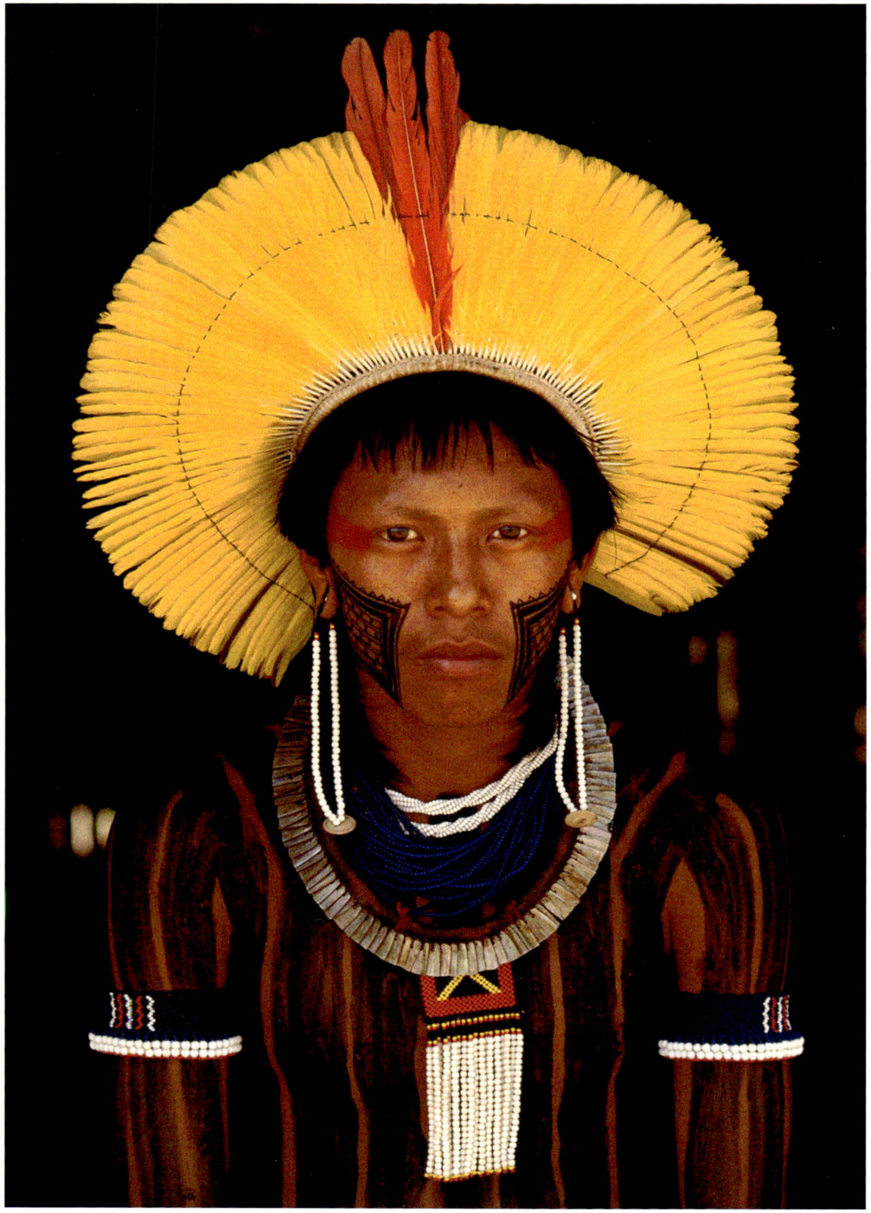

Kayapo Menõrõny-re, 1993, Kapoto Village, Para, Brazil

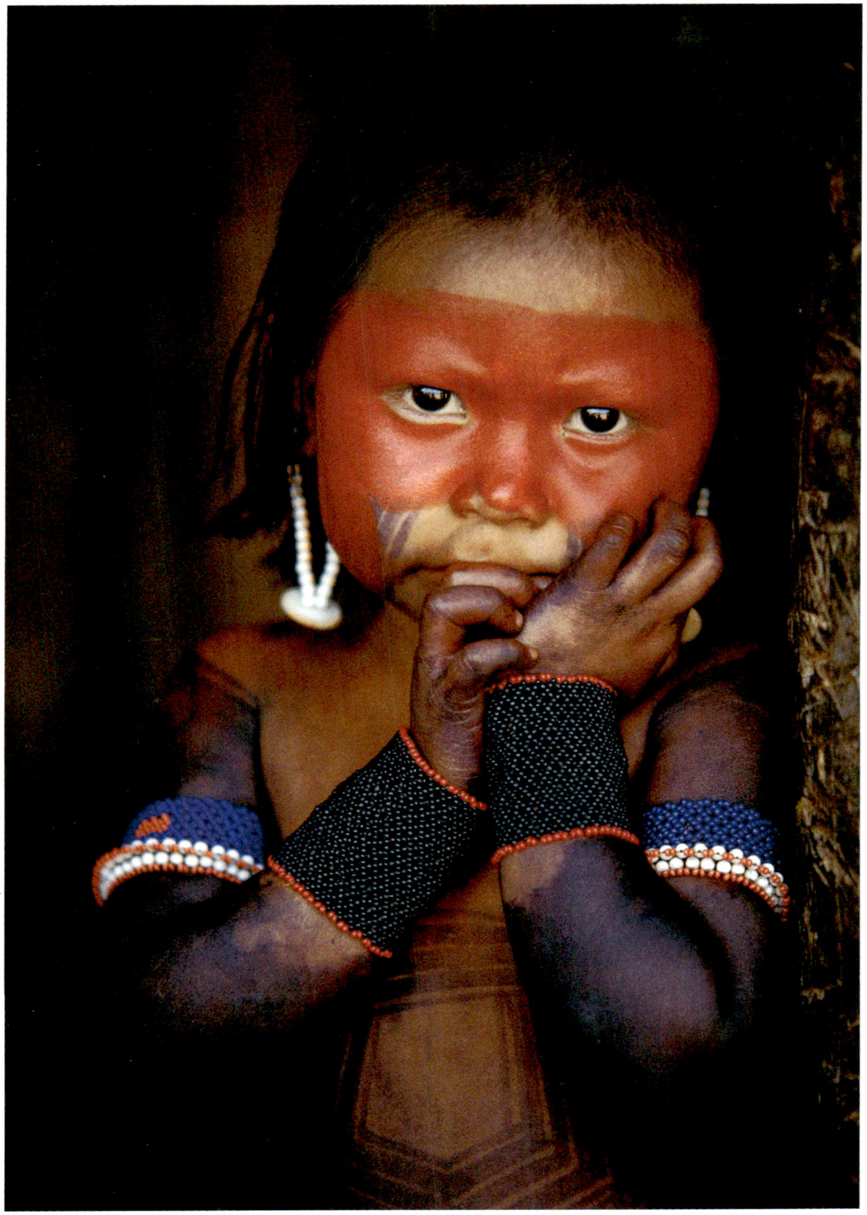

Kayapo Girl, 1993, Kapoto Village, Para, Brazil

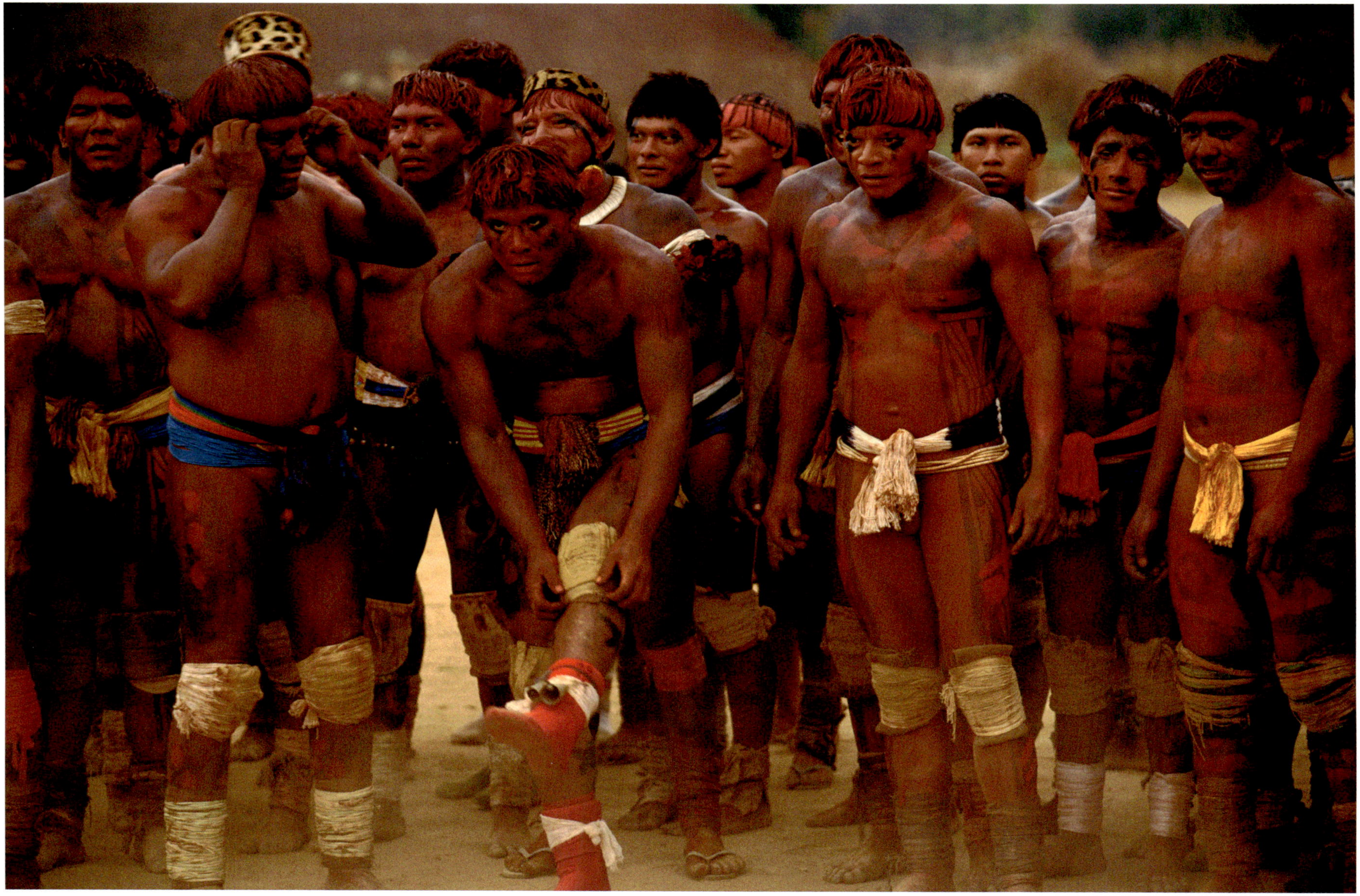

Kamayura Wrestlers, 1993, Mato Grosso, Brazil

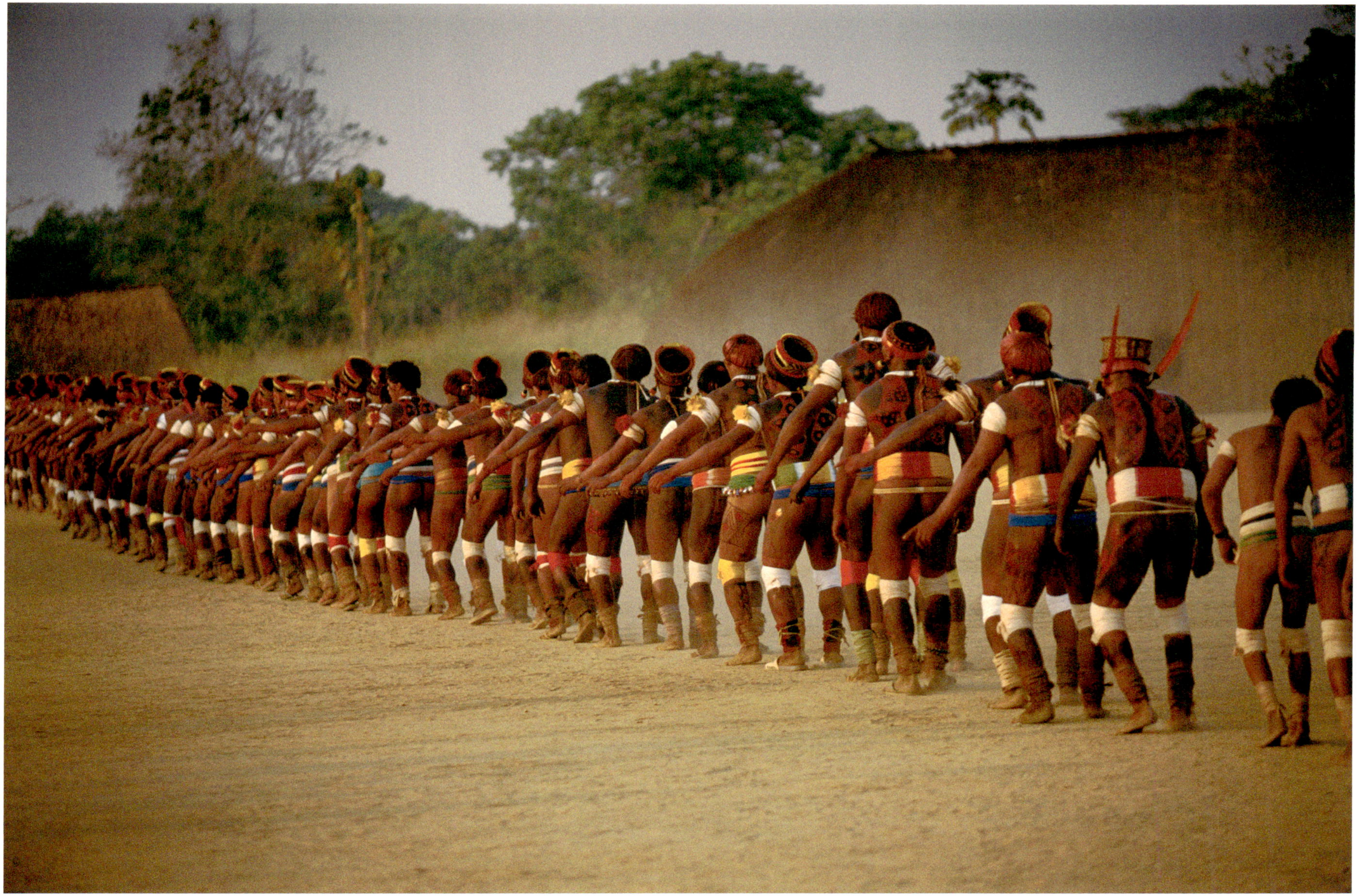

Xingu Kwarup Processional, 1993, Mato Grosso, Brazil

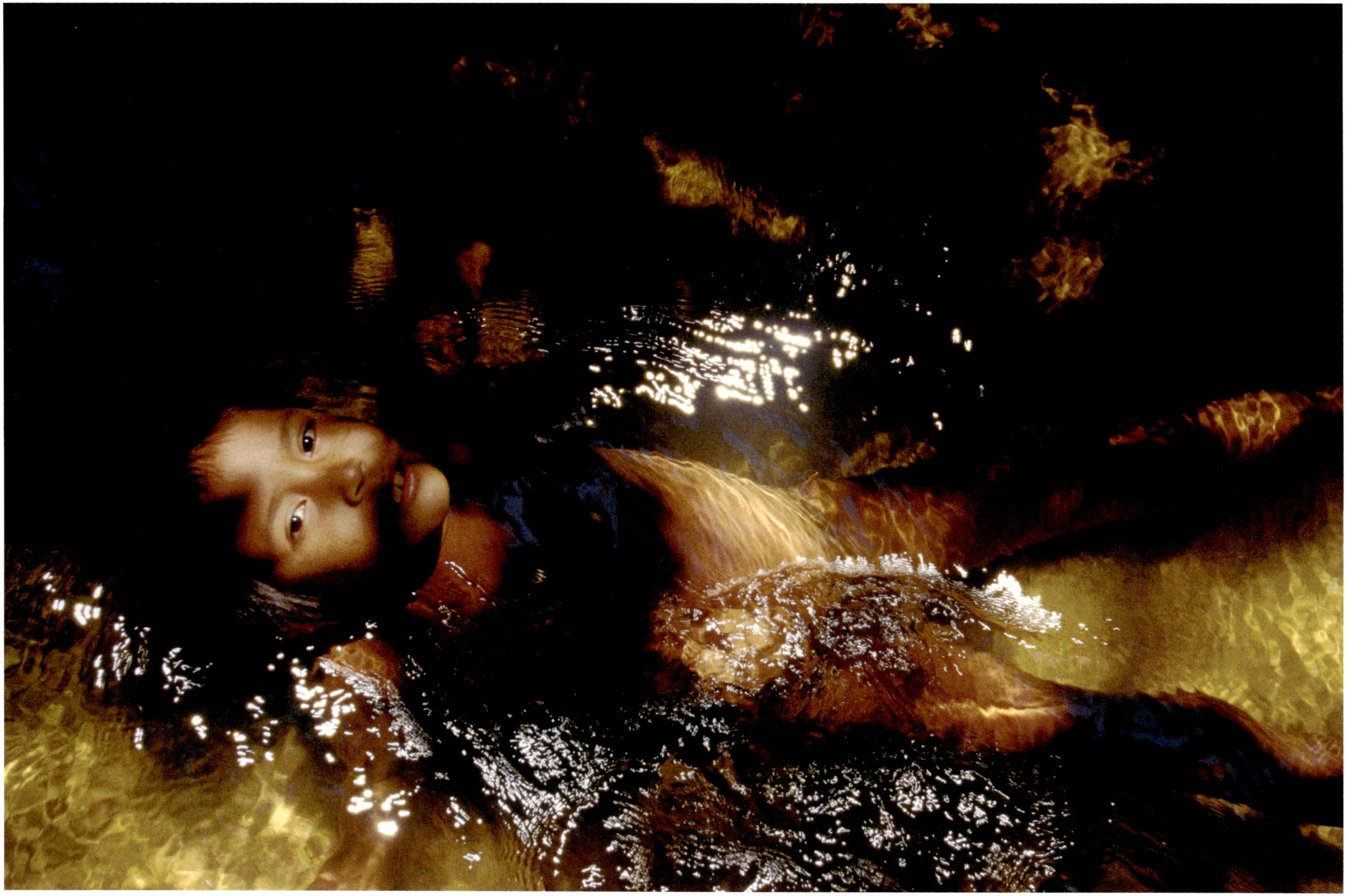

Yąnomamö Boy, 1996, Sierra Parima, Venezuela

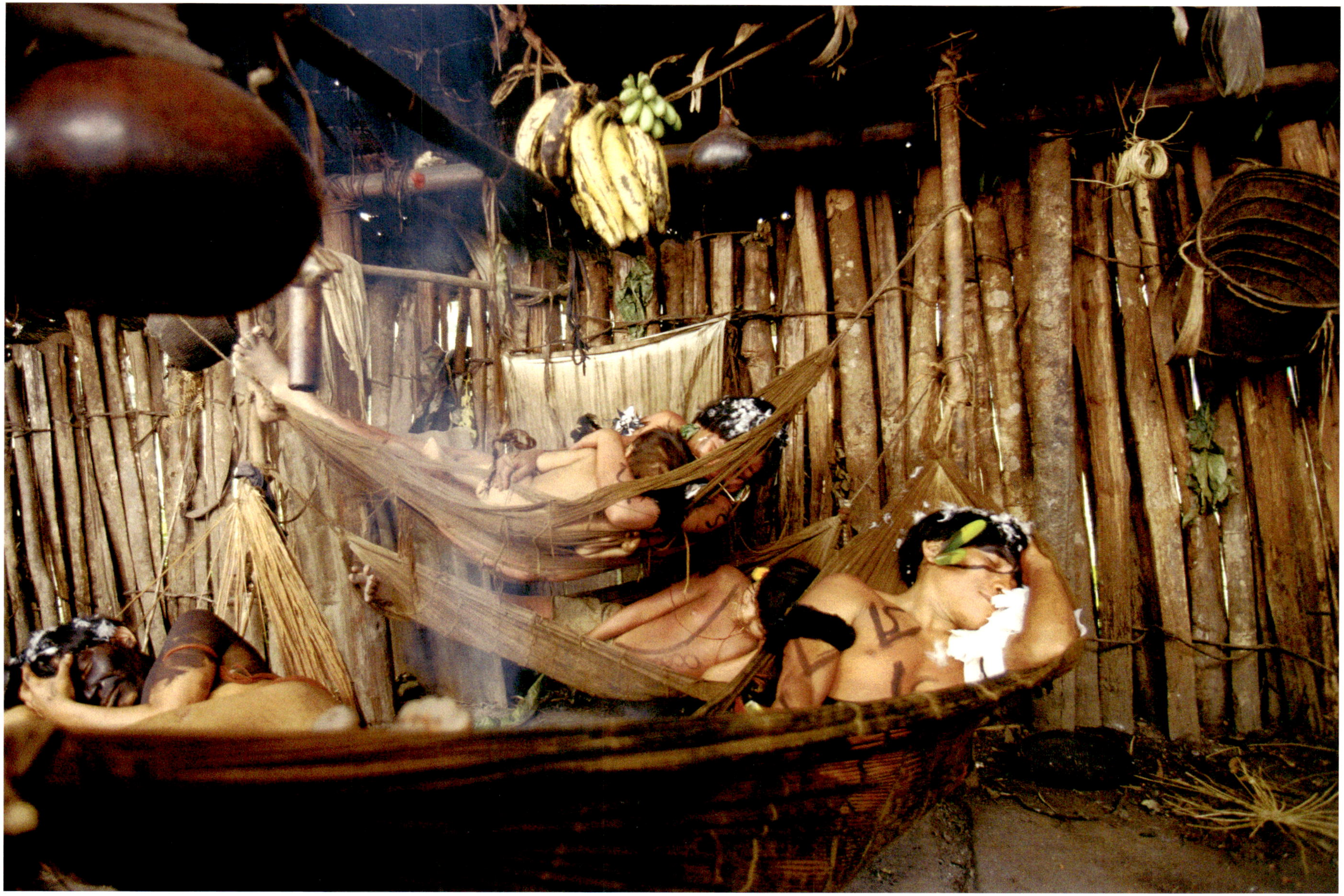

Yąnomamö Shabono, 1996, Sierra Parima, Venezuela

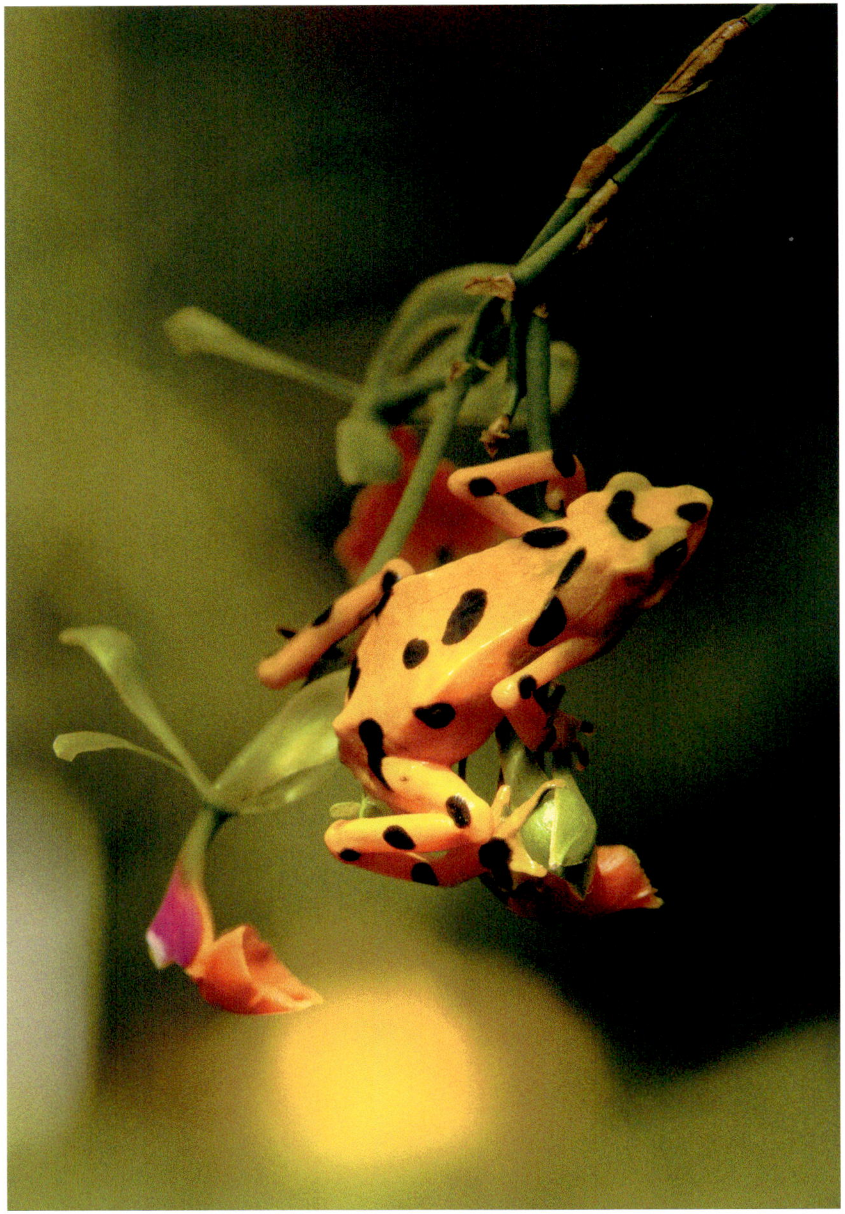

Golden Frog, 1996, Pacific Lowlands, Panama

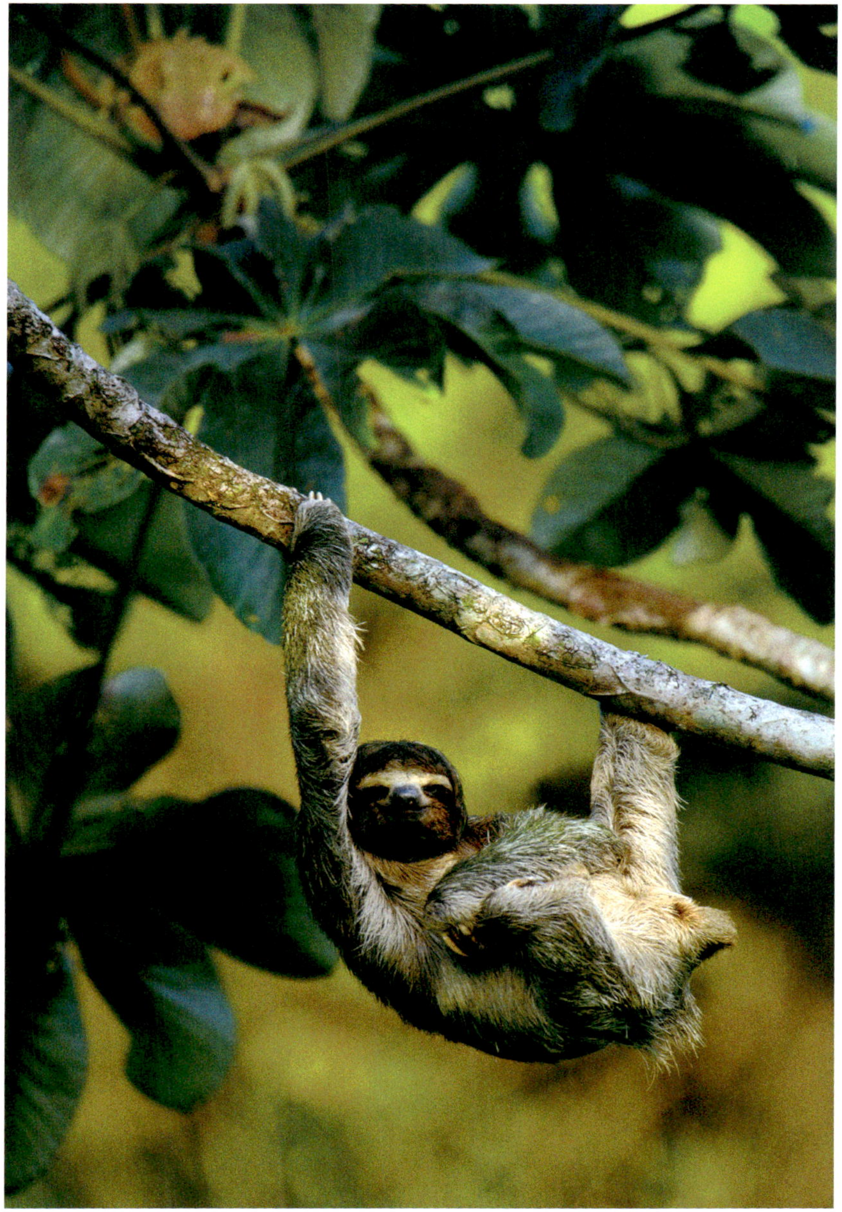

Three-toed Tree Sloth, 1996, Islas Bocas del Toro, Panama

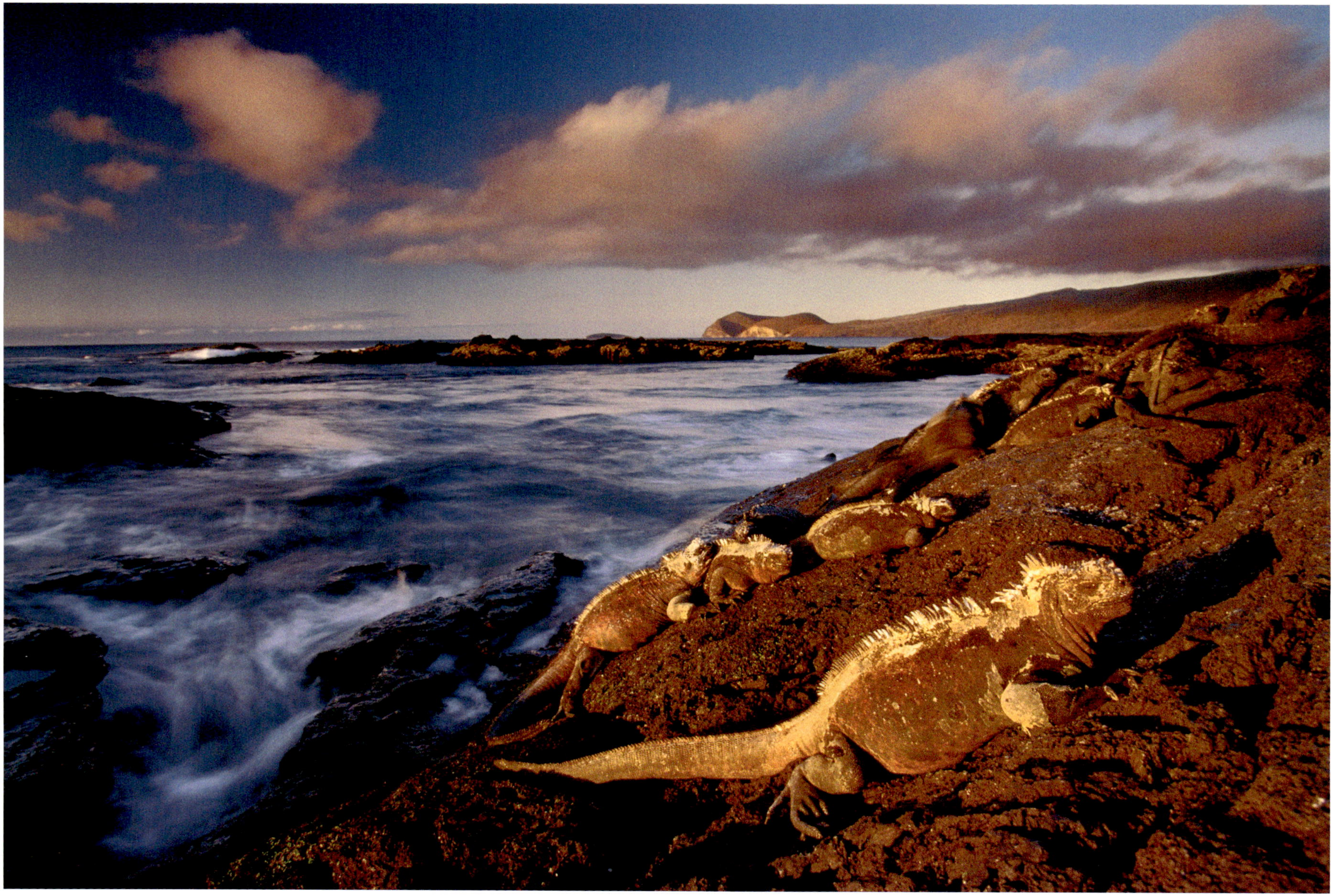

Marine Iguanas, 2000, Galapagos Islands, Ecuador

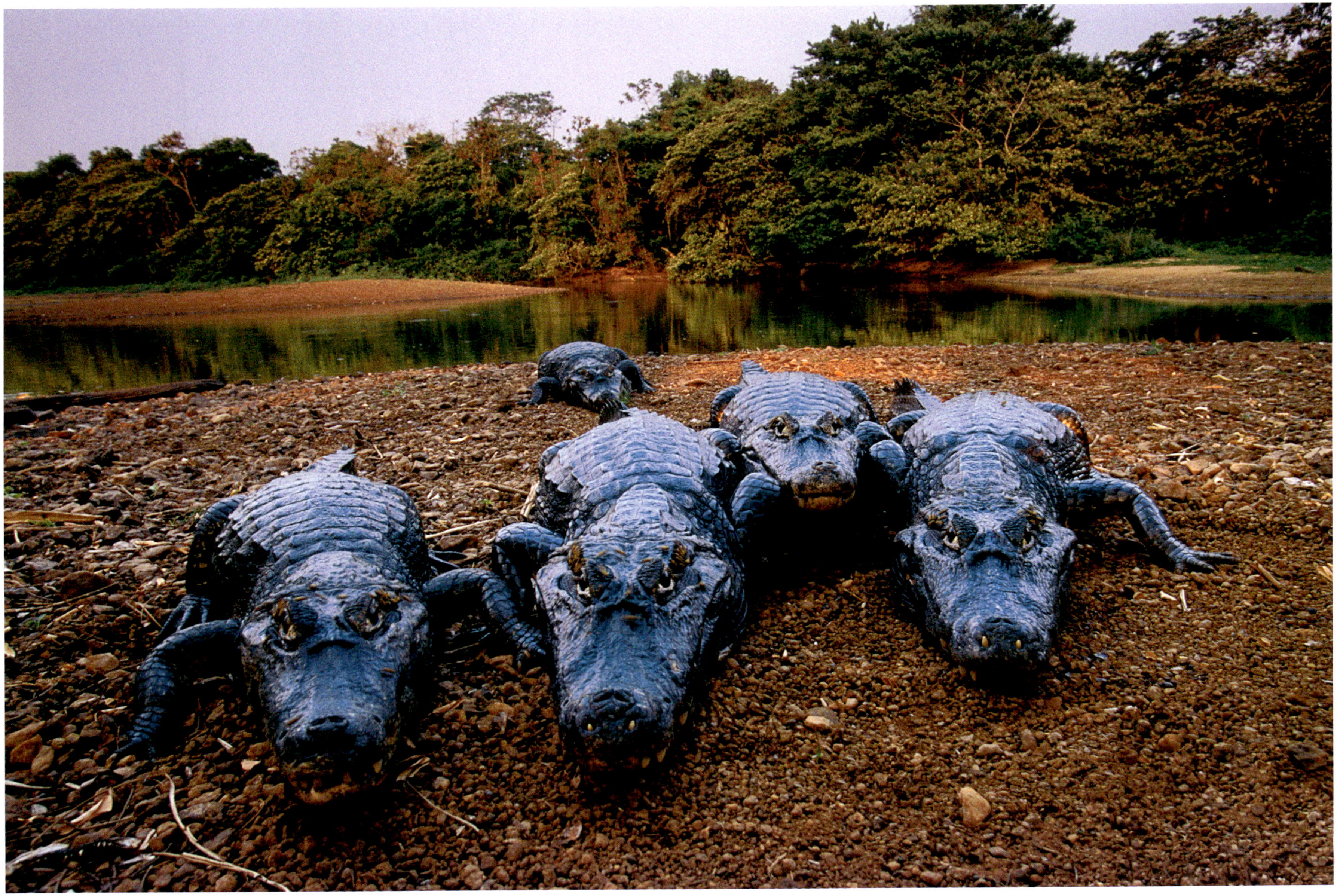

Yacare Caimans, 1999, Pantanal, Brazil

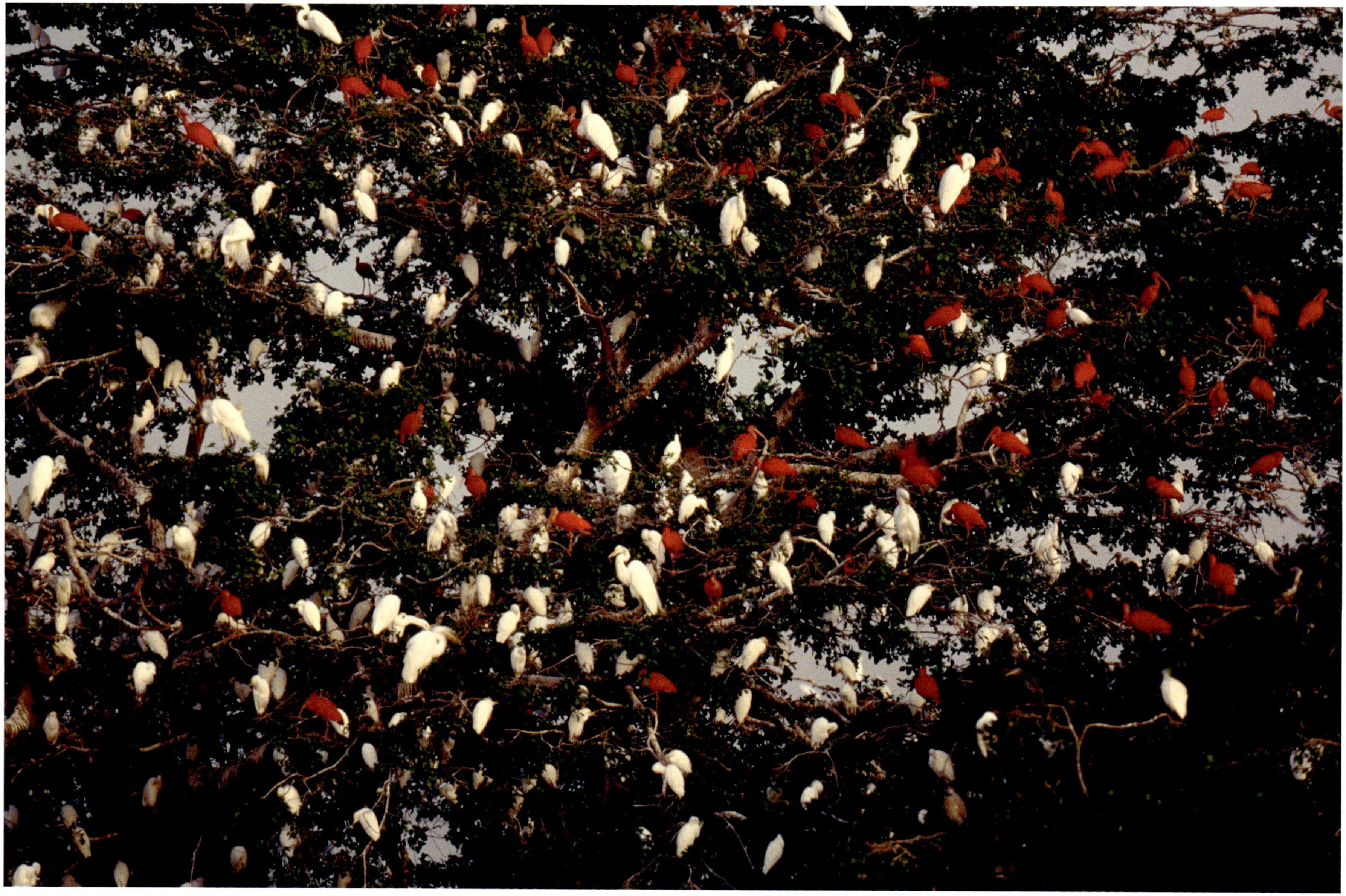

Scarlet Ibis and Cattle Egrets, 1994, Hato el Frio, Llanos, Venezuela

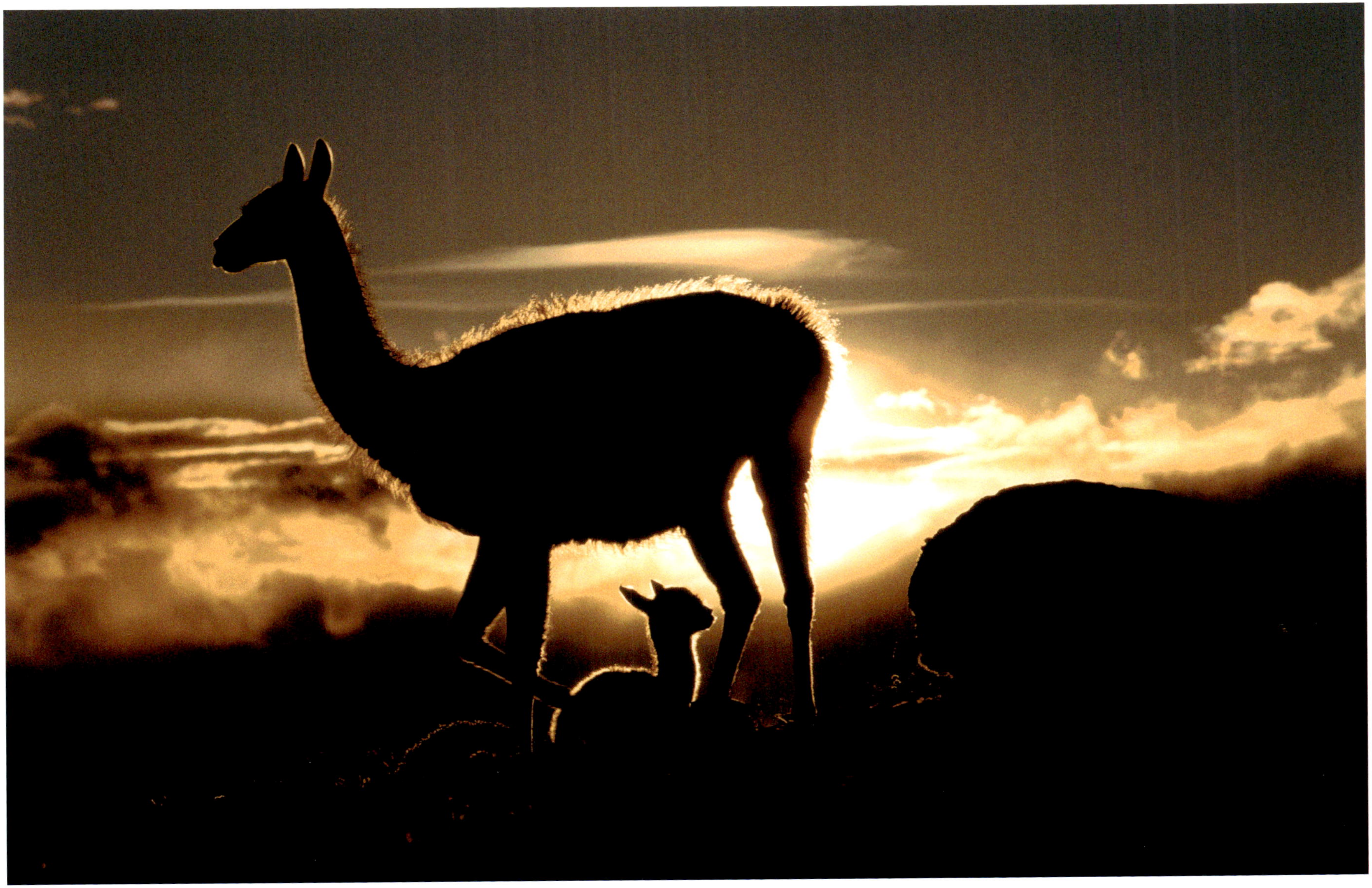

Guanaco and Chulengo, 1998, Torres del Paine National Park, Chile

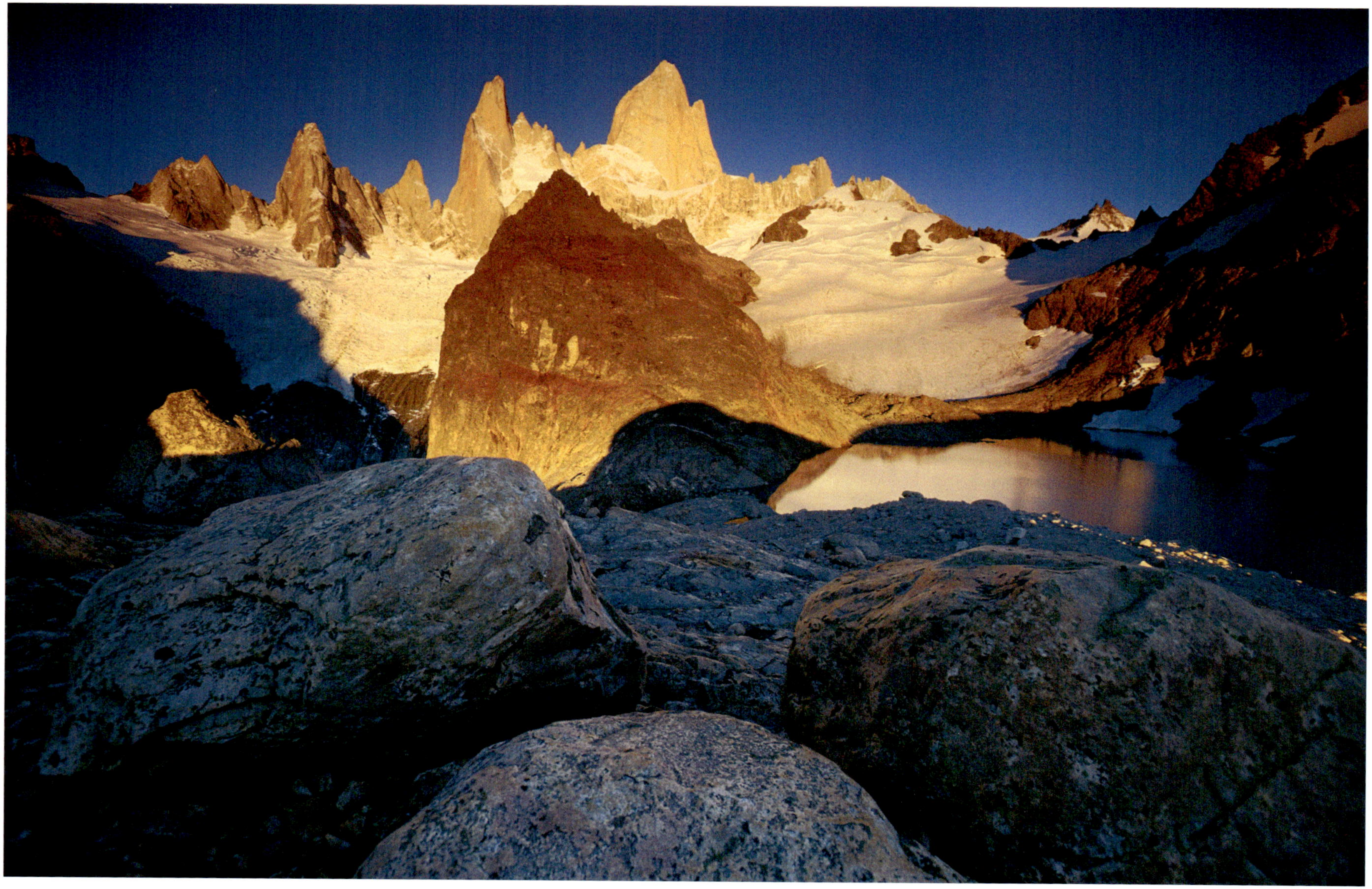

Mt. Fitzroy, 2002, Los Glaciares National Park, Argentina

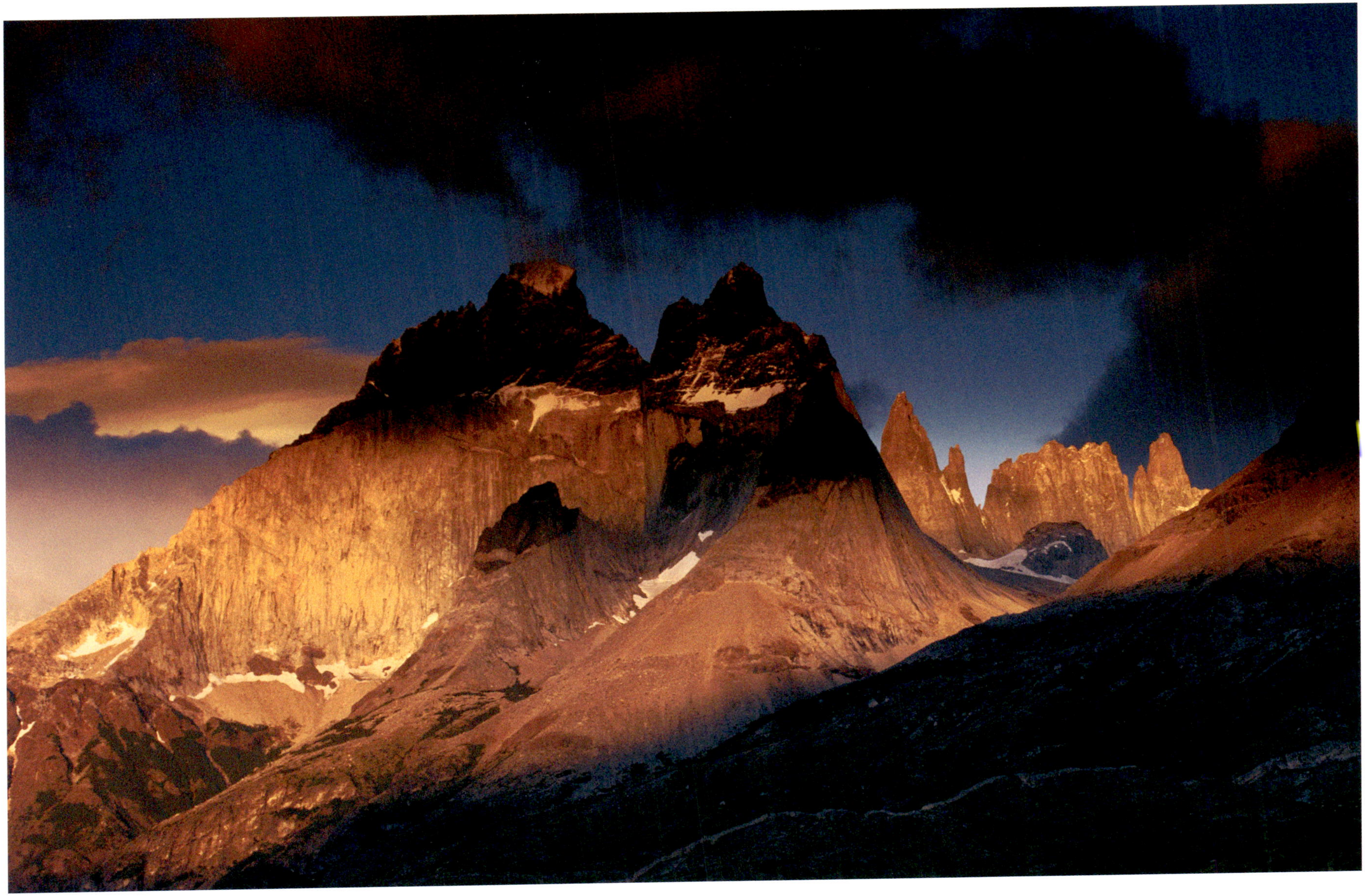

Cuernos del Diablo, 1998, Torres del Paine National Park, Chile

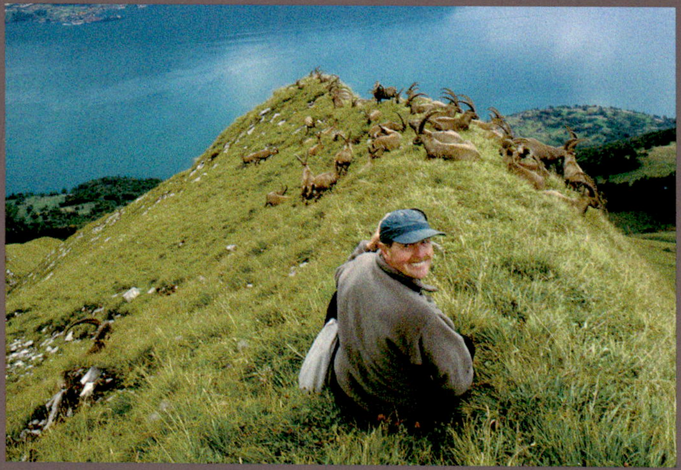

EUROPE

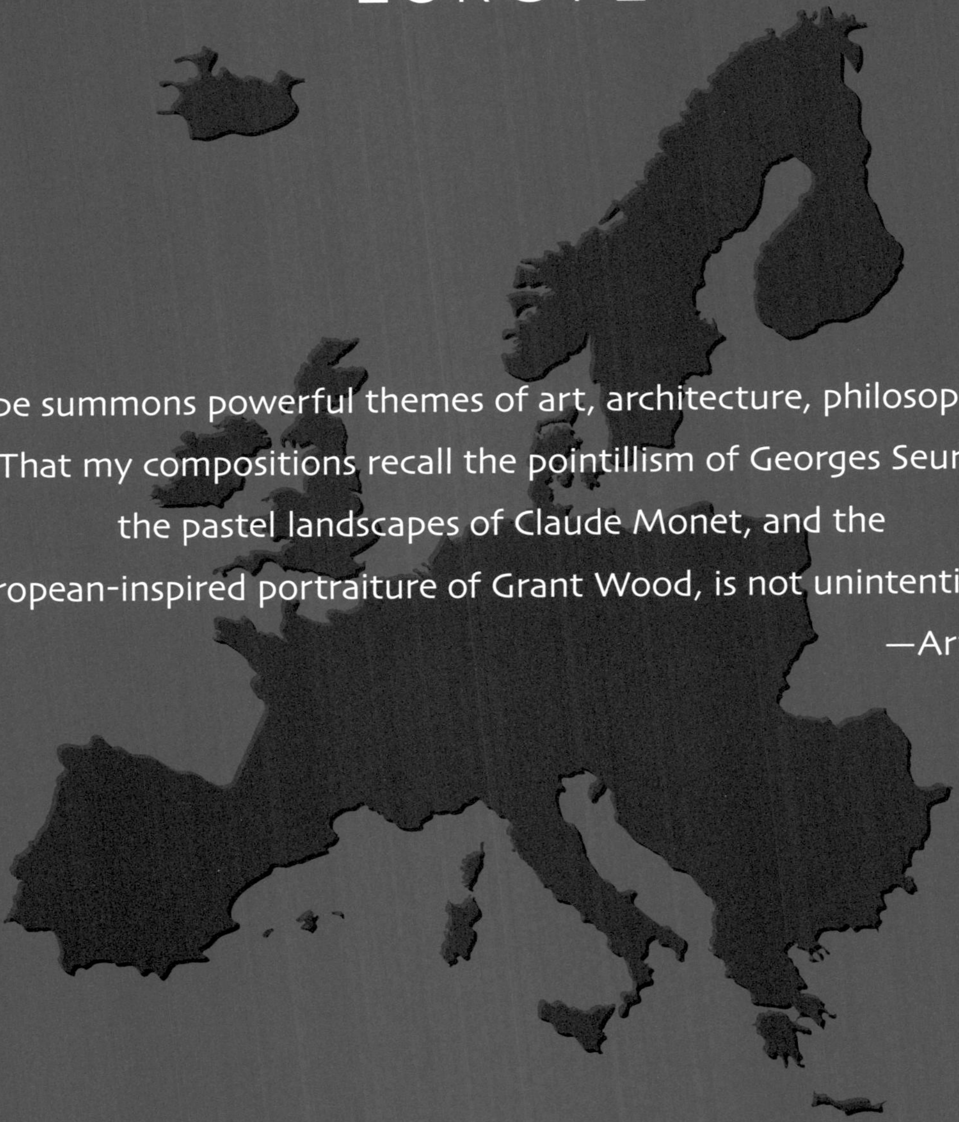

"For me, Europe summons powerful themes of art, architecture, philosophy, and ethnicity.
That my compositions recall the pointillism of Georges Seurat,
the pastel landscapes of Claude Monet, and the
European-inspired portraiture of Grant Wood, is not unintentional."

—Art Wolfe

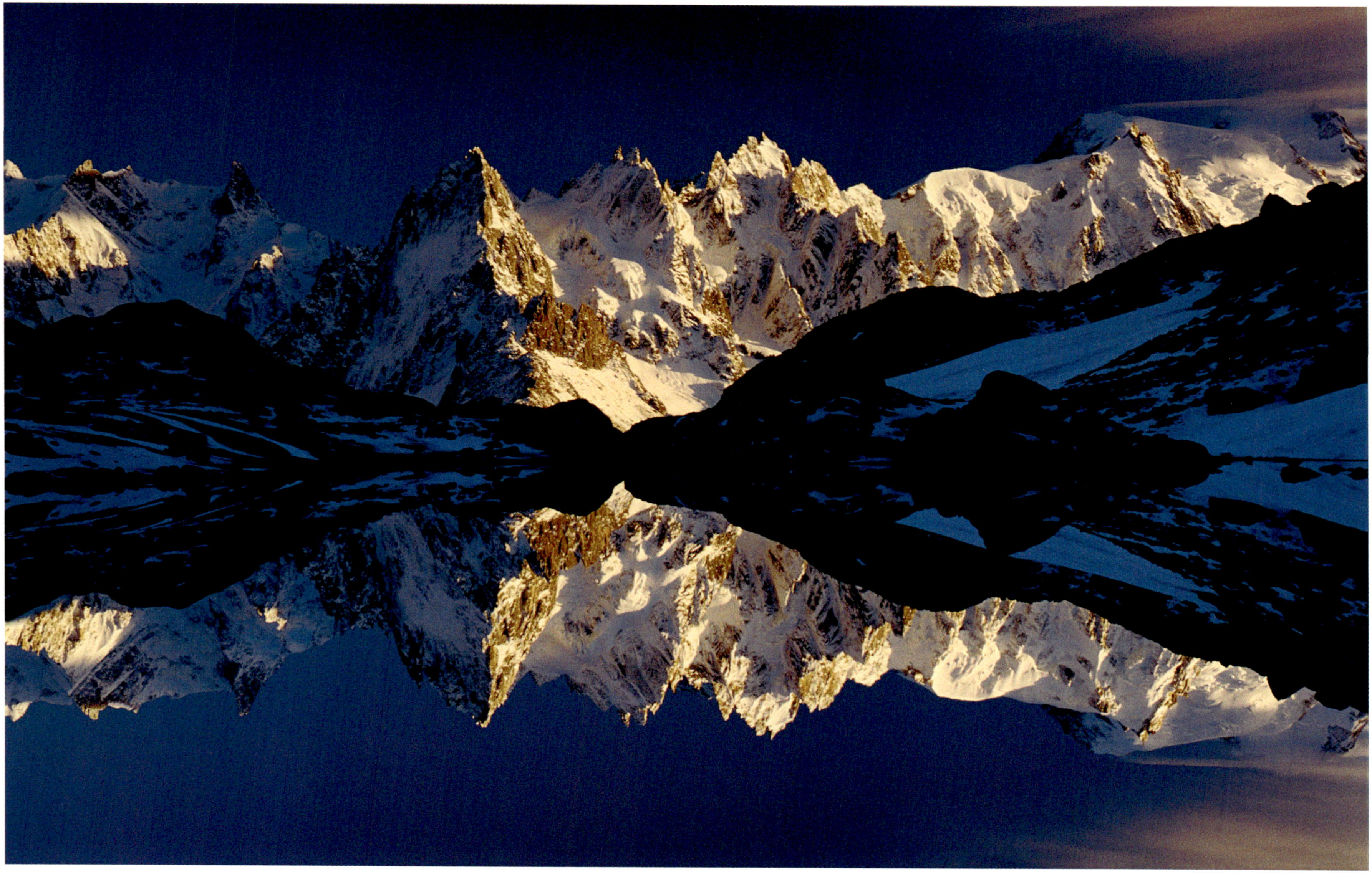

Les Aiguilles, 1995, Chamonix, France

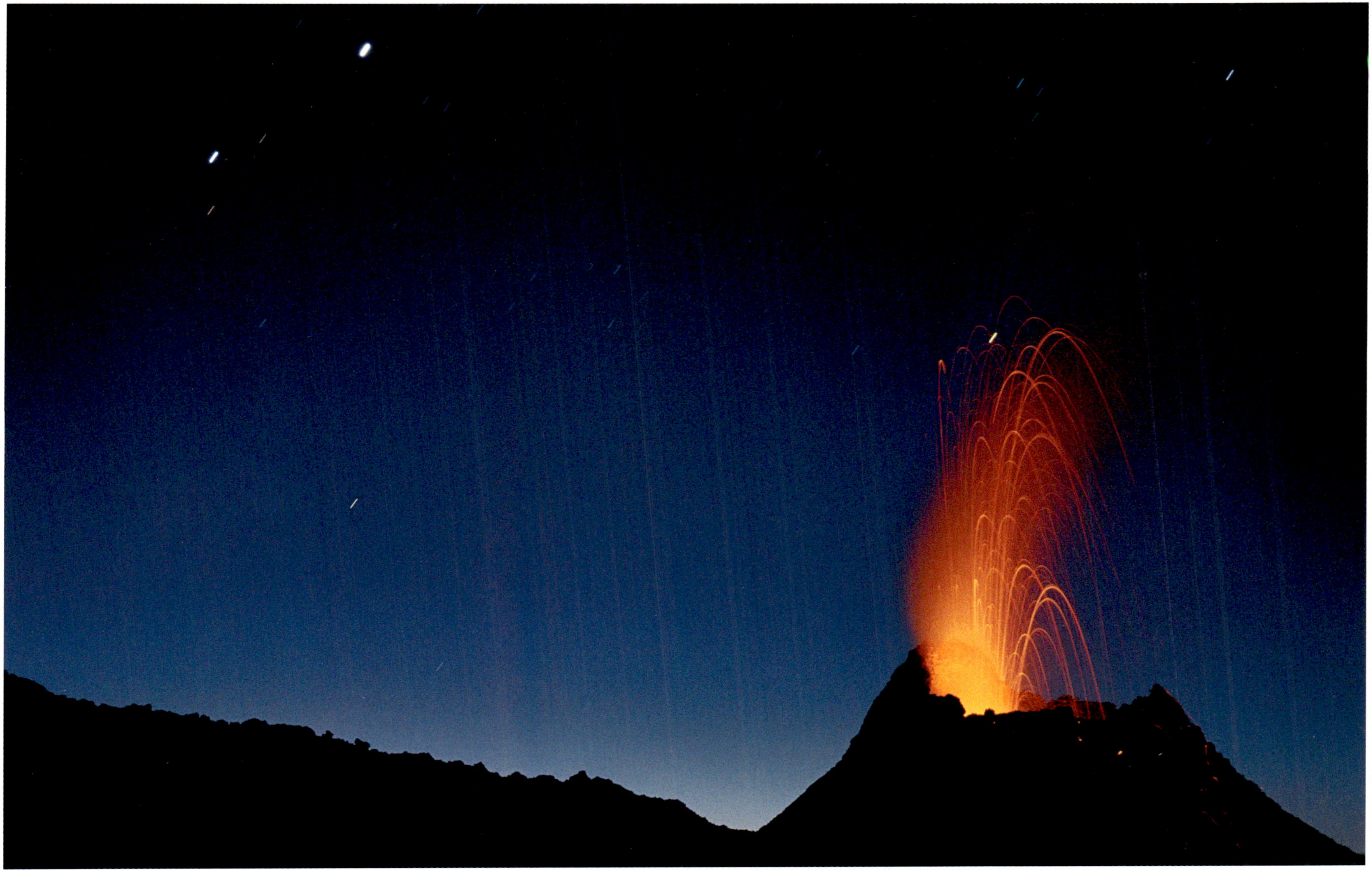

Cinder Cone, 2001, Mt. Etna, Sicily, Italy

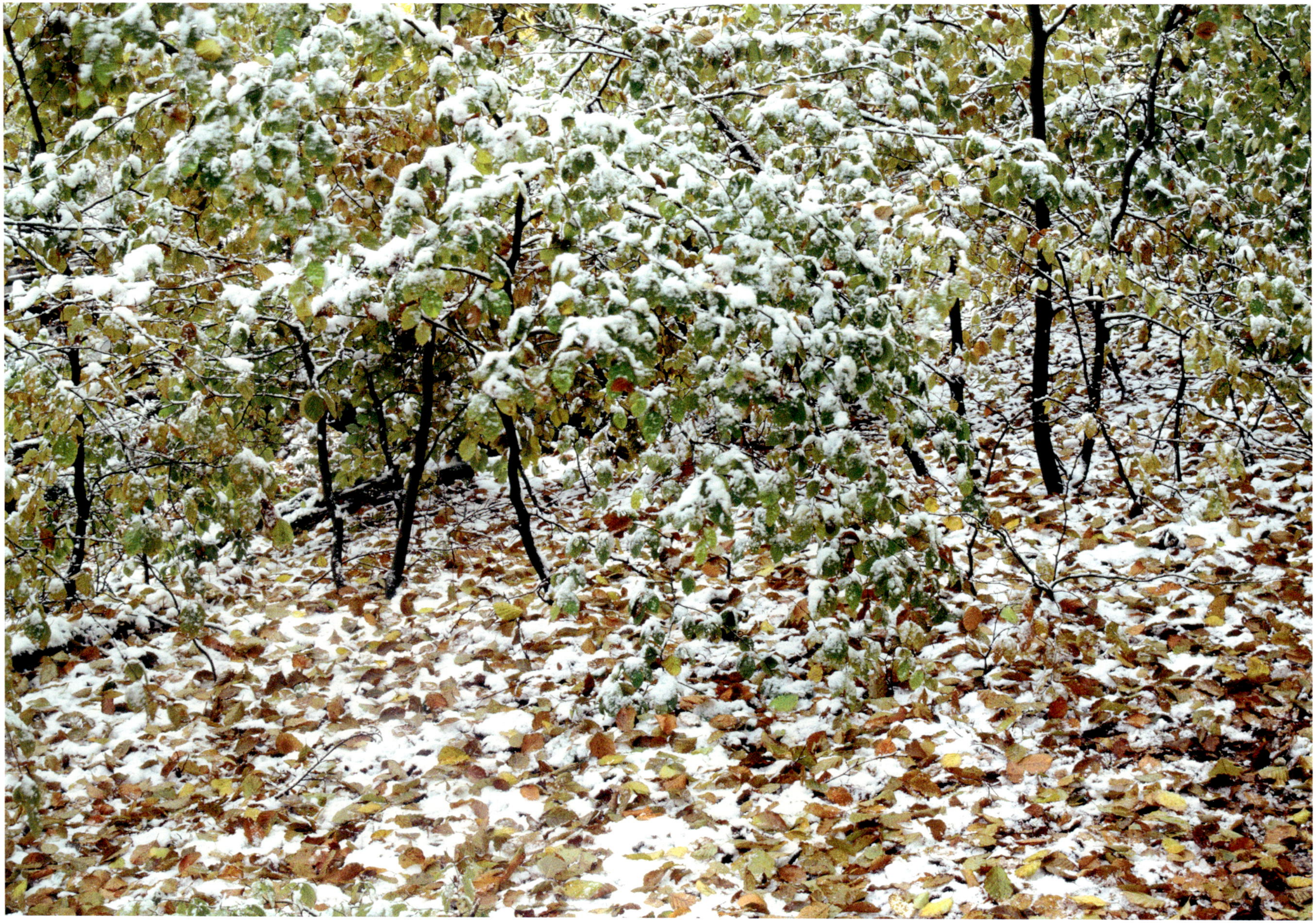

Winterscape, 1997, Sweden

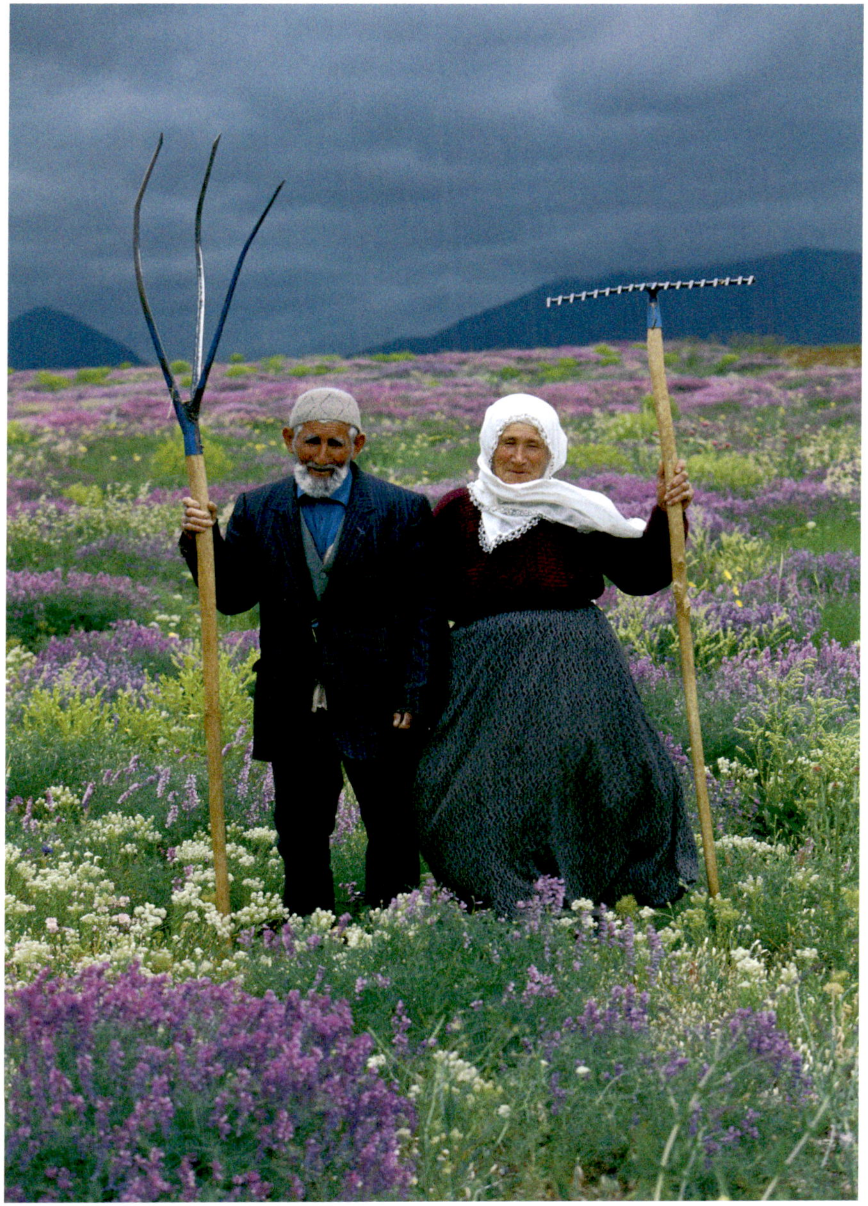

Farmers, 2002, Cappadocia, Turkey

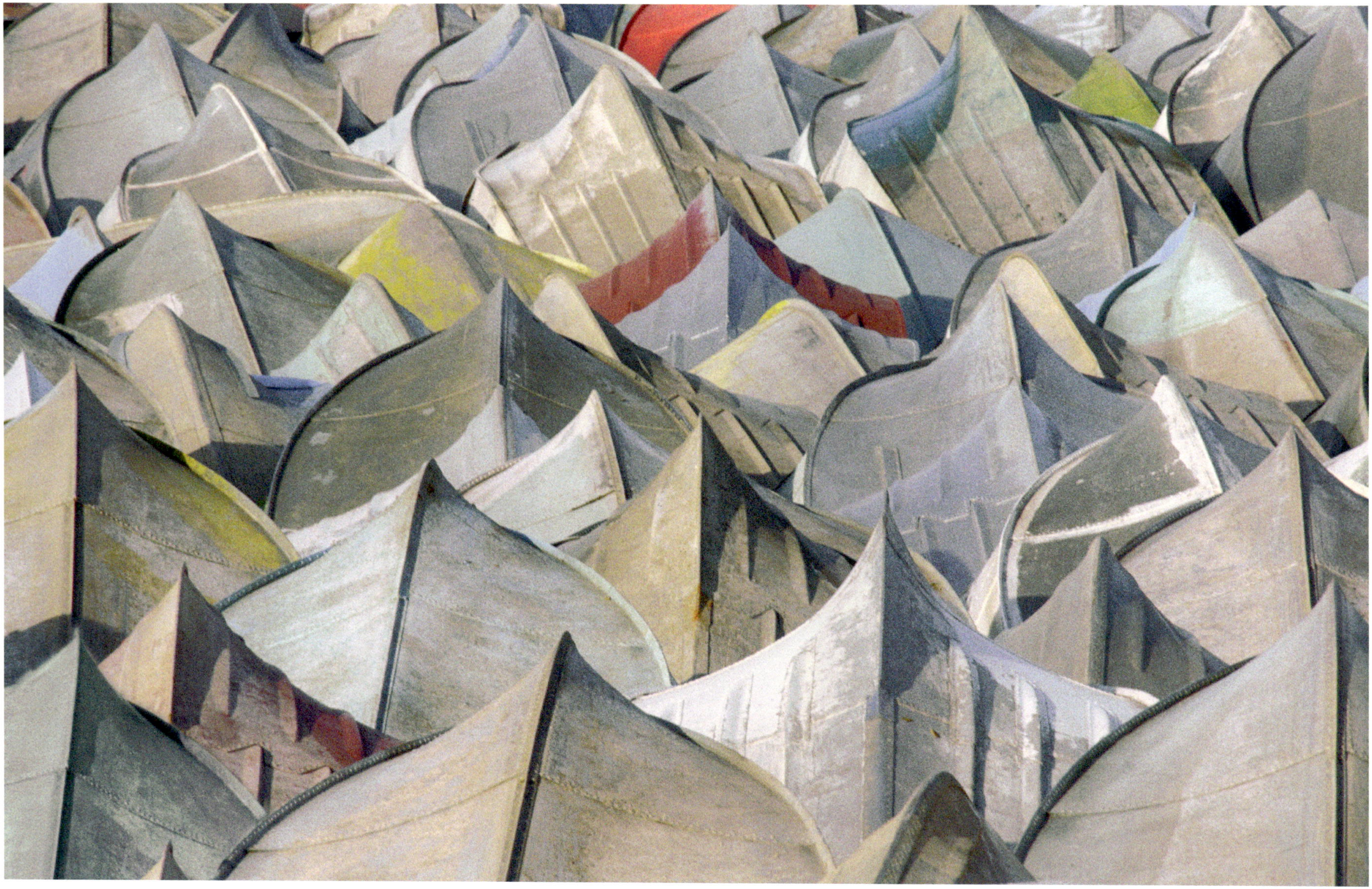

Boats, 1990, Lake Baikal, Siberia, Russia

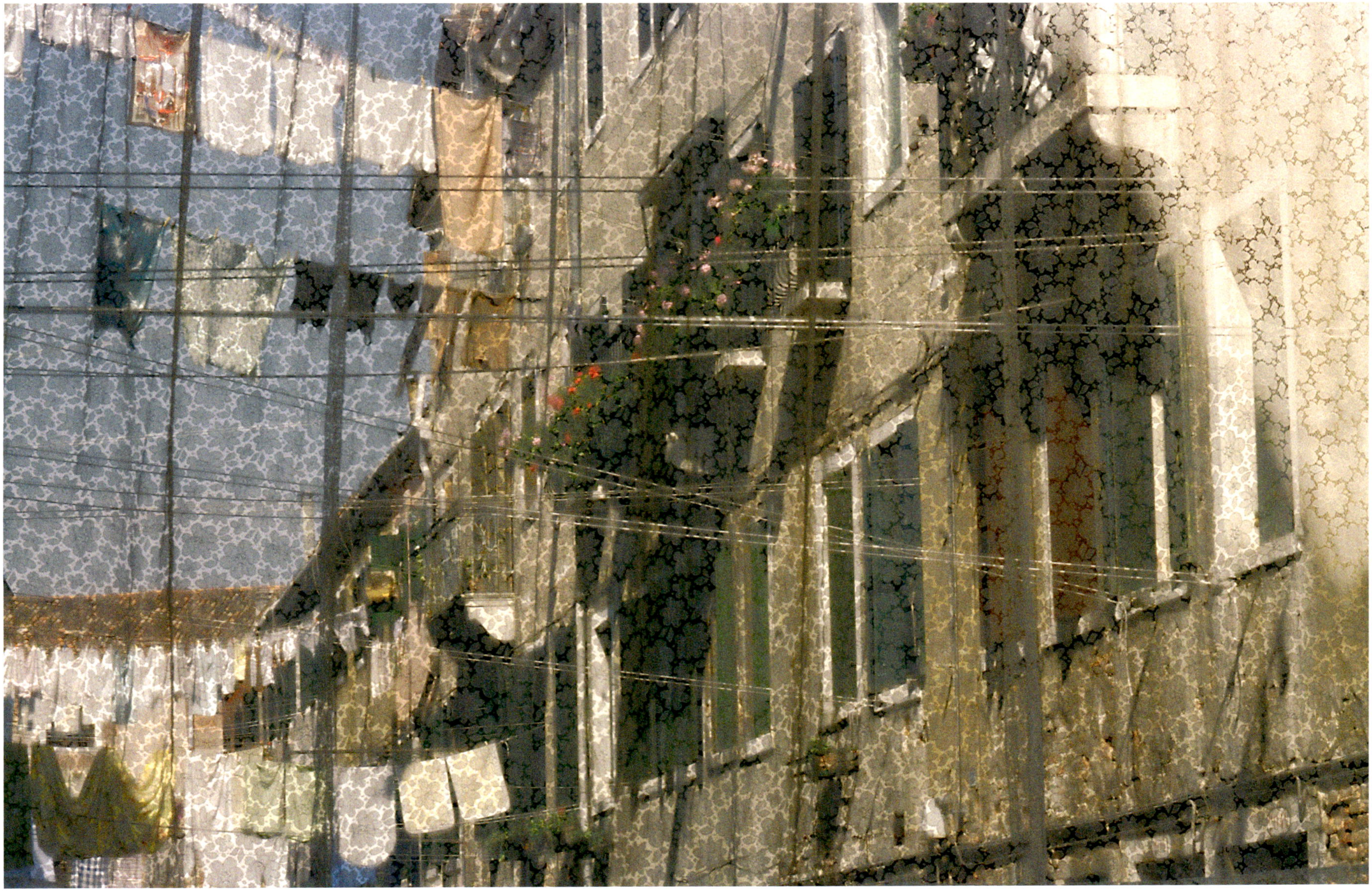

Hanging Laundry, 1989, Venice, Italy

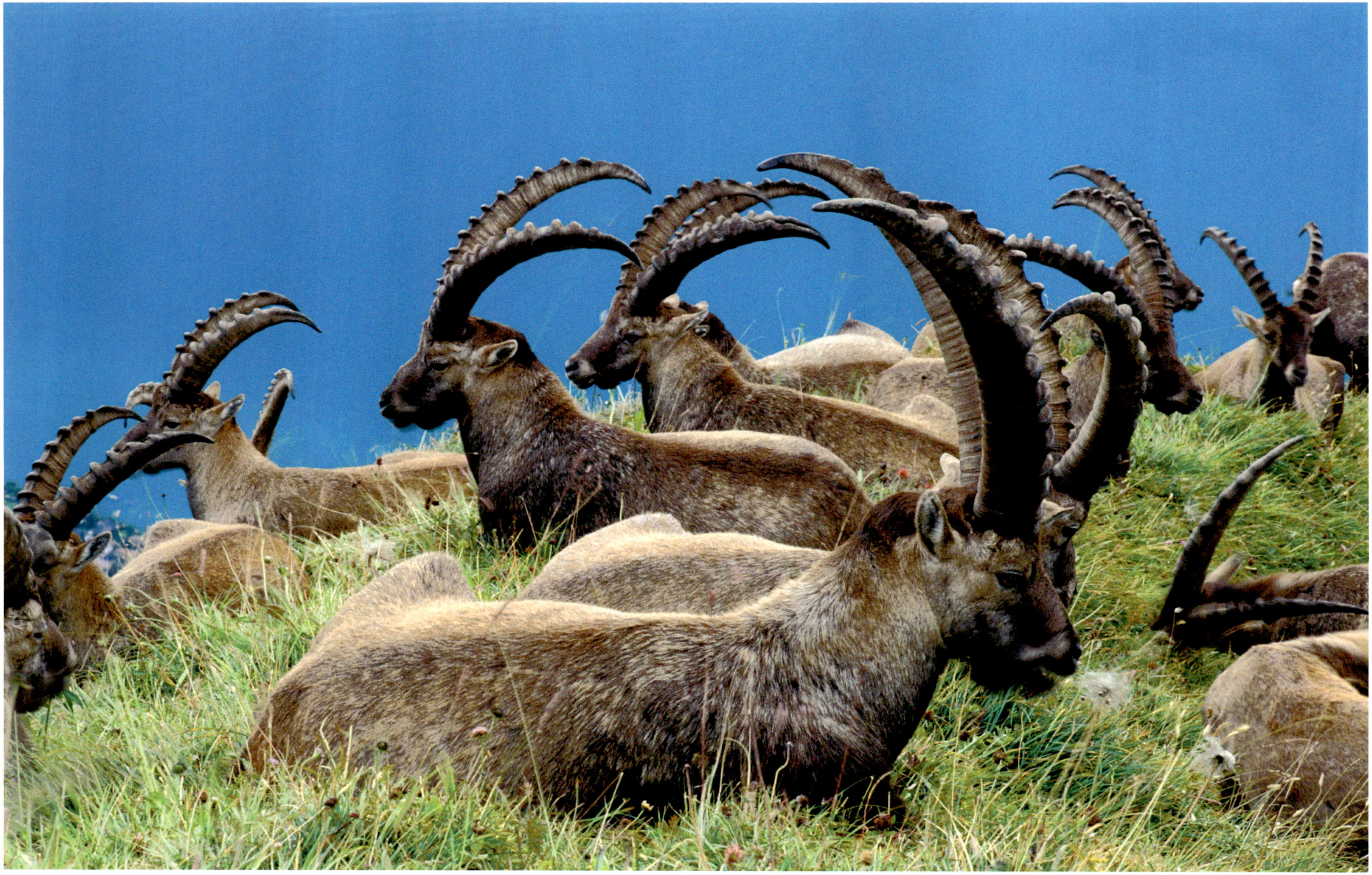

Alpine Ibex, 1995, Bernese Alps, Switzerland

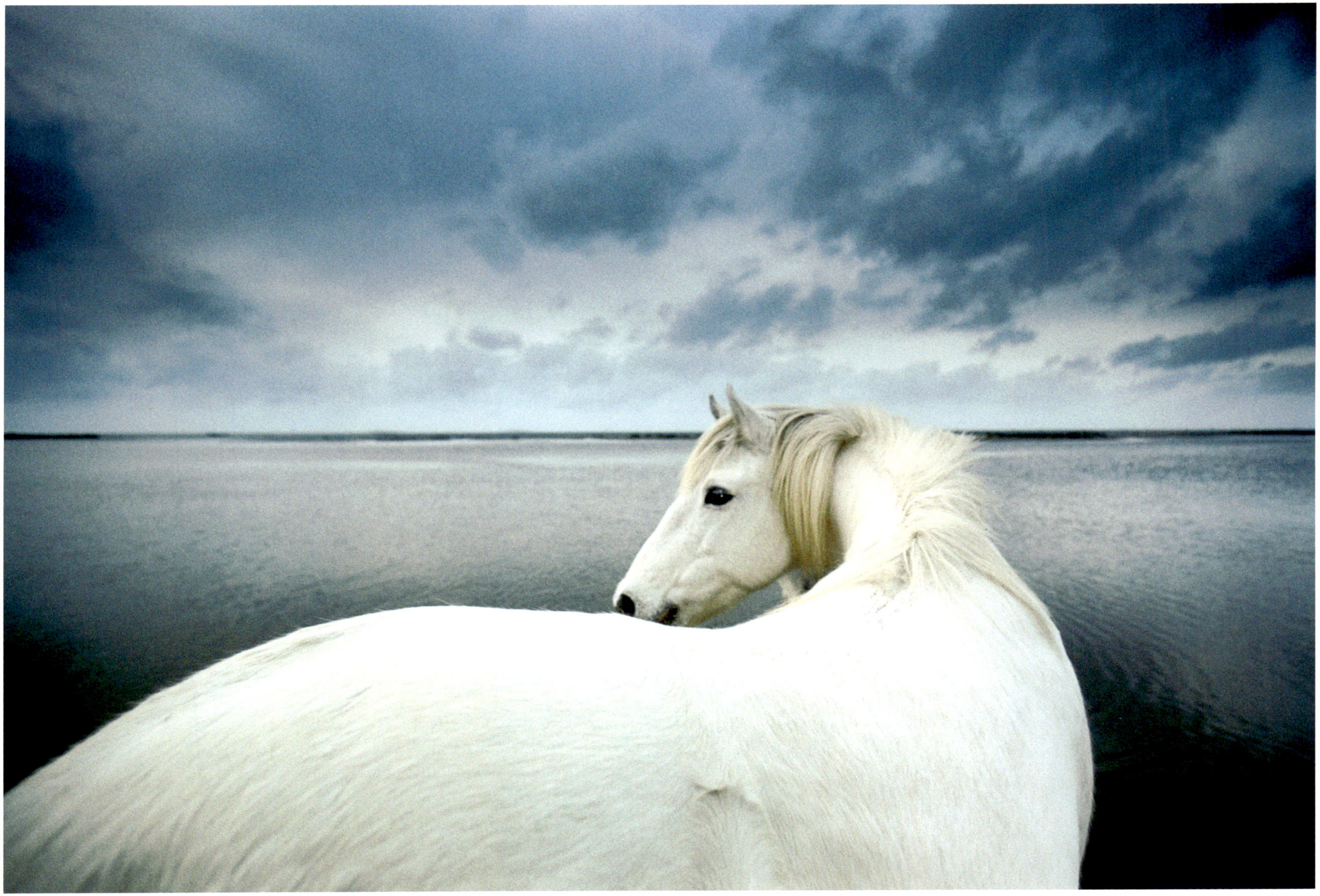

Camargue Horse, 2001, Camargue National Reserve, France

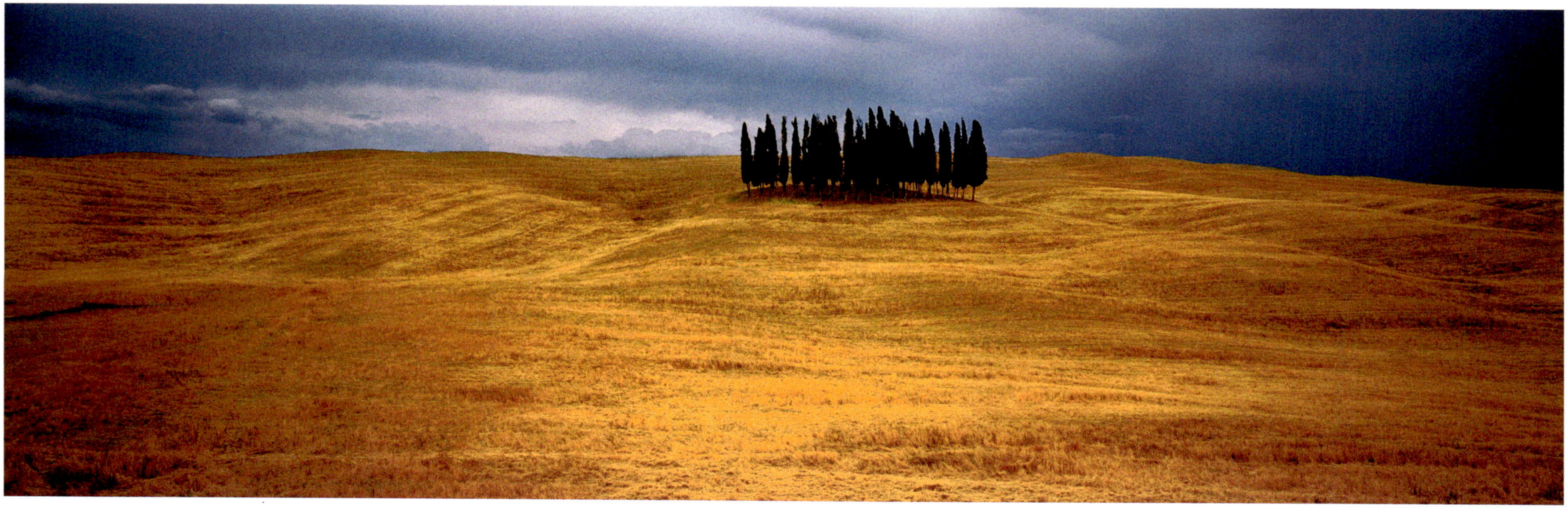

Cypress Stand, 2002, Tuscany, Italy

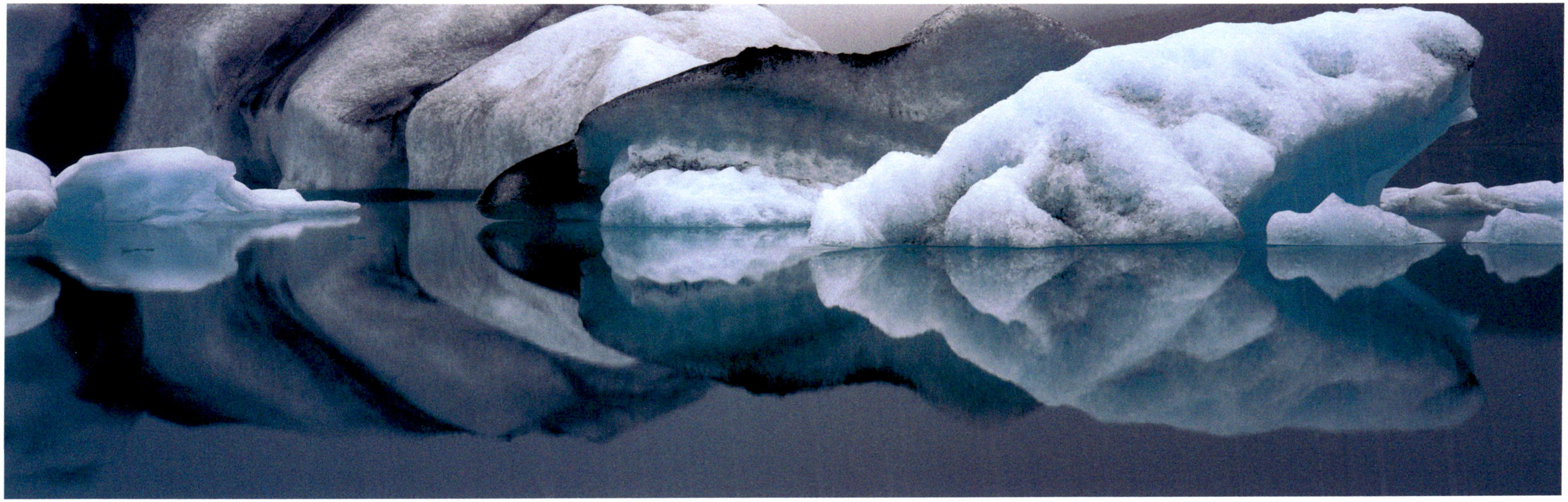

Icebergs, 1998, Jokulsarlon, Iceland

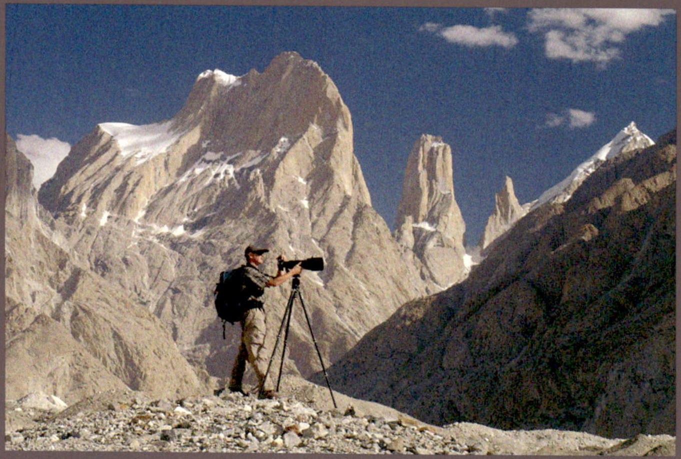

ASIA

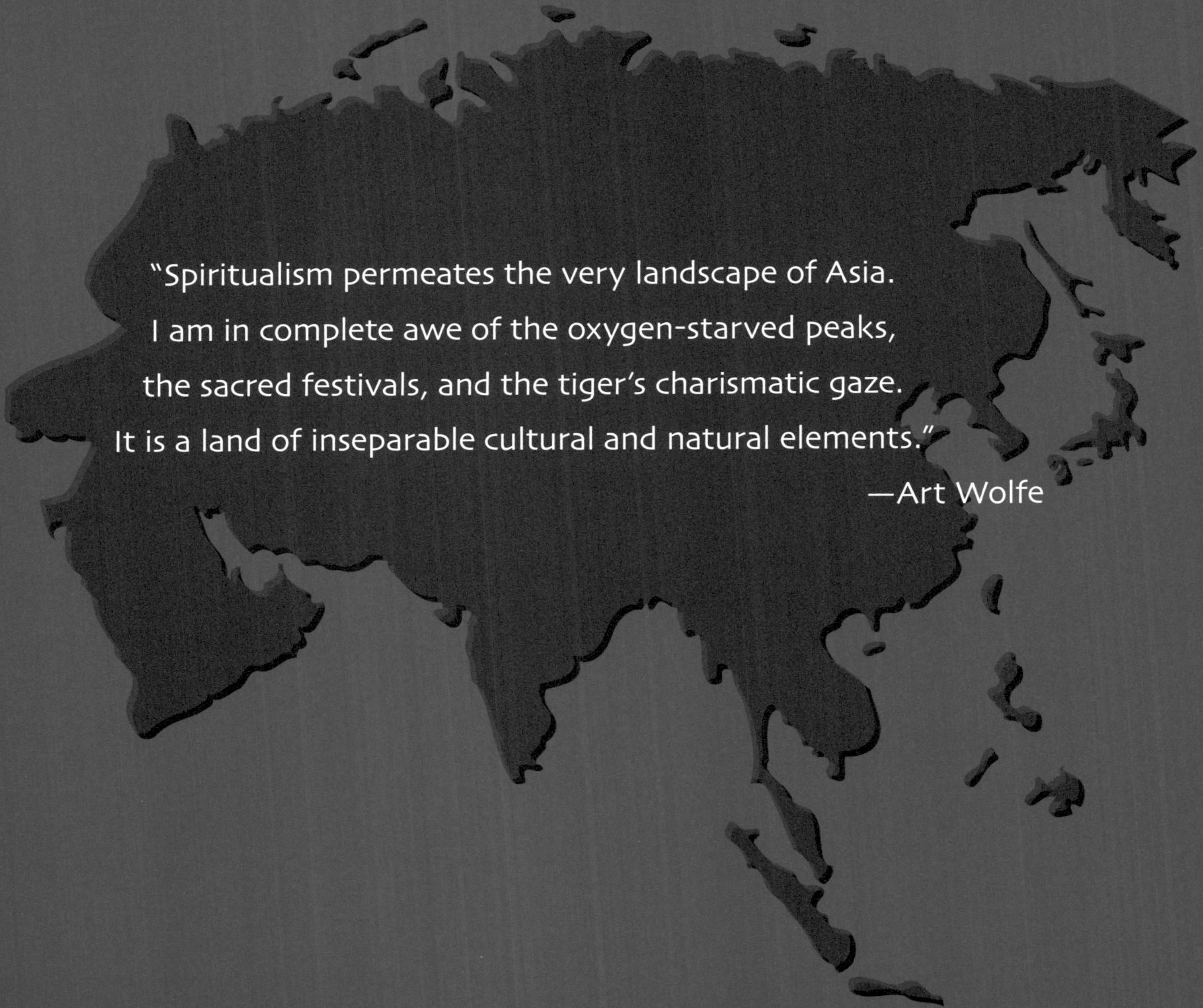

"Spiritualism permeates the very landscape of Asia.
I am in complete awe of the oxygen-starved peaks,
the sacred festivals, and the tiger's charismatic gaze.
It is a land of inseparable cultural and natural elements."

—Art Wolfe

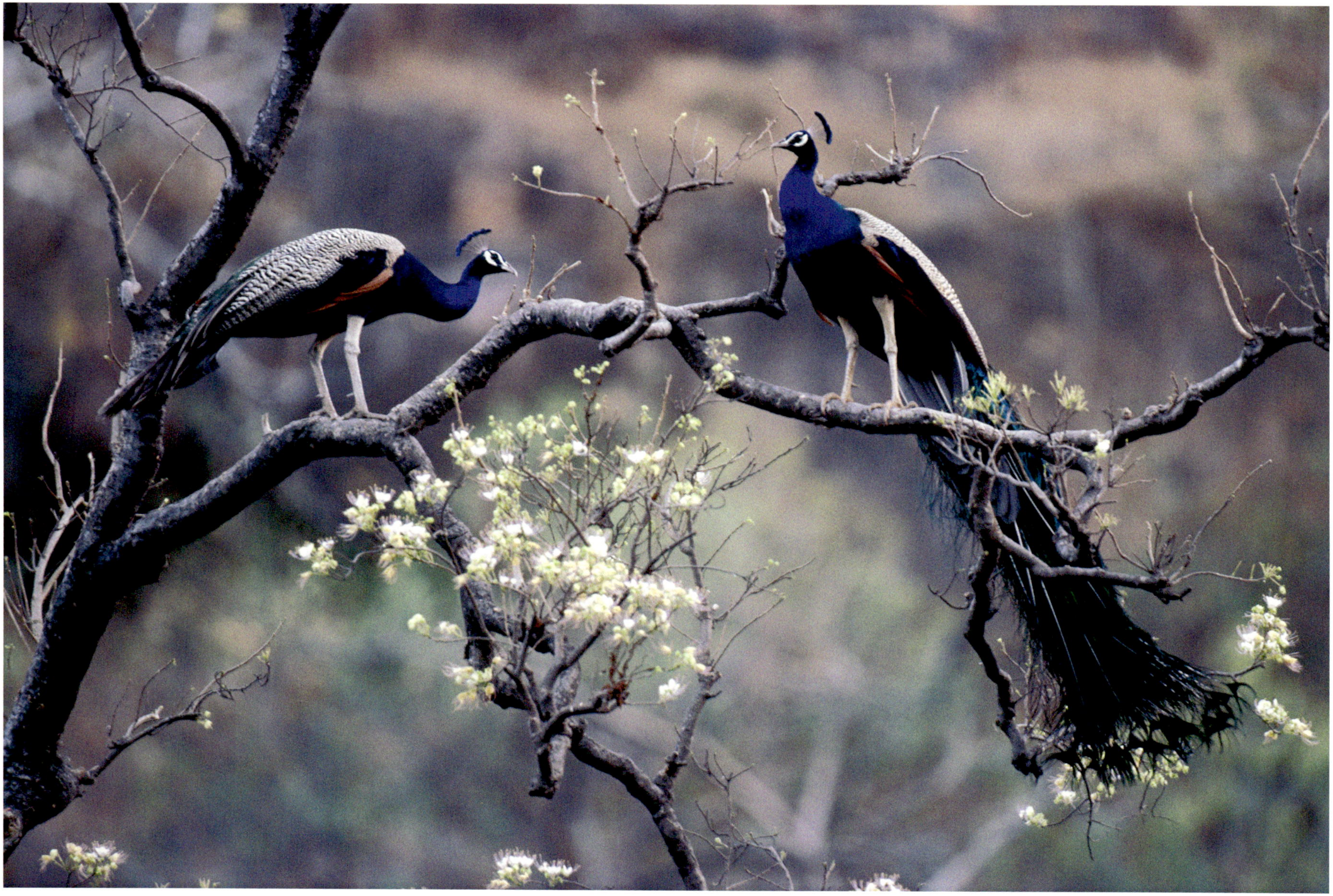

Indian Peafowl, 1999, Ranthambore National Park, Rajasthan, India

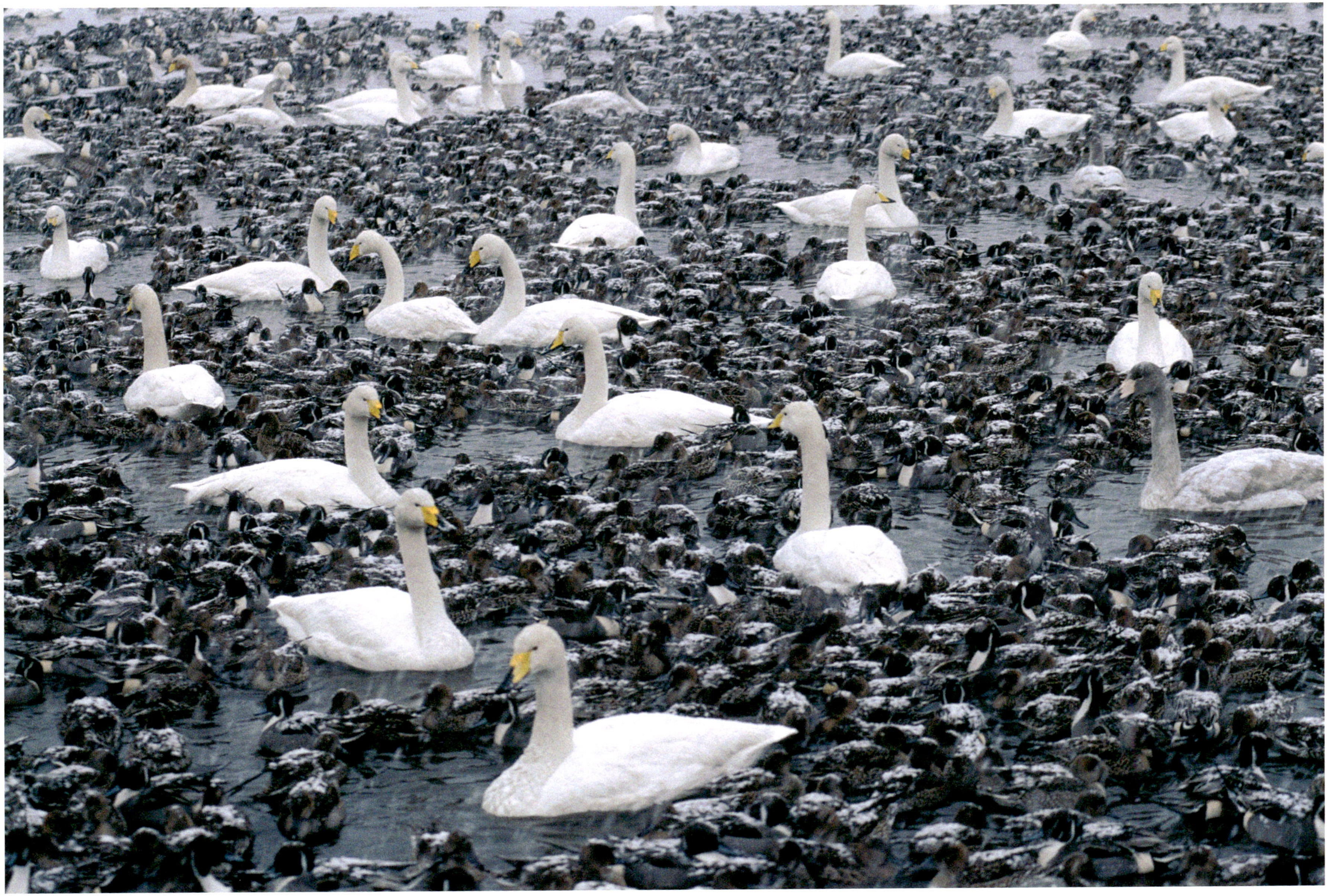

Whooper Swans and Northern Pintail Ducks, 1990, Hokkaido, Japan

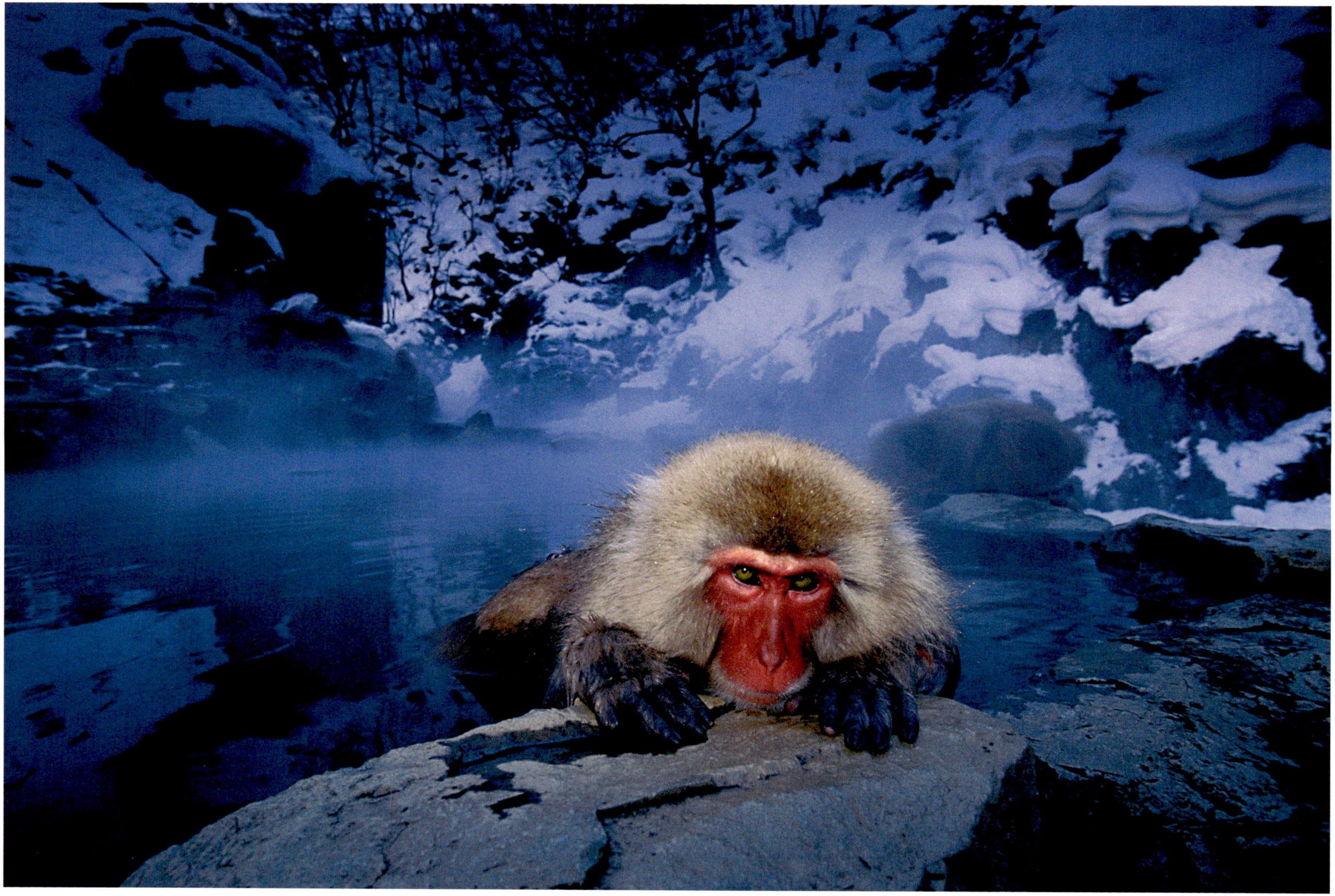

Japanese Macaque in Thermal Pool, 1999, Japanese Alps, Honshu Island, Japan

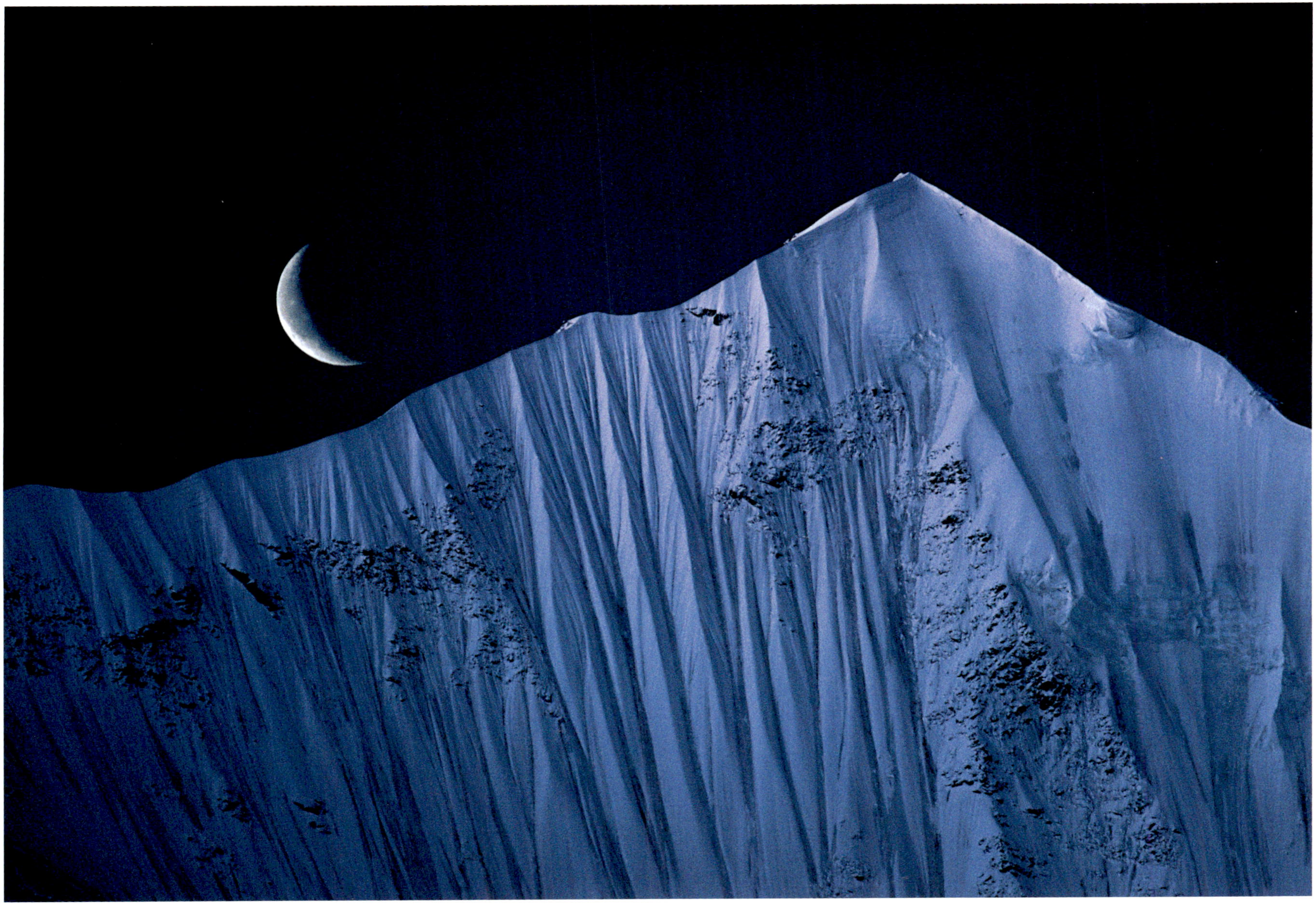

Moon over Lingtrin, 1984, Tibet, China

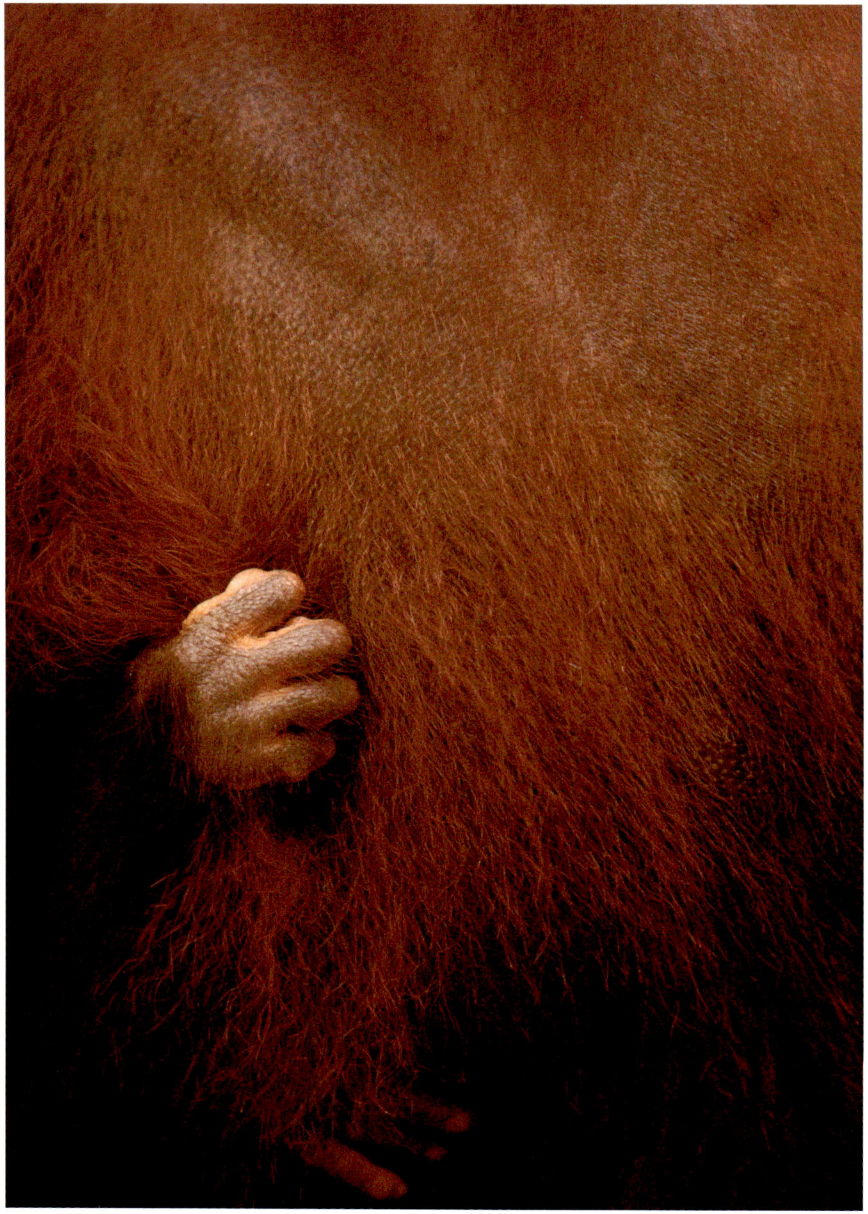

Baby Orangutan, 2000, Gunung Leuser National Park, Sumatra, Indonesia

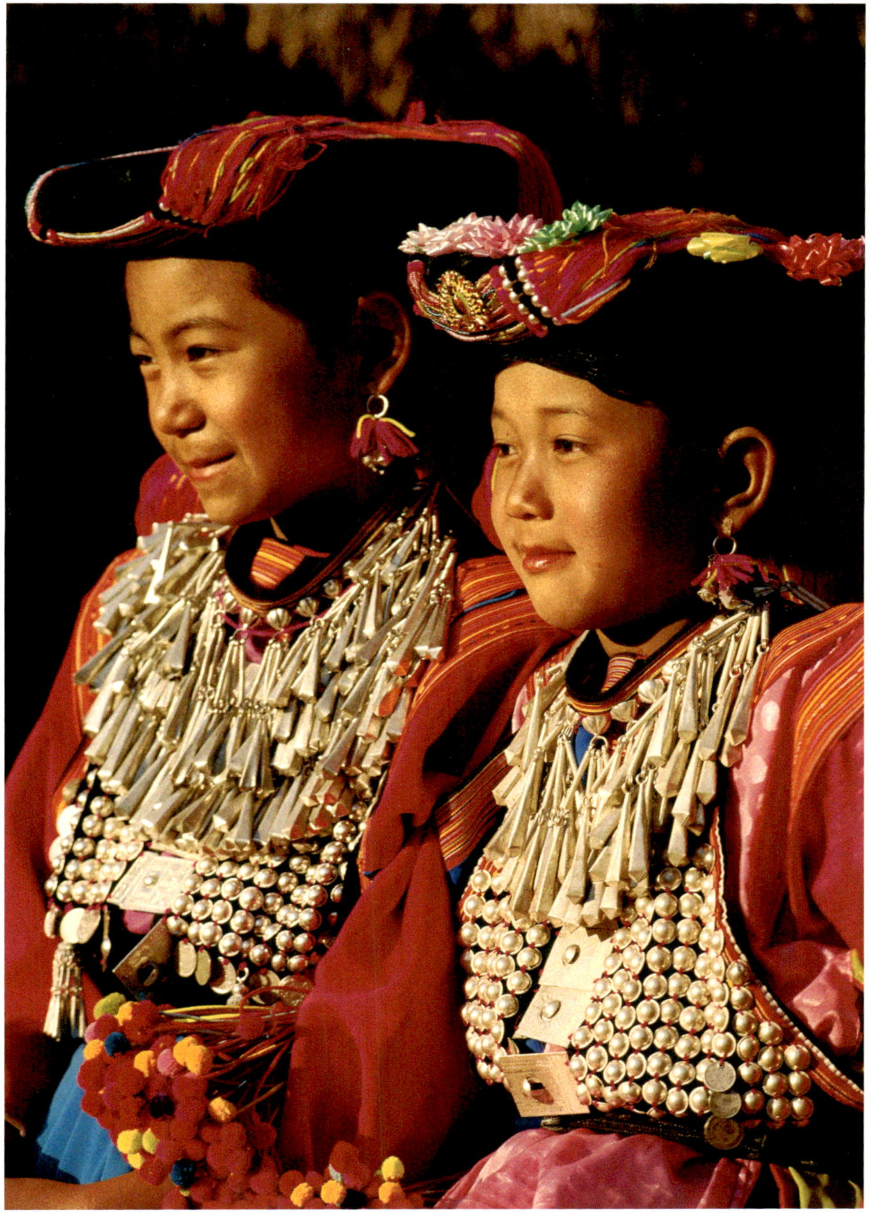

Lisu Girls, 1995, Doichang Village, Thailand

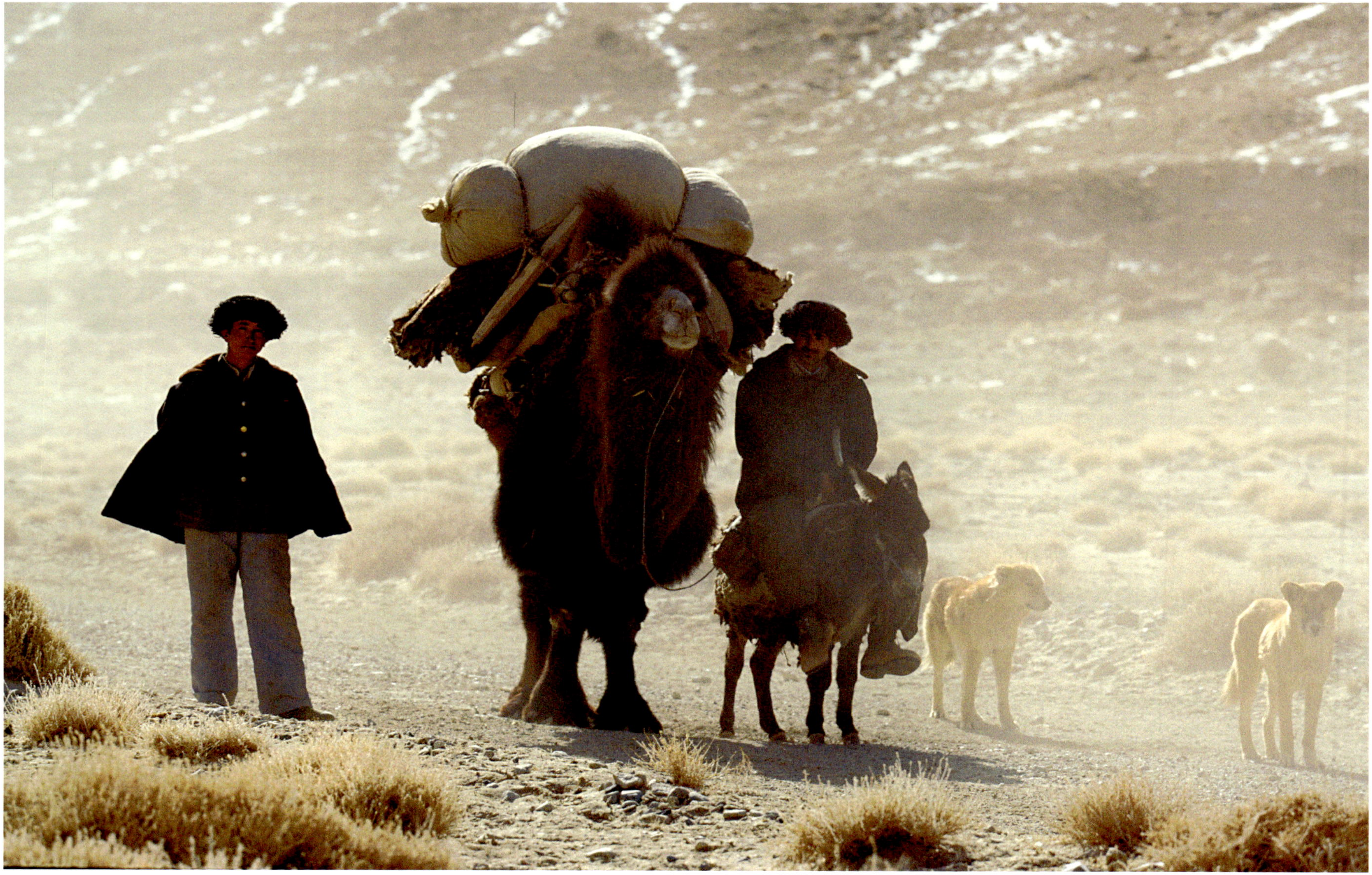

High Country Herders, 1990, Pamir Plateau, China

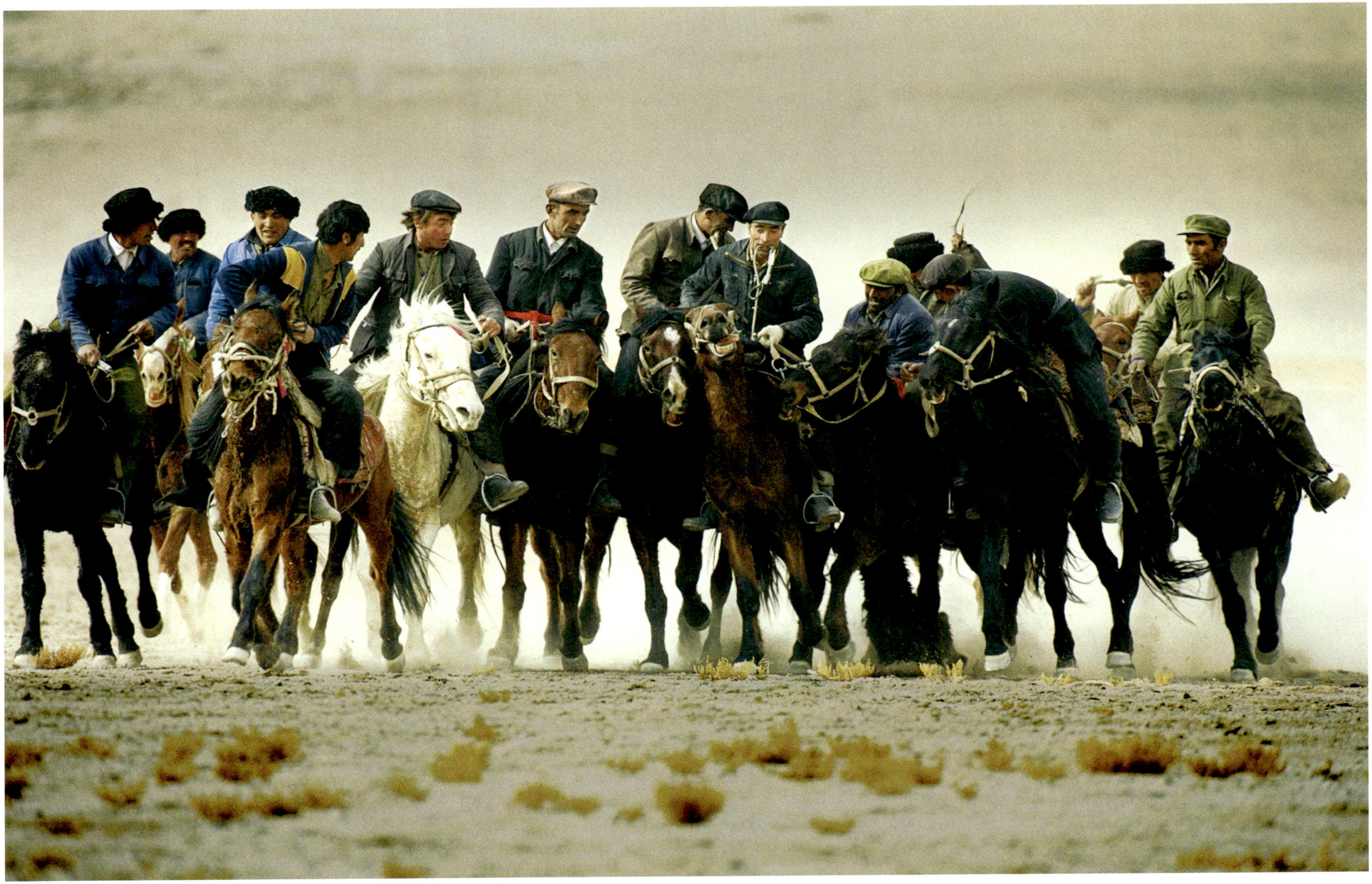

Kazakhs Playing Buzkashi, 1990, Pamir Plateau, China

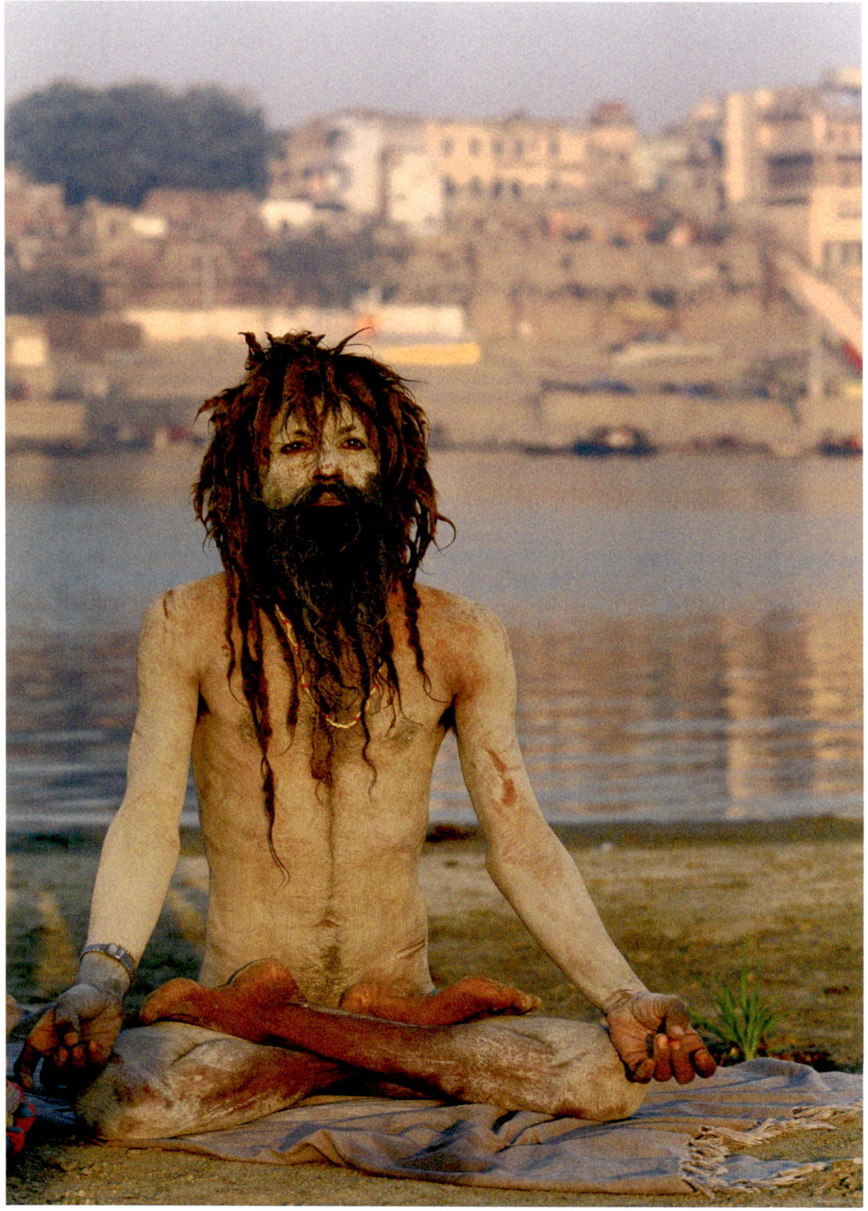

Naga Sadhu, 2001, Varanasi, Uttar Pradesh, India

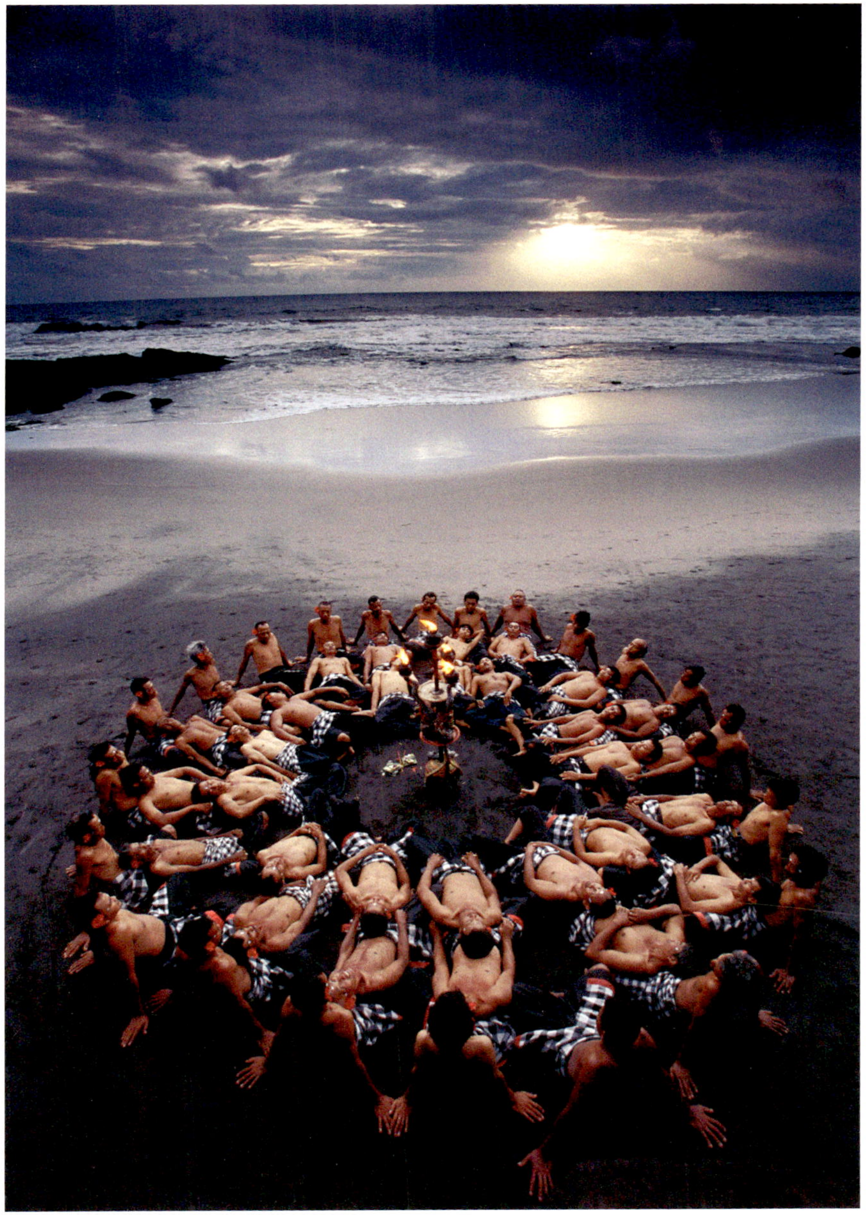

Kecak Dance, 2000, Bali, Indonesia

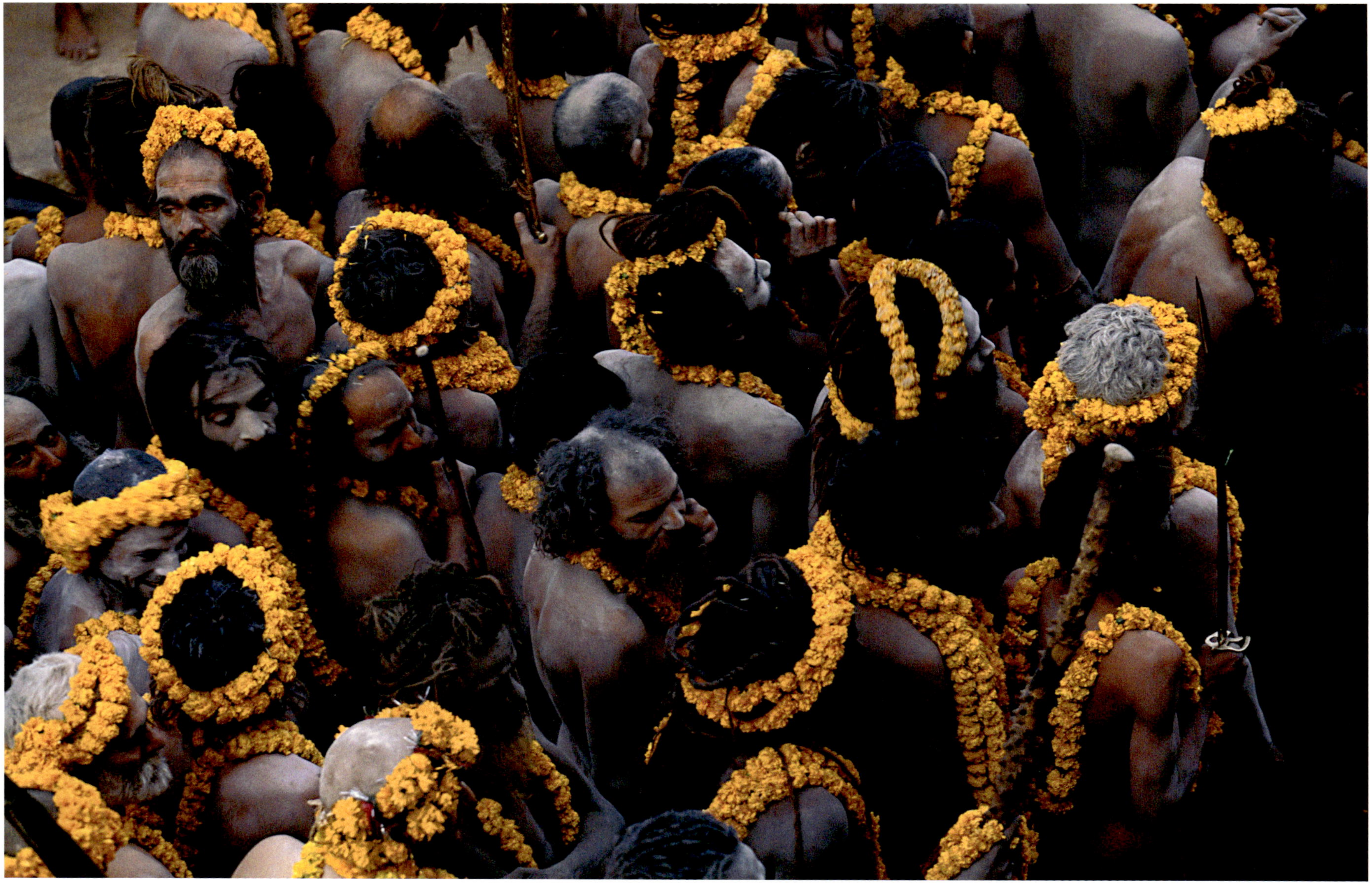

Procession of Naga Sadhus, 2001, Varanasi, Uttar Pradesh, India

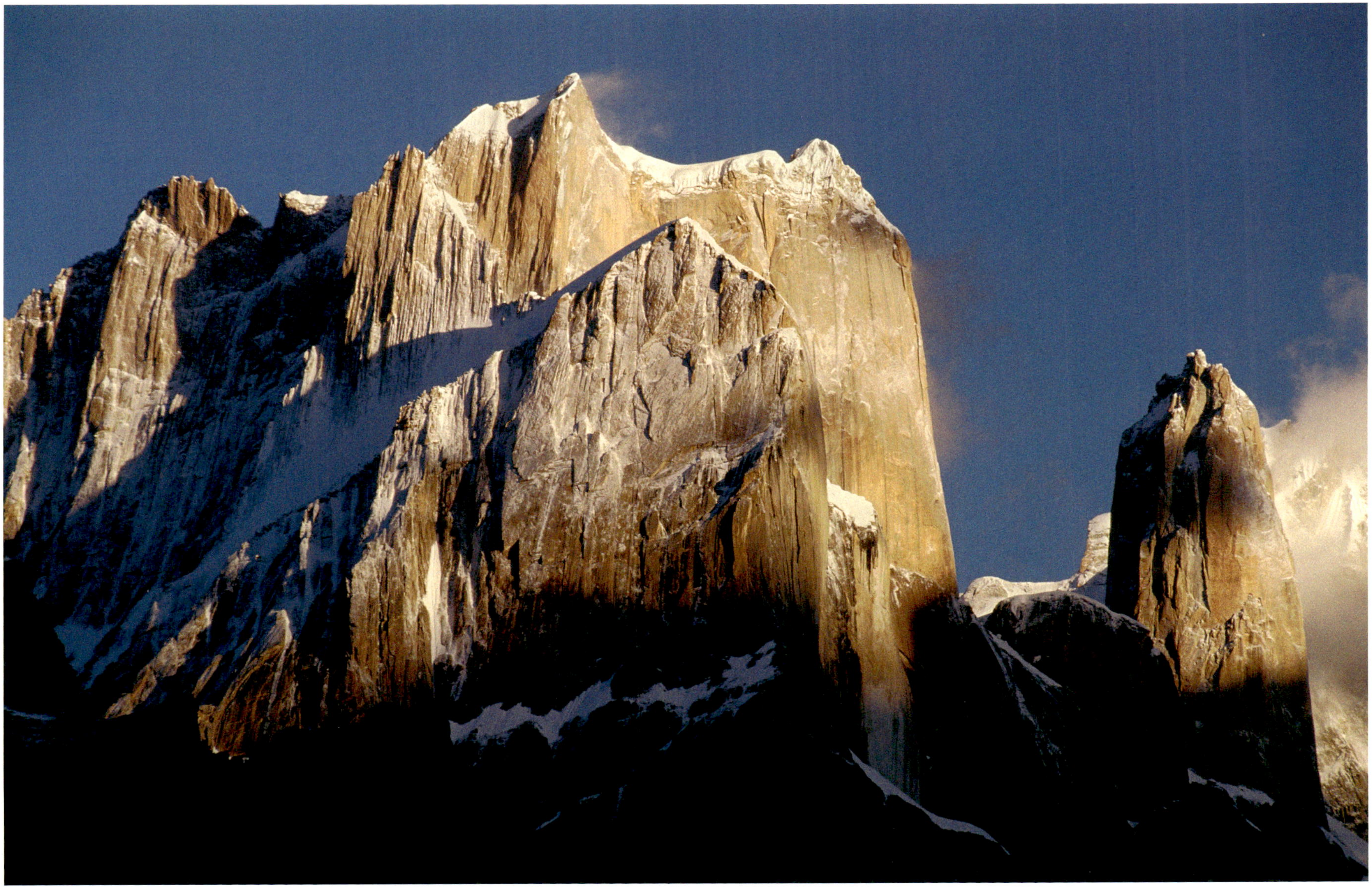

Great Trango Tower, 1996, Baltoro Muztagh Range, Pakistan

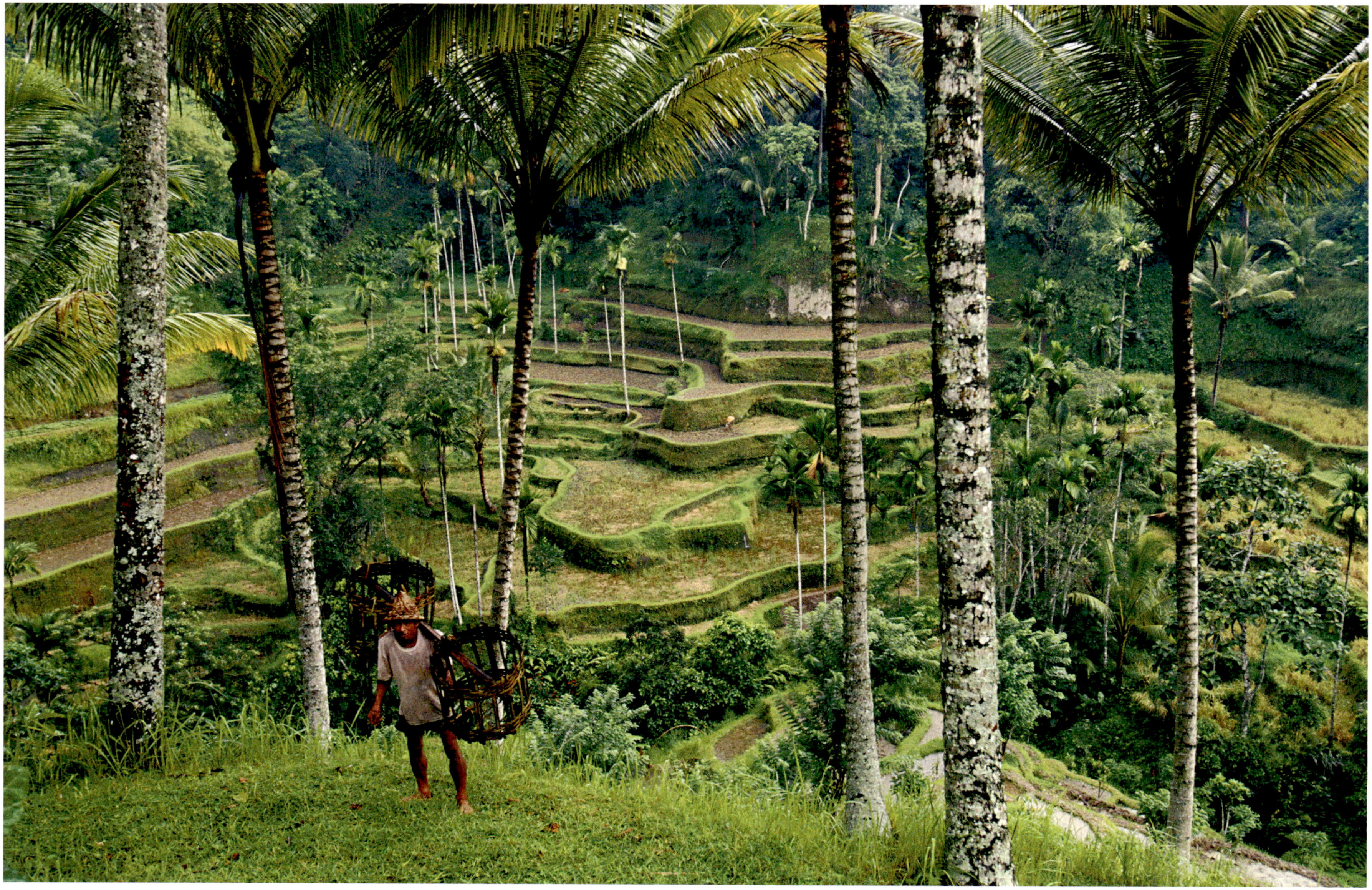

Terraces, 1995, Bali, Indonesia

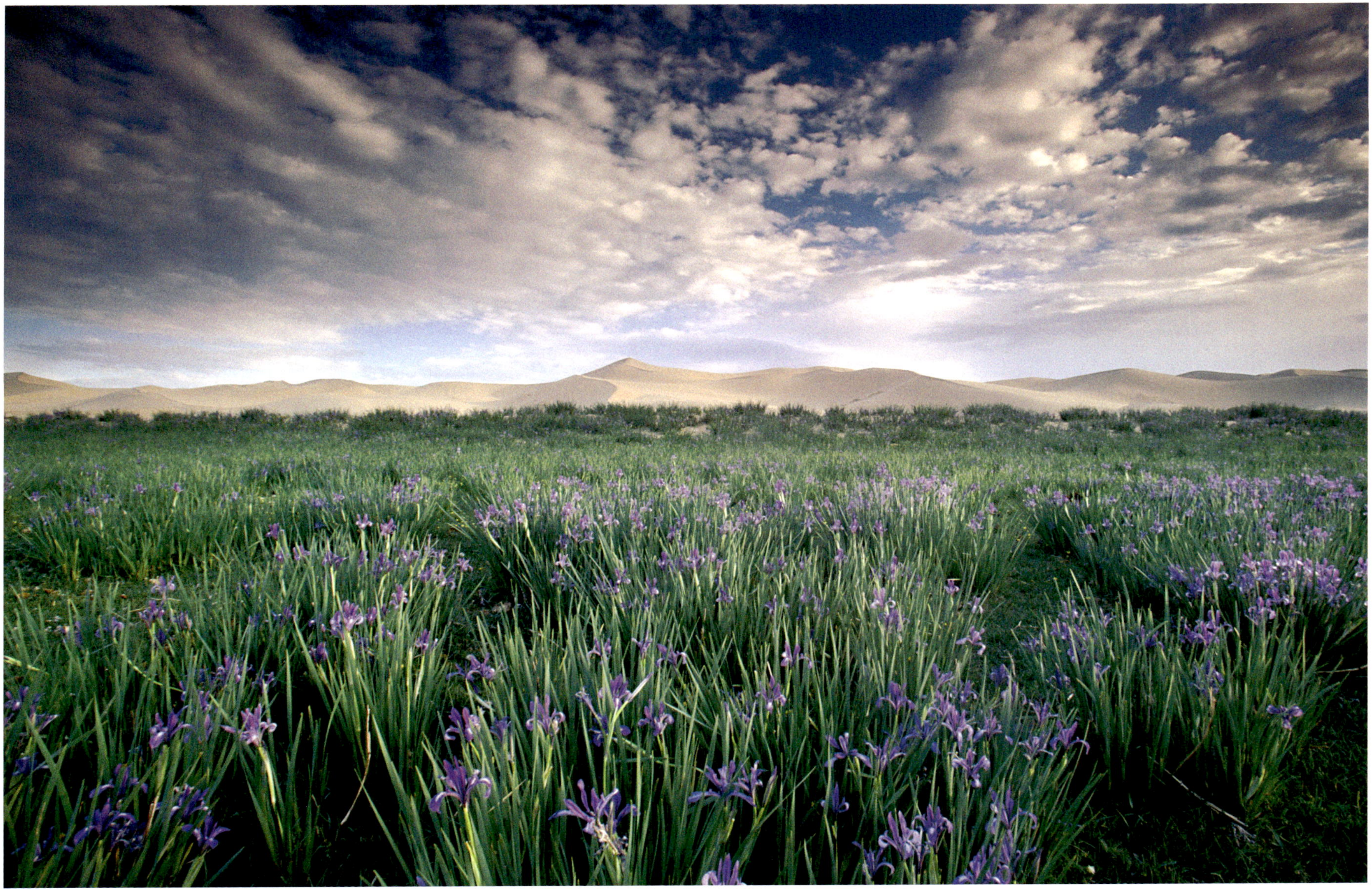

Siberian Iris, 1998, Gurvansaikhan National Park, Mongolia

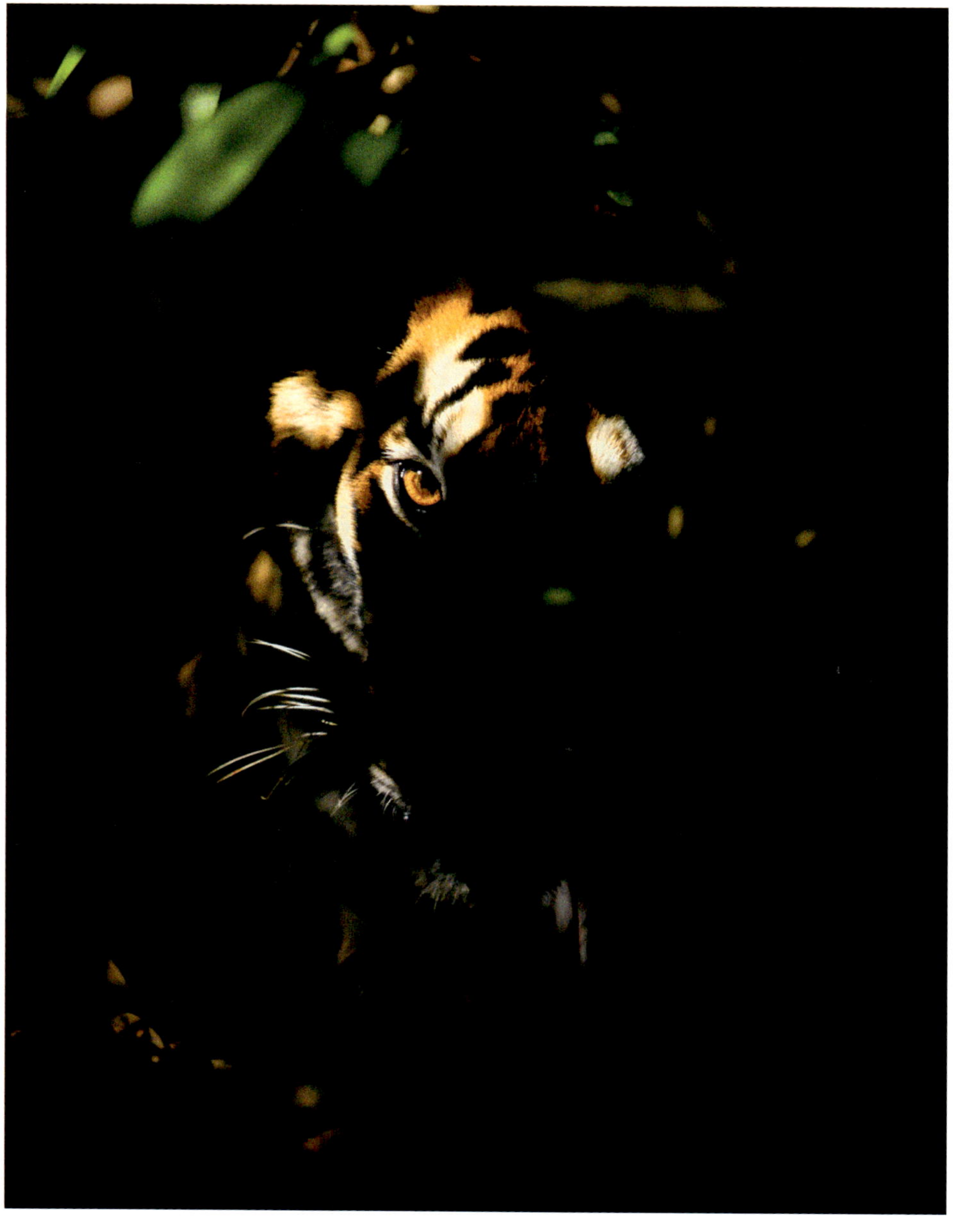

Bengal Tiger, 1999, Kanha National Park, Madhaya Pradesh, India

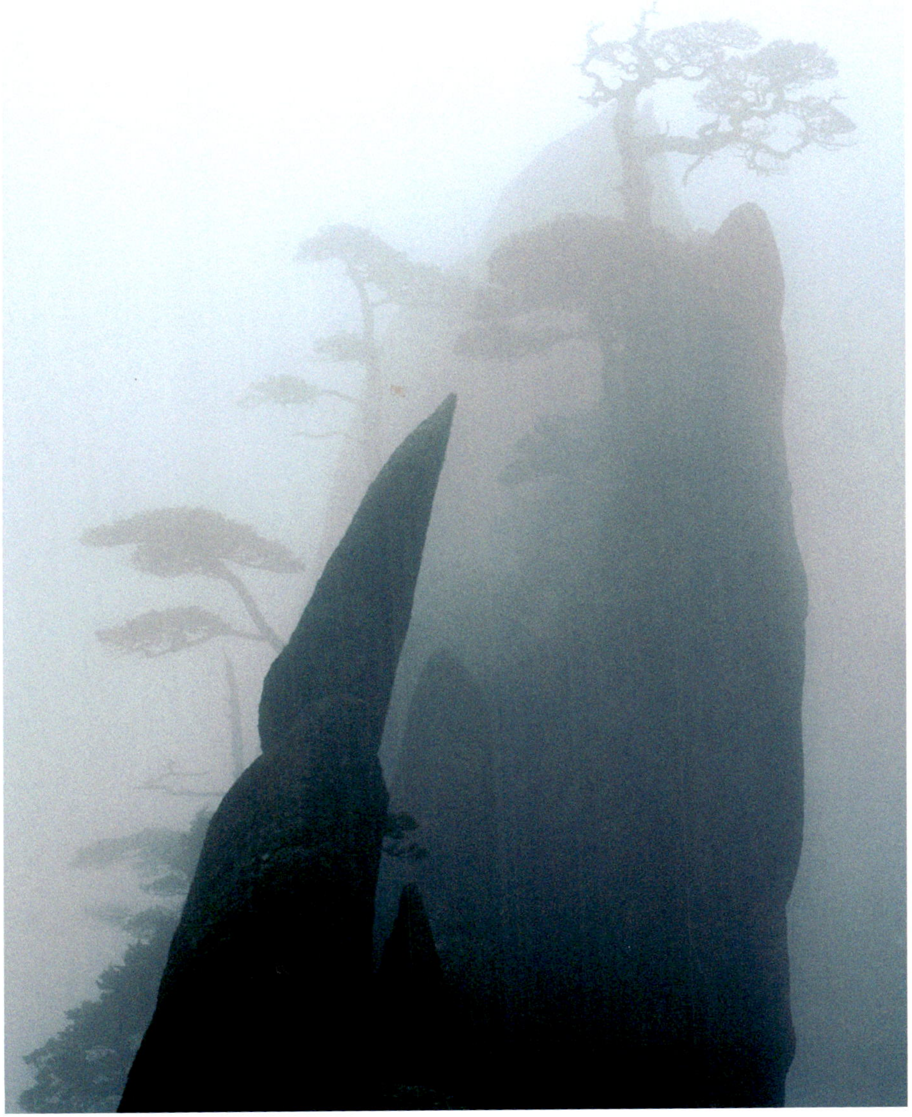

Huanshan, 1986, Anhui Province, China

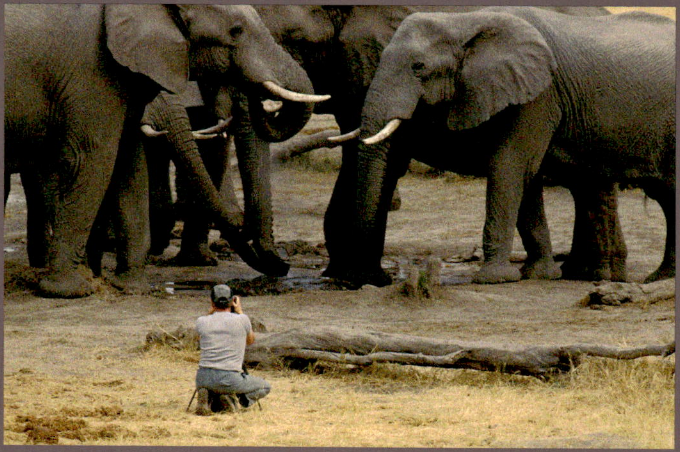

AFRICA

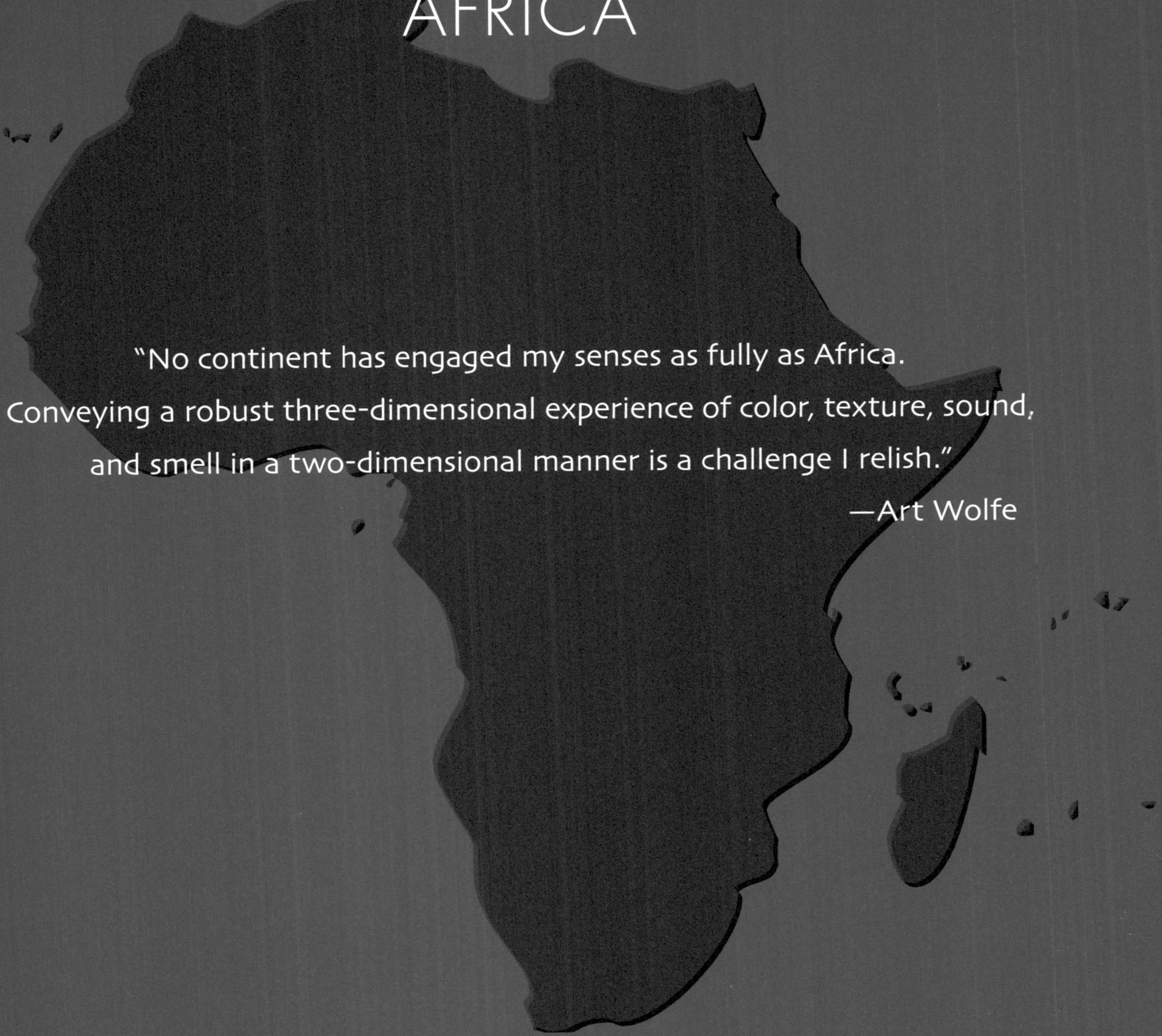

"No continent has engaged my senses as fully as Africa. Conveying a robust three-dimensional experience of color, texture, sound, and smell in a two-dimensional manner is a challenge I relish."

—Art Wolfe

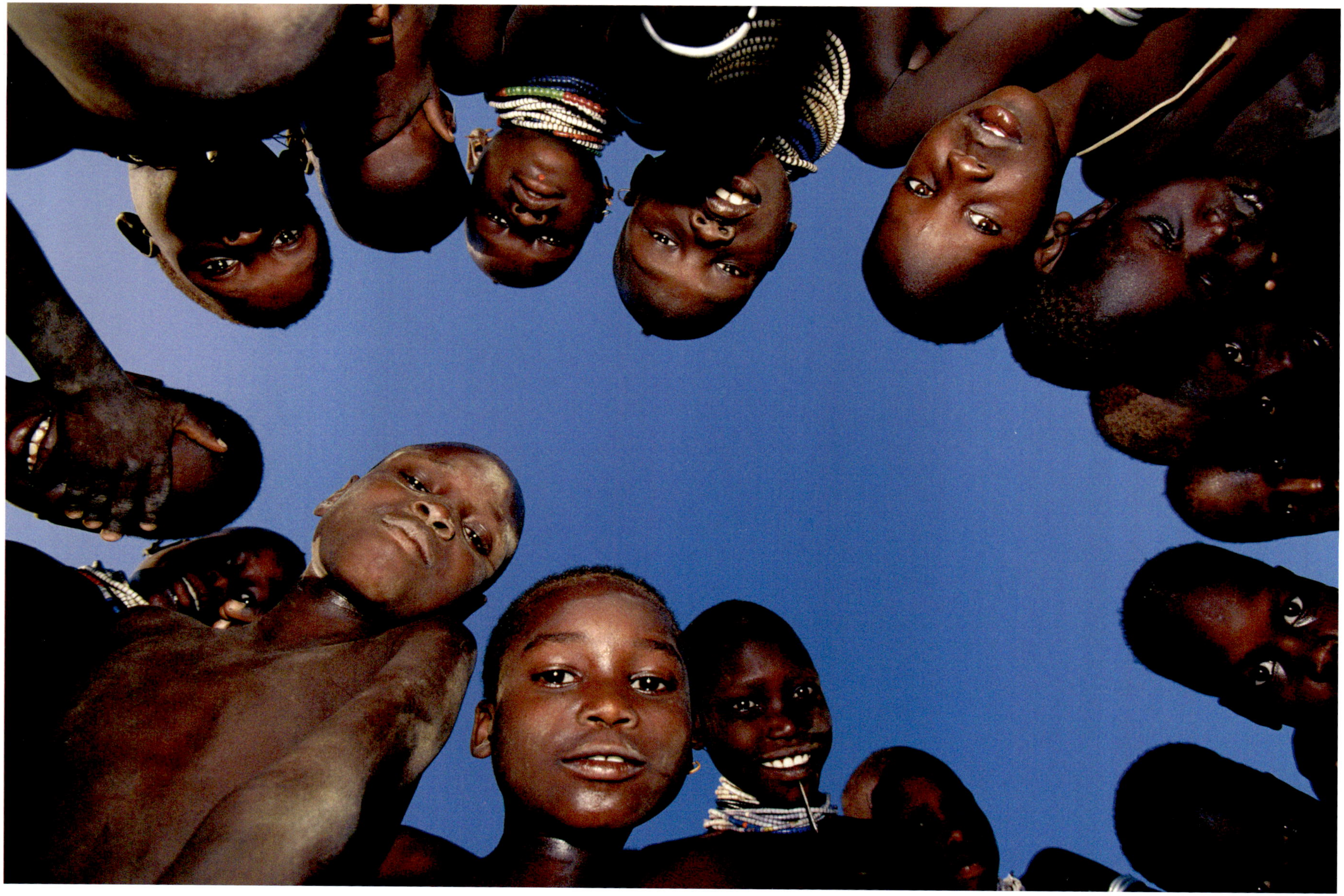

Bumi Children, 1995, Lower Omo River, Ethiopia

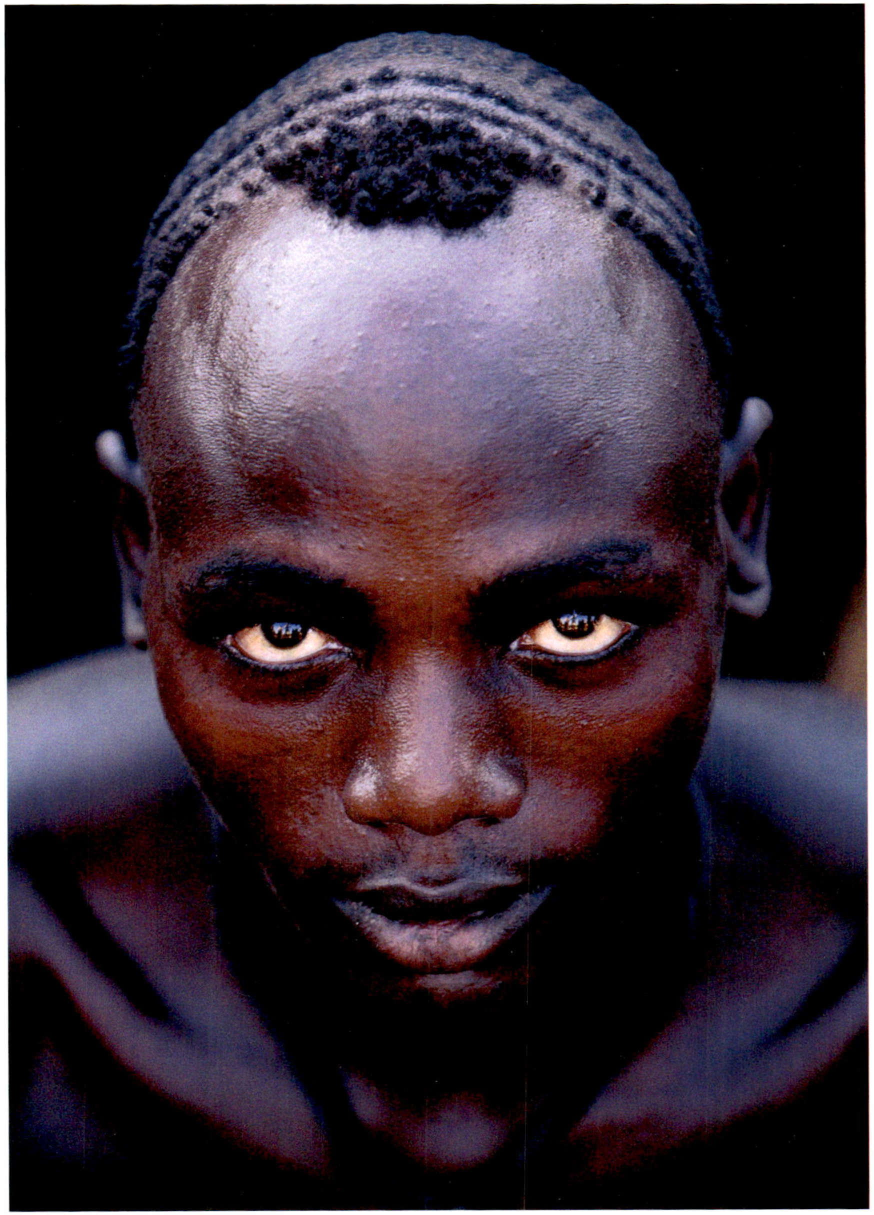

Mursi Man, 1995, Lower Omo River, Ethiopia

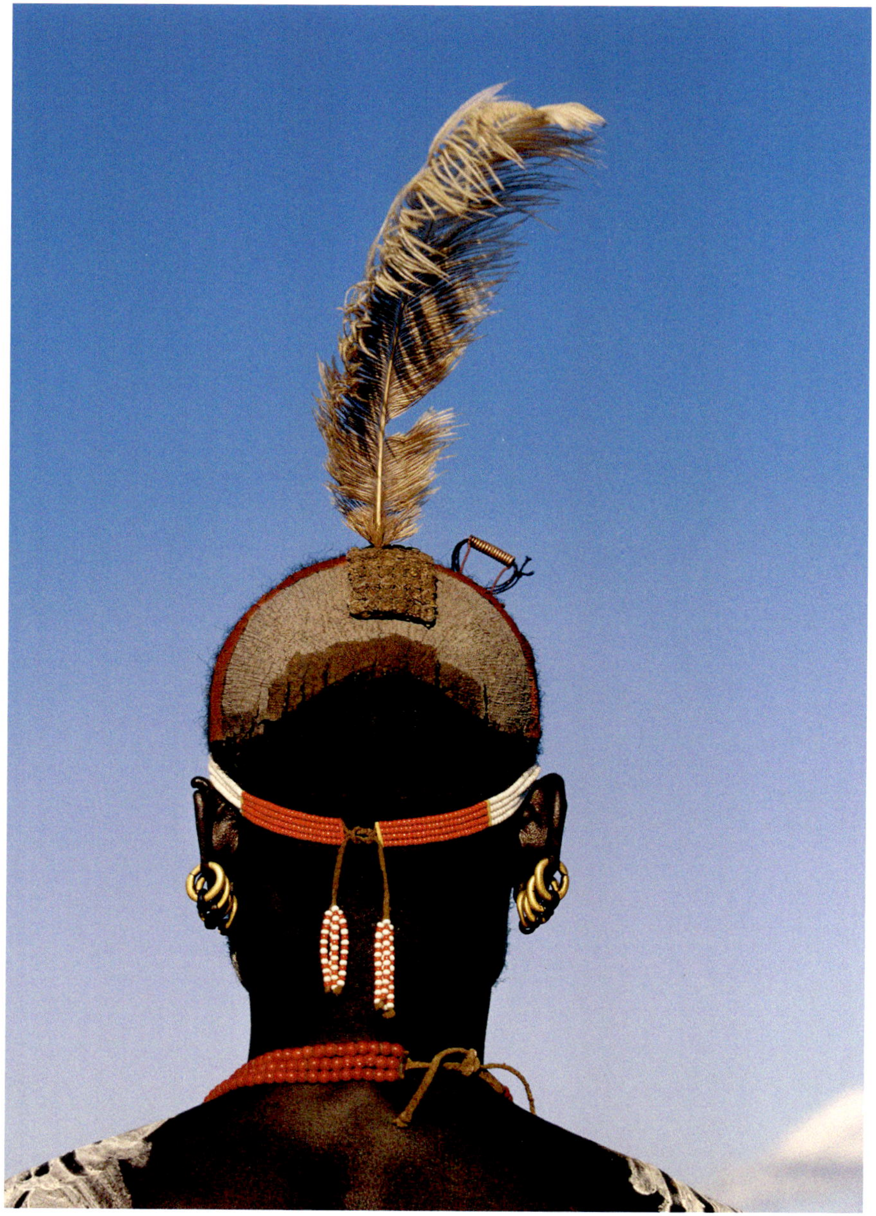

Karo Man, 1995, Lower Omo River, Ethiopia

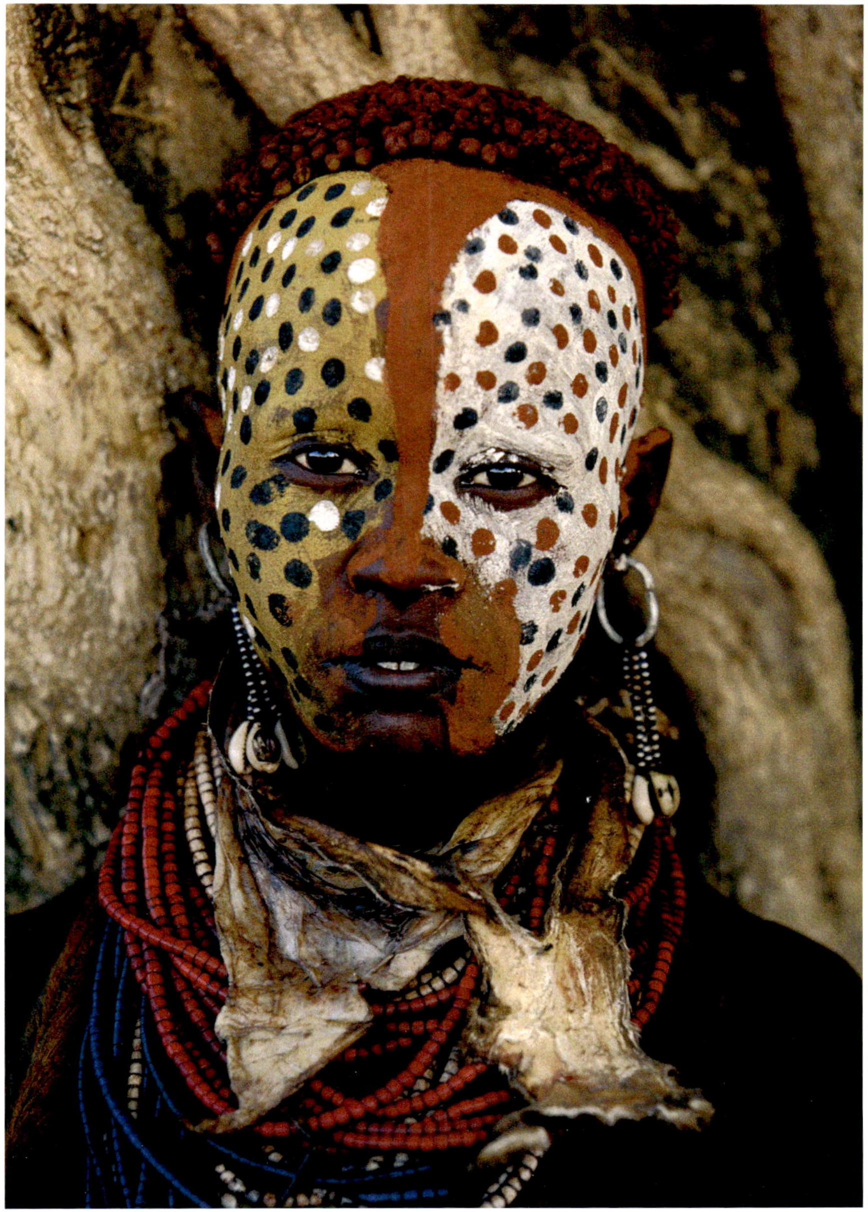

Karo Woman, 1995, Lower Omo River, Ethiopia

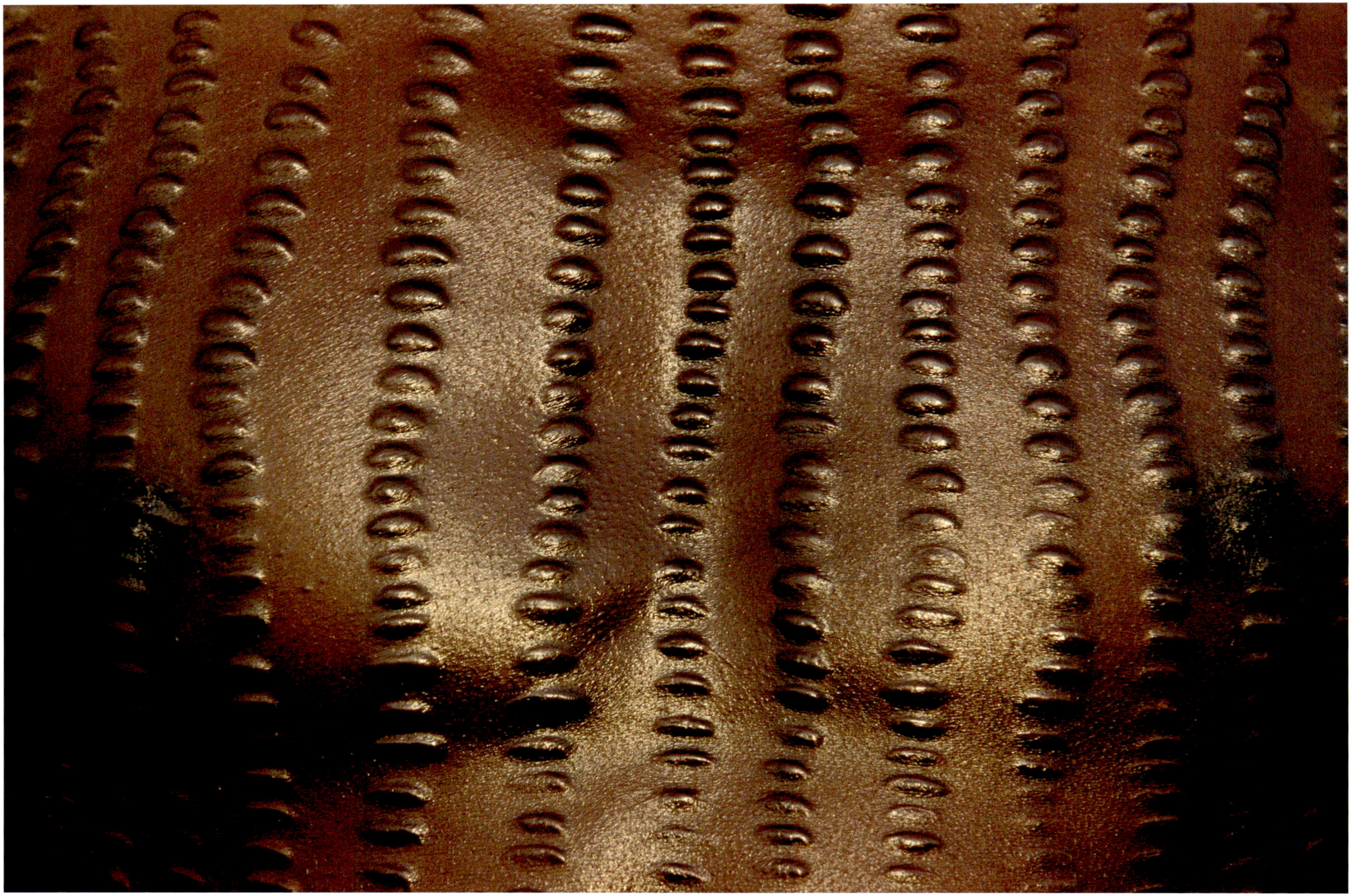

Bumi Male Scarification, 1995, Lower Omo River, Ethiopia

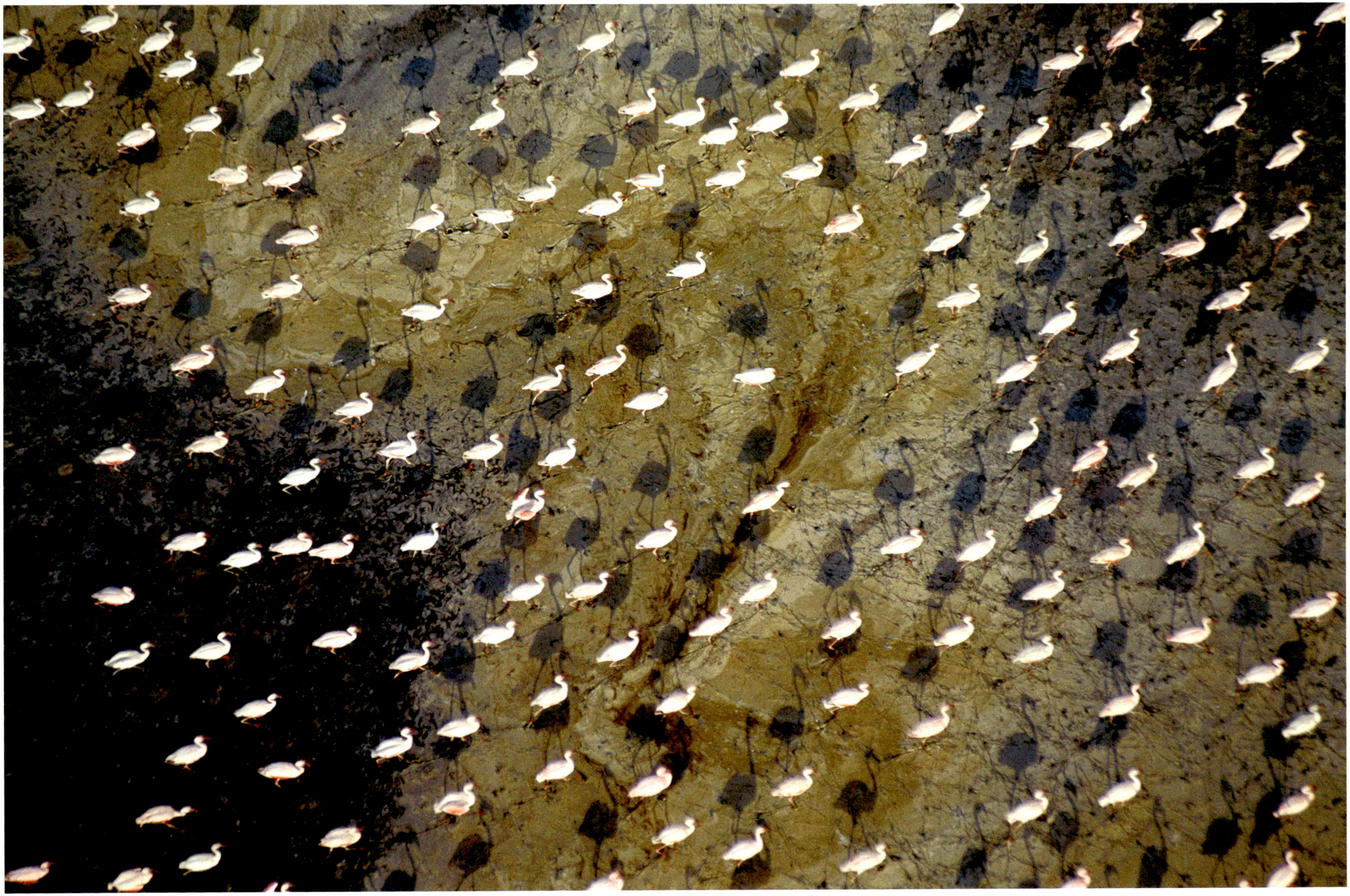

Lesser Flamingos, 1993, Lake Magadi, Kenya

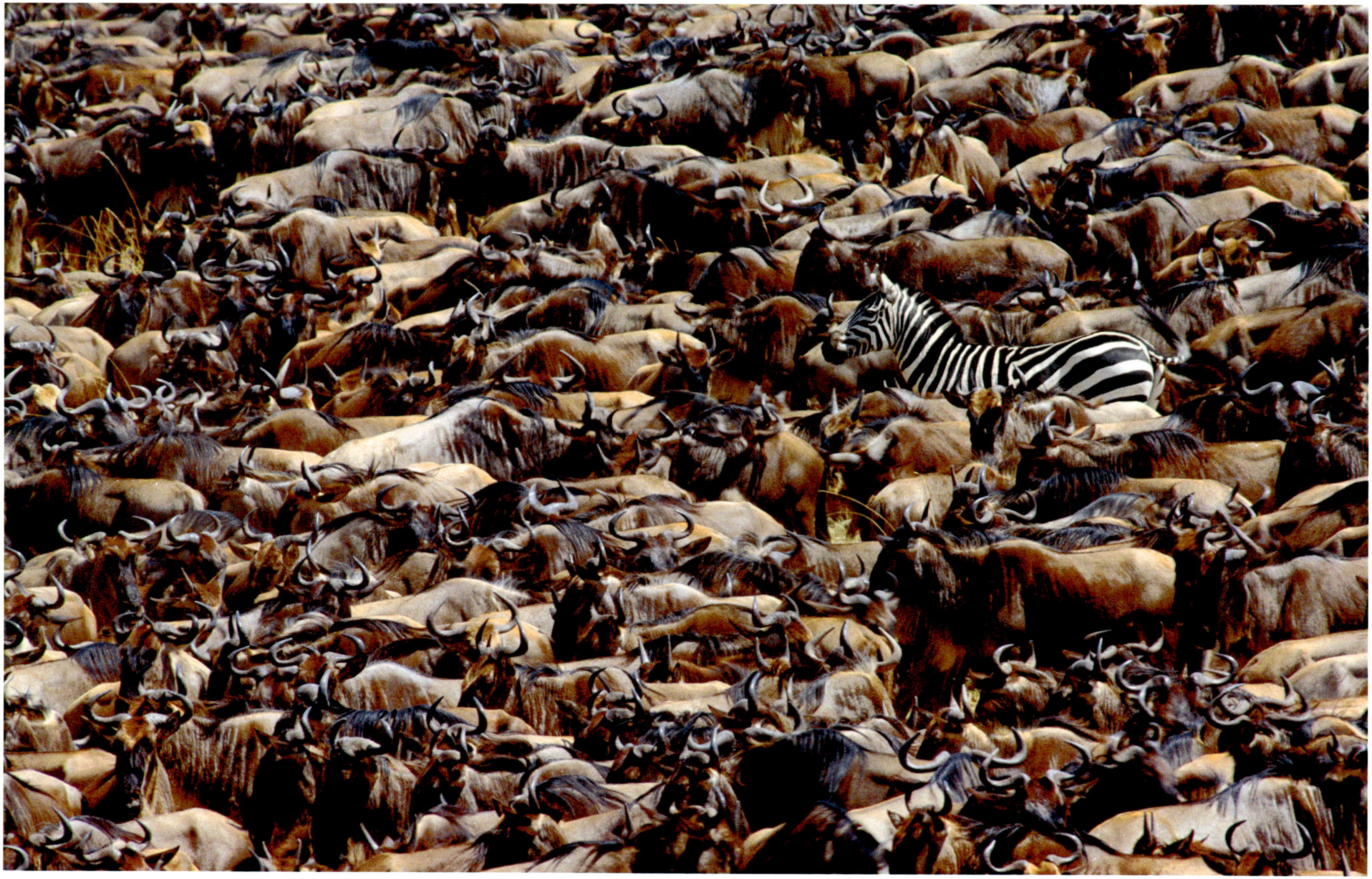

Zebra Amidst Wildebeest Herd, 1992, Masai Mara National Reserve, Kenya

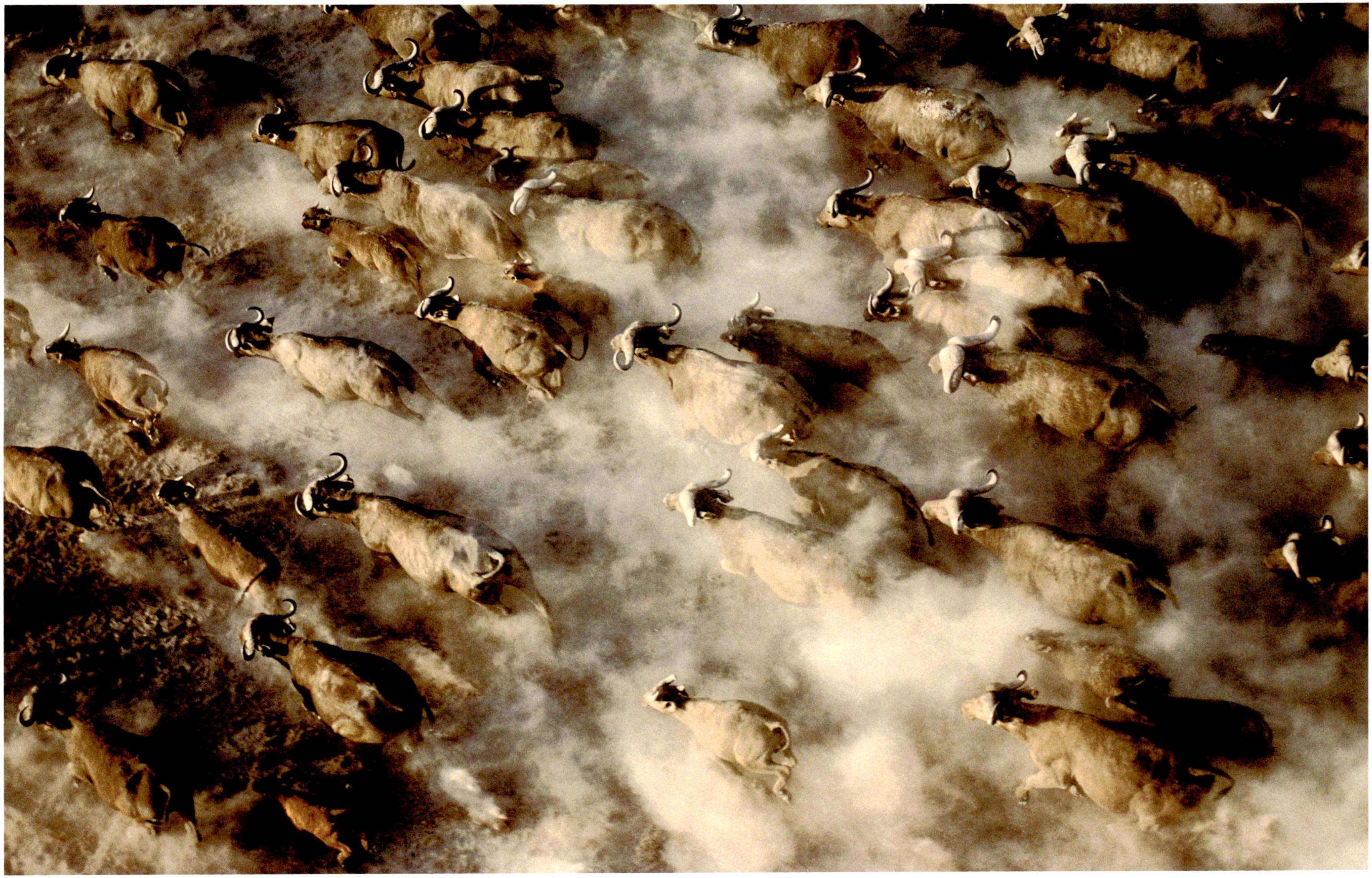

African Buffalo, 1993, Amboseli National Park, Kenya

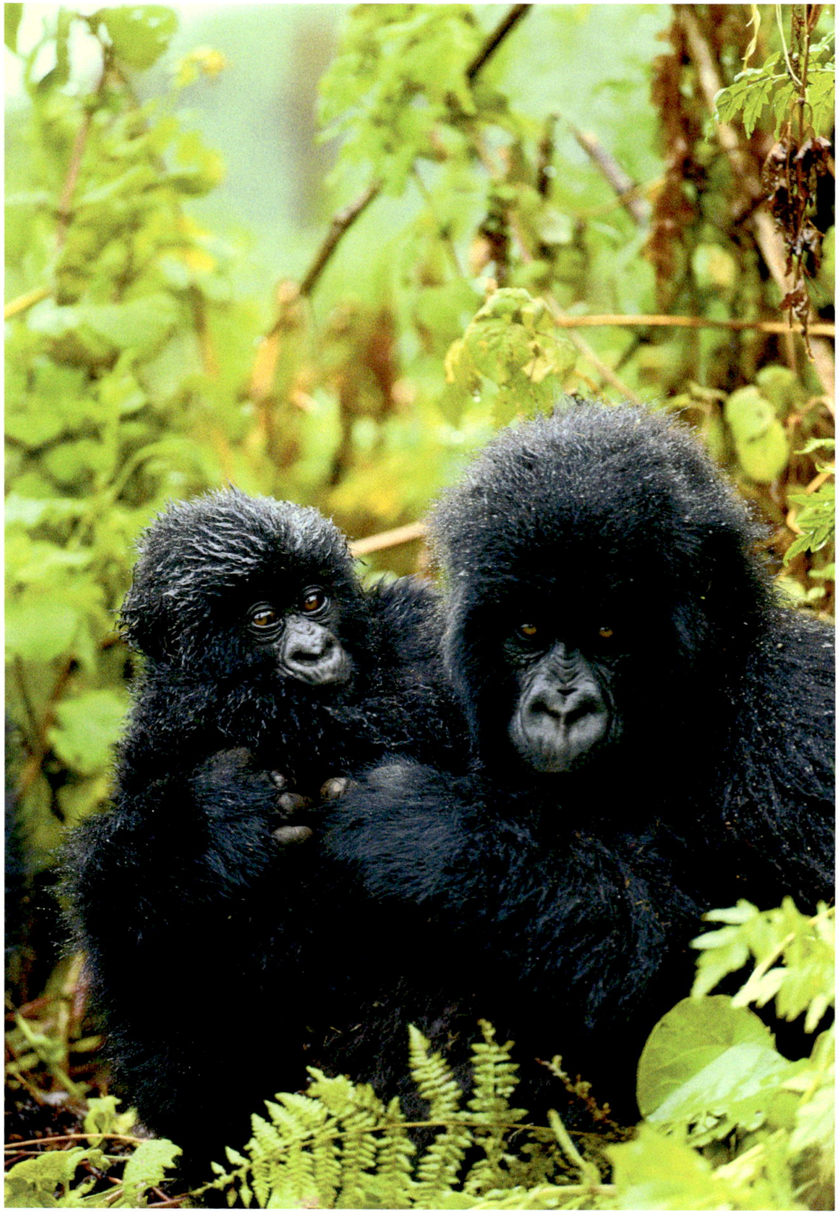

Mountain Gorilla and Baby, 1992, Parc National des Volcans, Rwanda

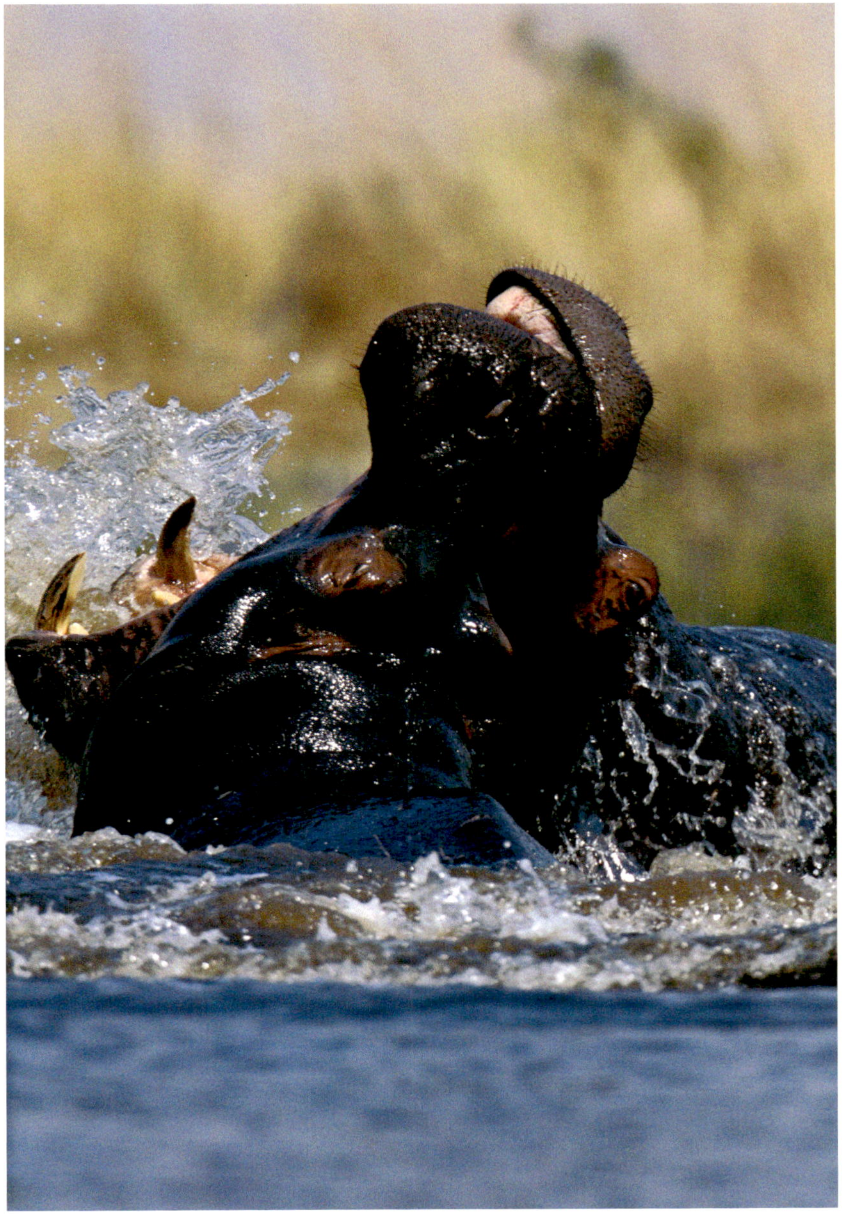

Hippopotamuses in Territorial Dispute, 2001, Okavango Delta, Botswana

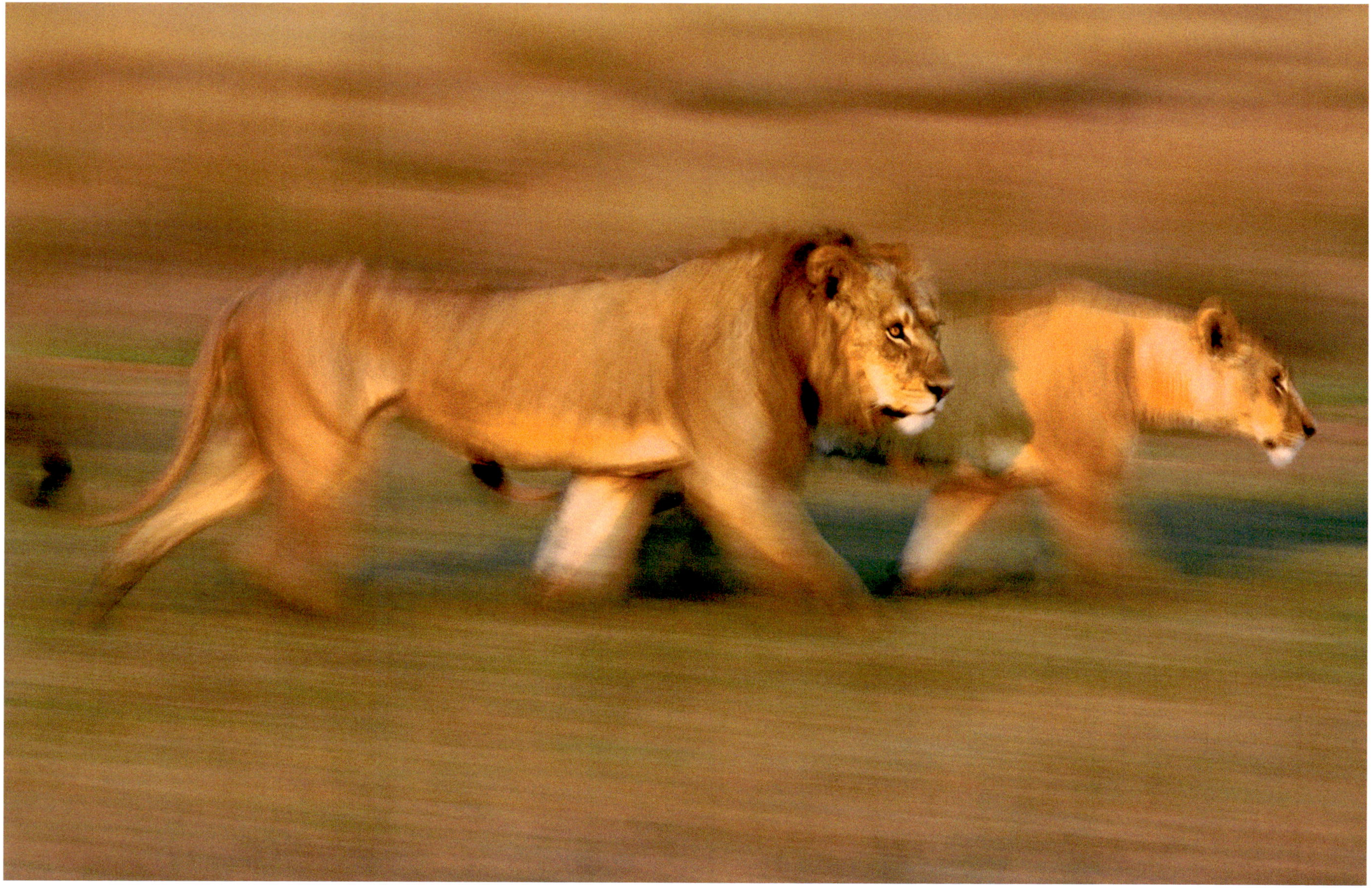

Lion Pair, 2001, Okavango Delta, Botswana

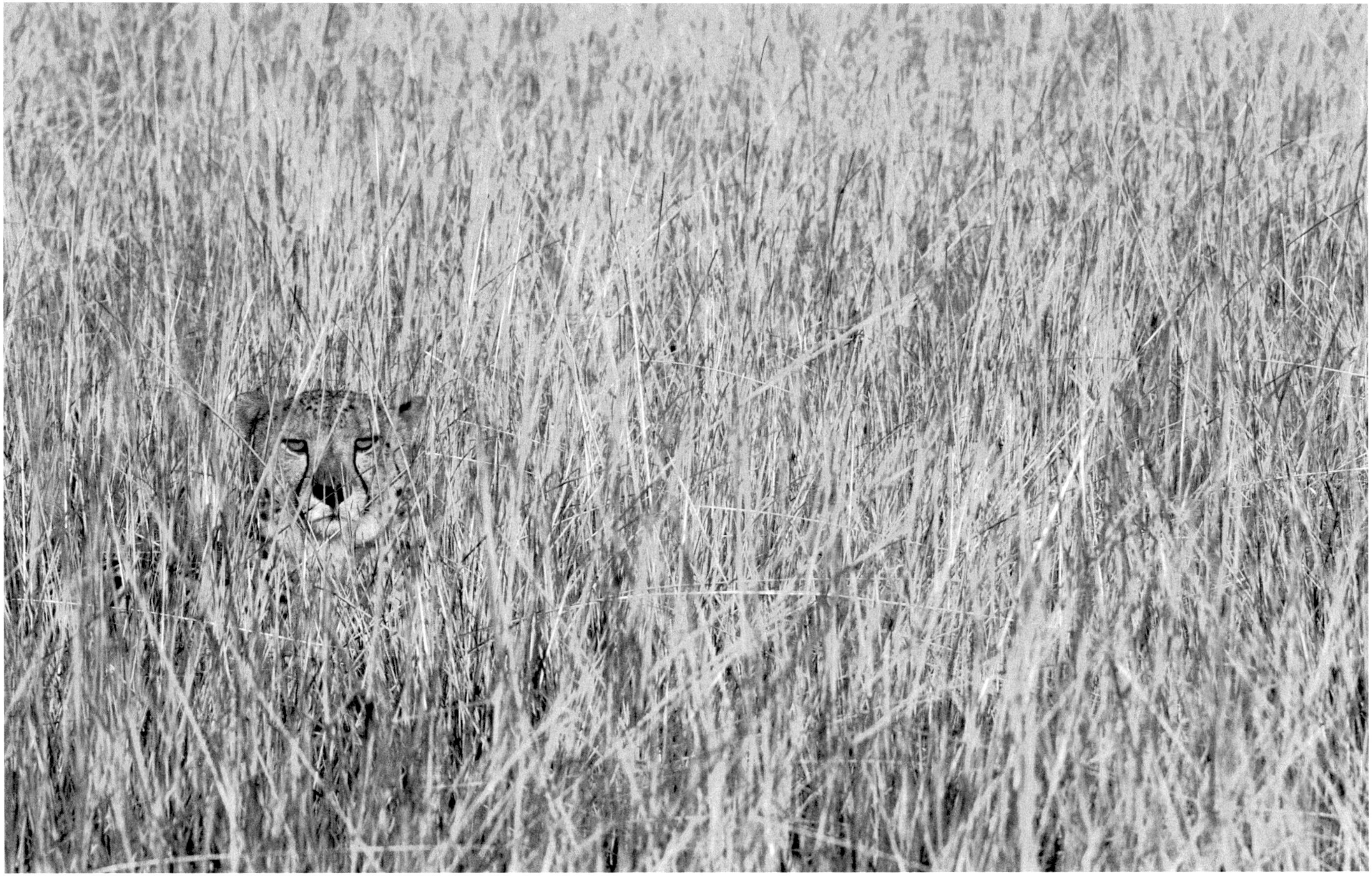

Cheetah in Grass, 1997, Phinda Reserve, South Africa

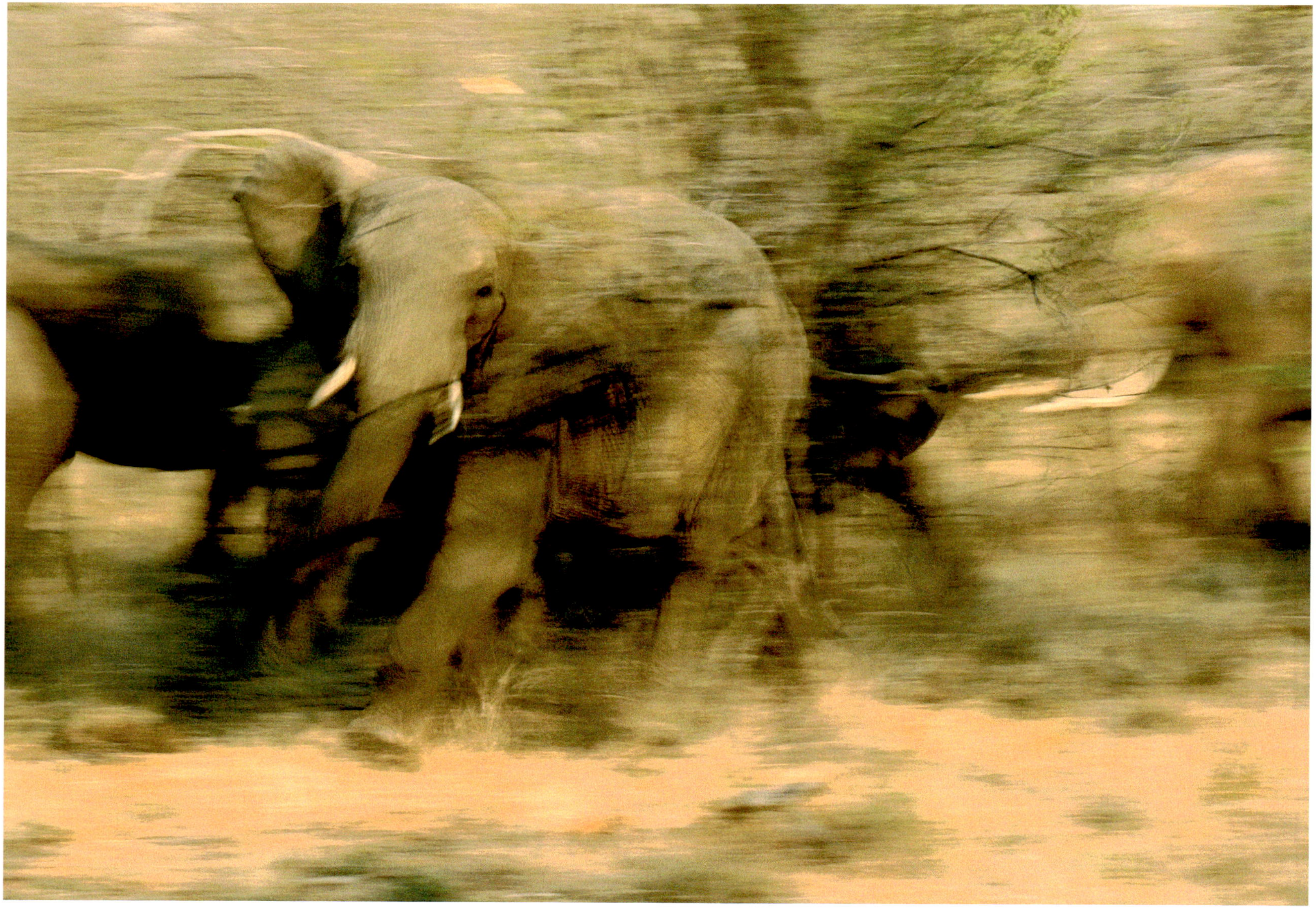

Charging Elephant, 1996, Matetsi Reserve, Zimbabwe

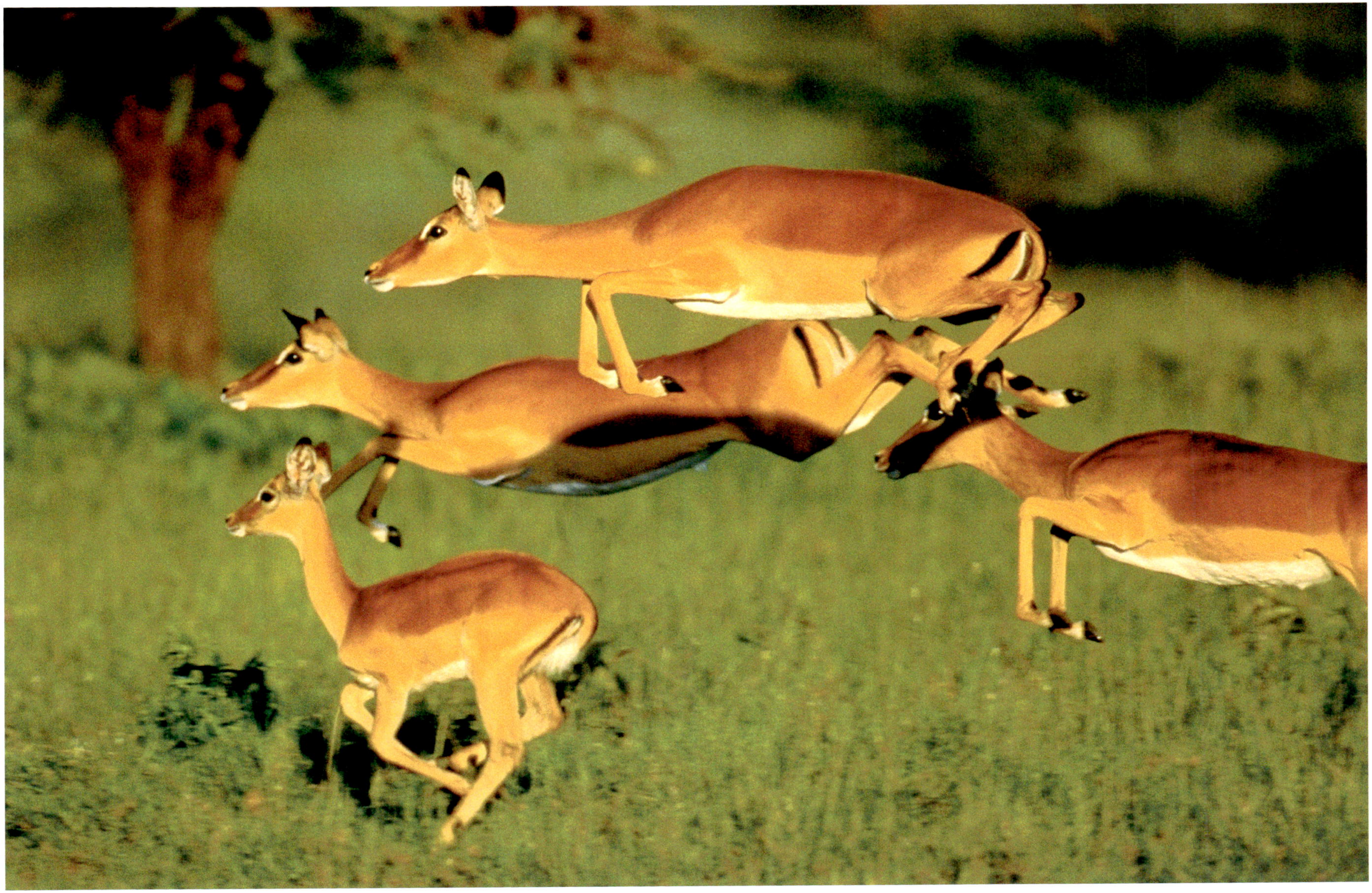

Pronking Impala, 1995, Masai Mara National Reserve, Kenya

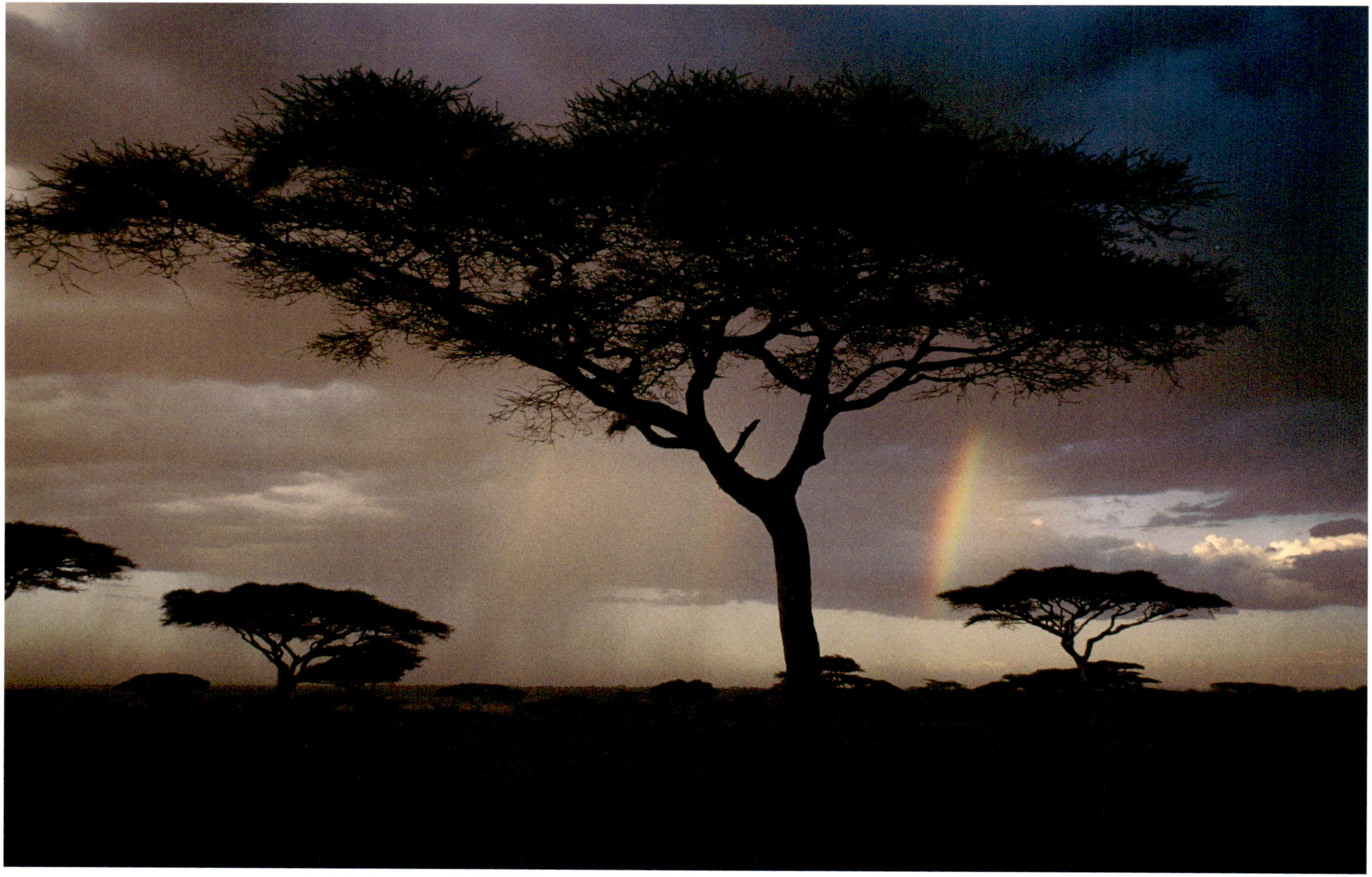

Acacias and Rainbow, 1997, Serengeti National Park, Tanzania

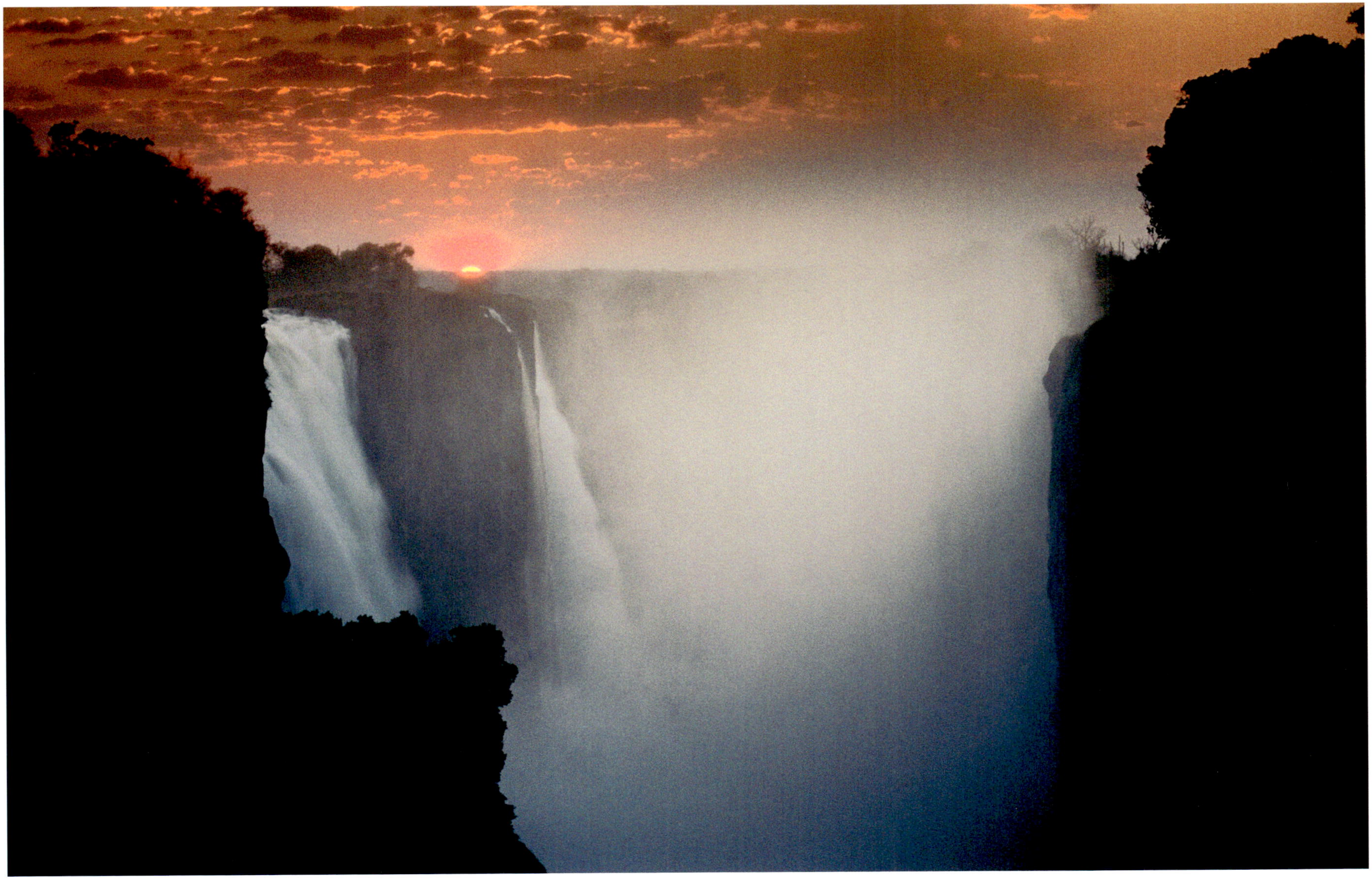

Sunrise Over Victoria Falls, 1996, Zambezi River, Zimbabwe

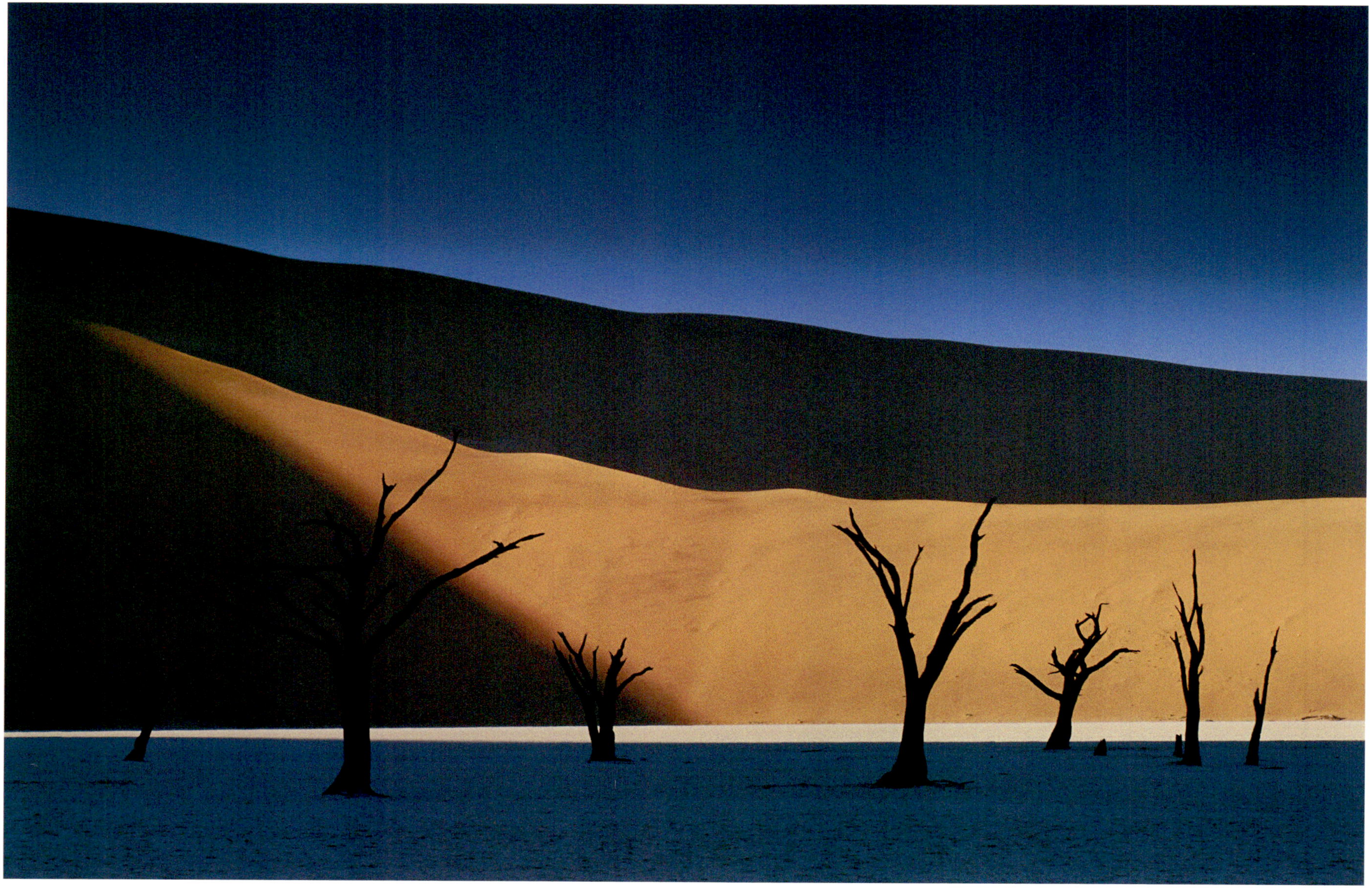

Acacia Trees, 1997, Sossusvlei, Namib-Naukluft Park, Namibia

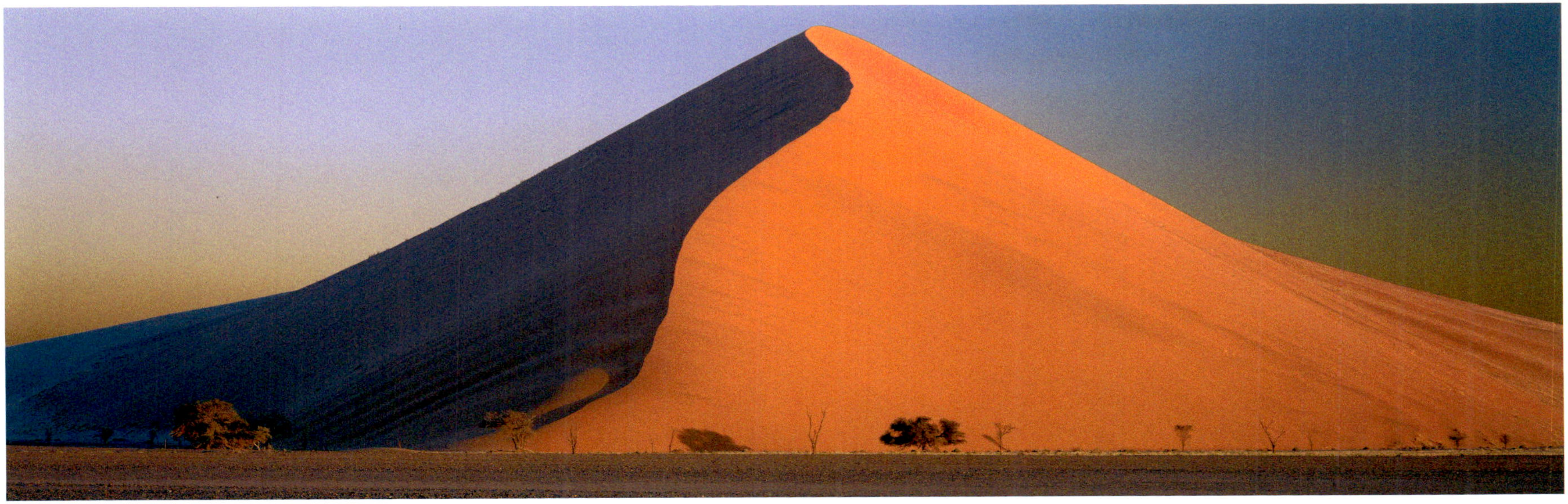

Great Dune, 1997, Namib-Naukluft Park, Namibia

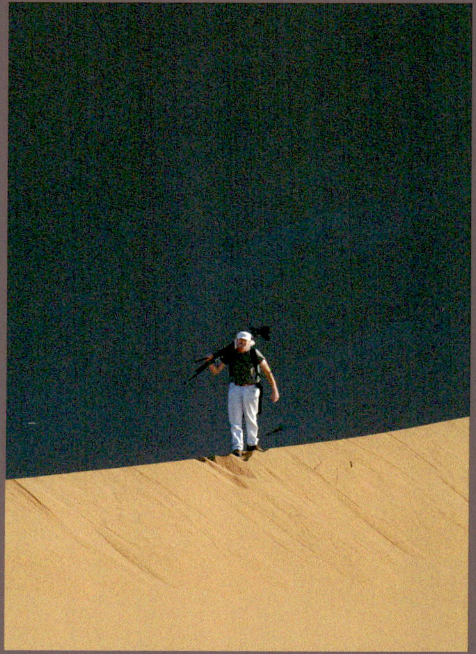

AUSTRALIA/OCEANIA

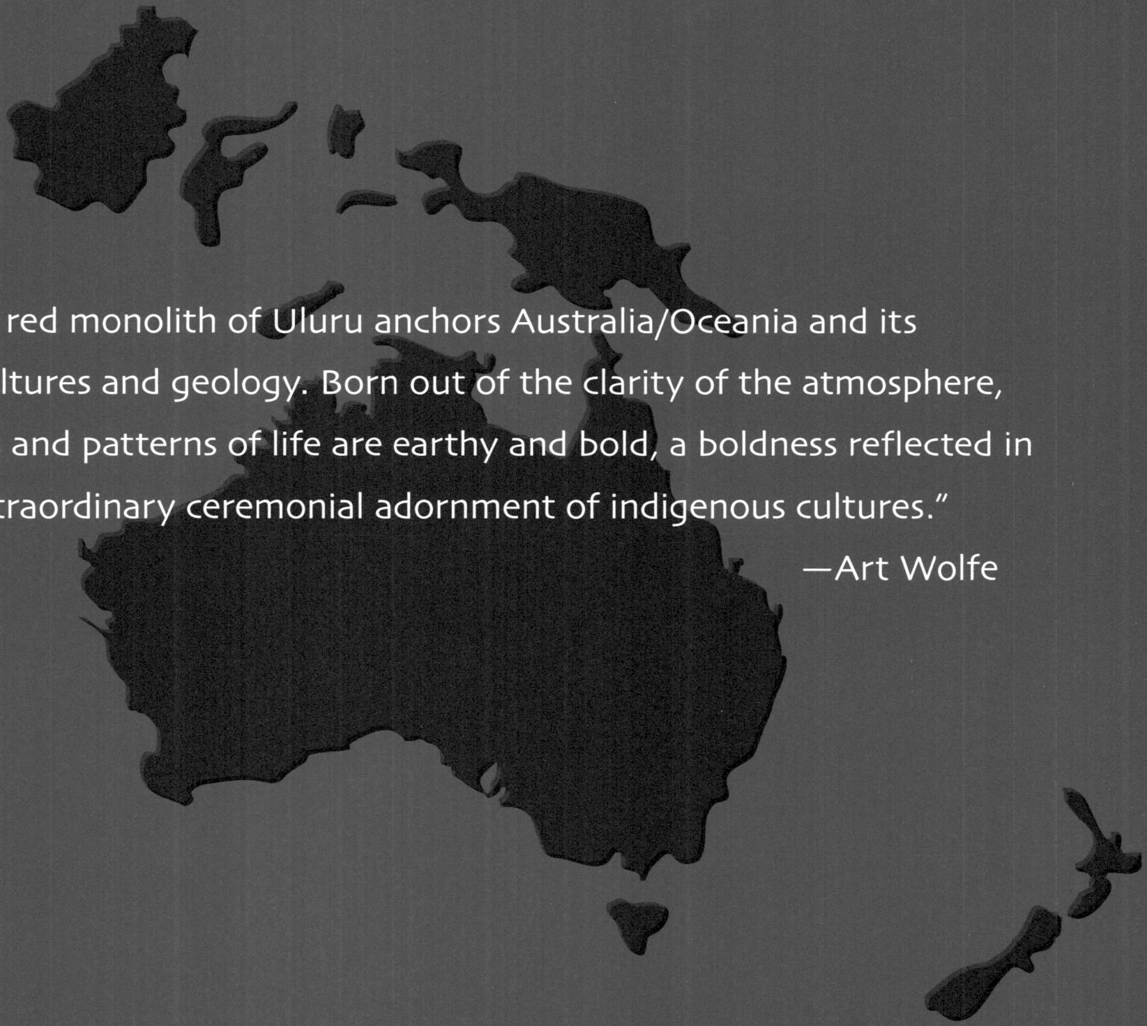

"The red monolith of Uluru anchors Australia/Oceania and its ancient cultures and geology. Born out of the clarity of the atmosphere, the textures and patterns of life are earthy and bold, a boldness reflected in the extraordinary ceremonial adornment of indigenous cultures."

—Art Wolfe

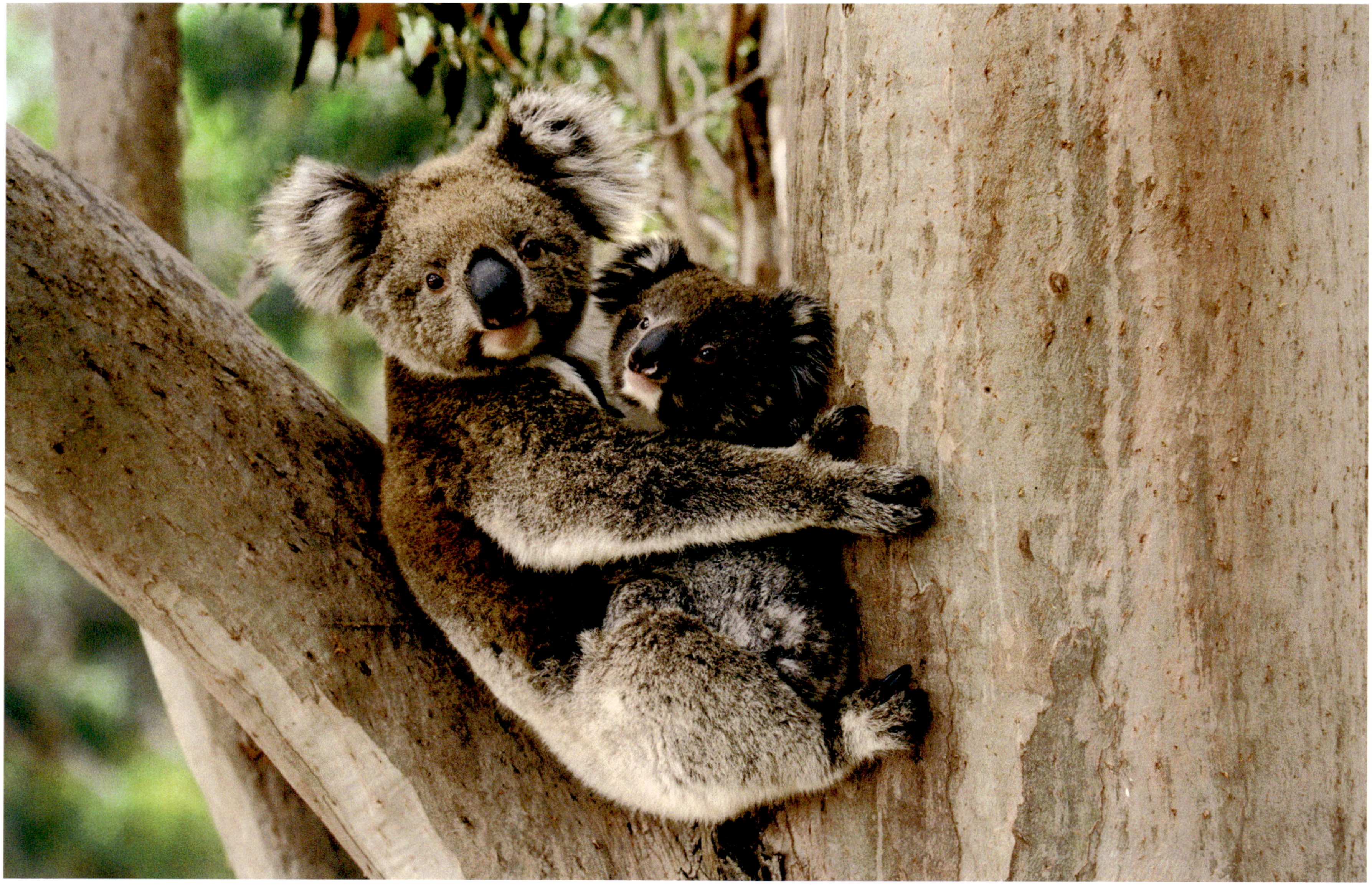

Koala and Young, 1999, Kangaroo Island, South Australia

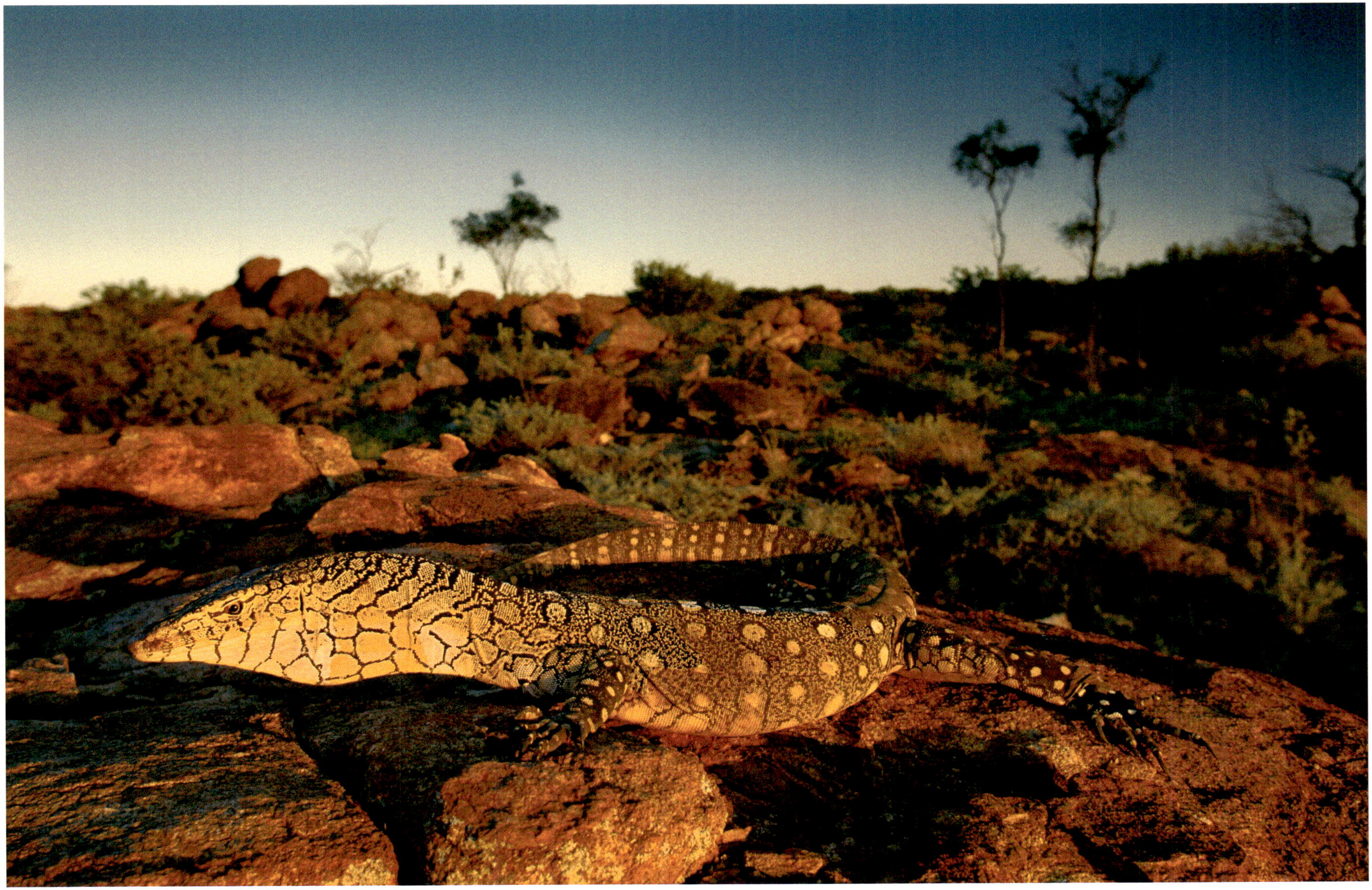

Perentie Goanna, 2000, MacDonnell Ranges, Northern Territory, Australia

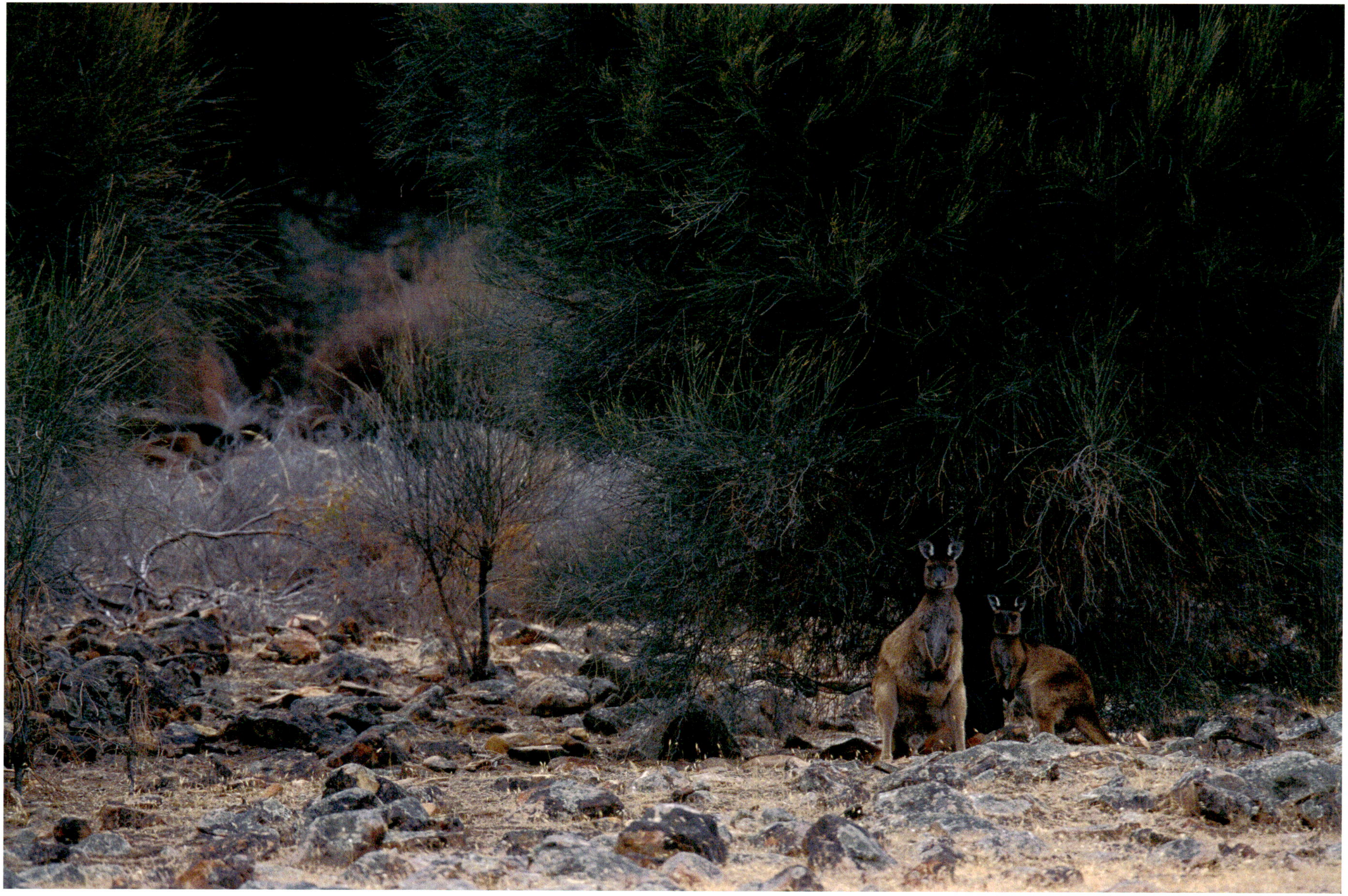

Western Gray Kangaroo, 1999, Flinders Chase National Park, South Australia

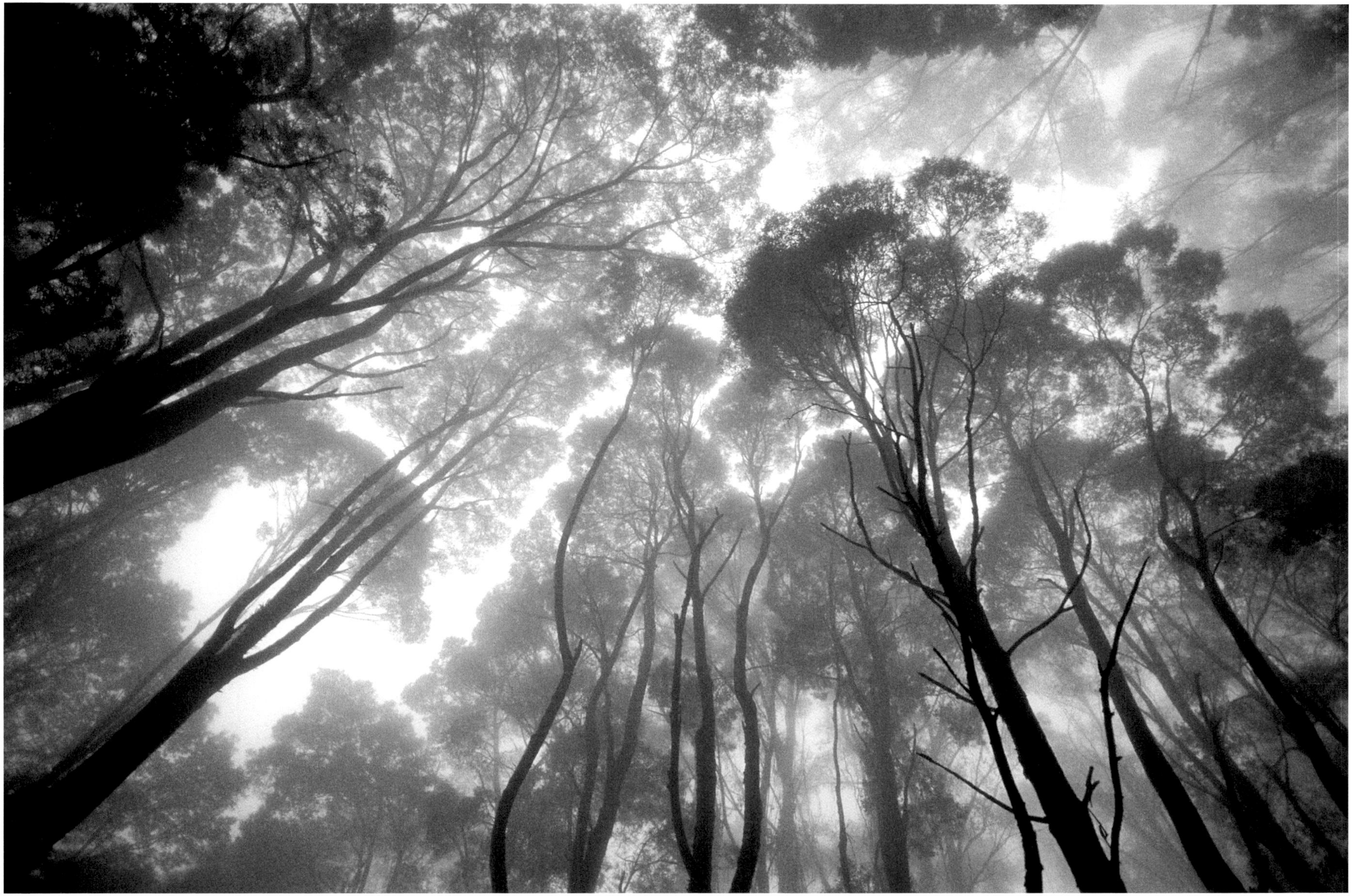

Eucalyptus Trees, 1990, Victoria, Australia

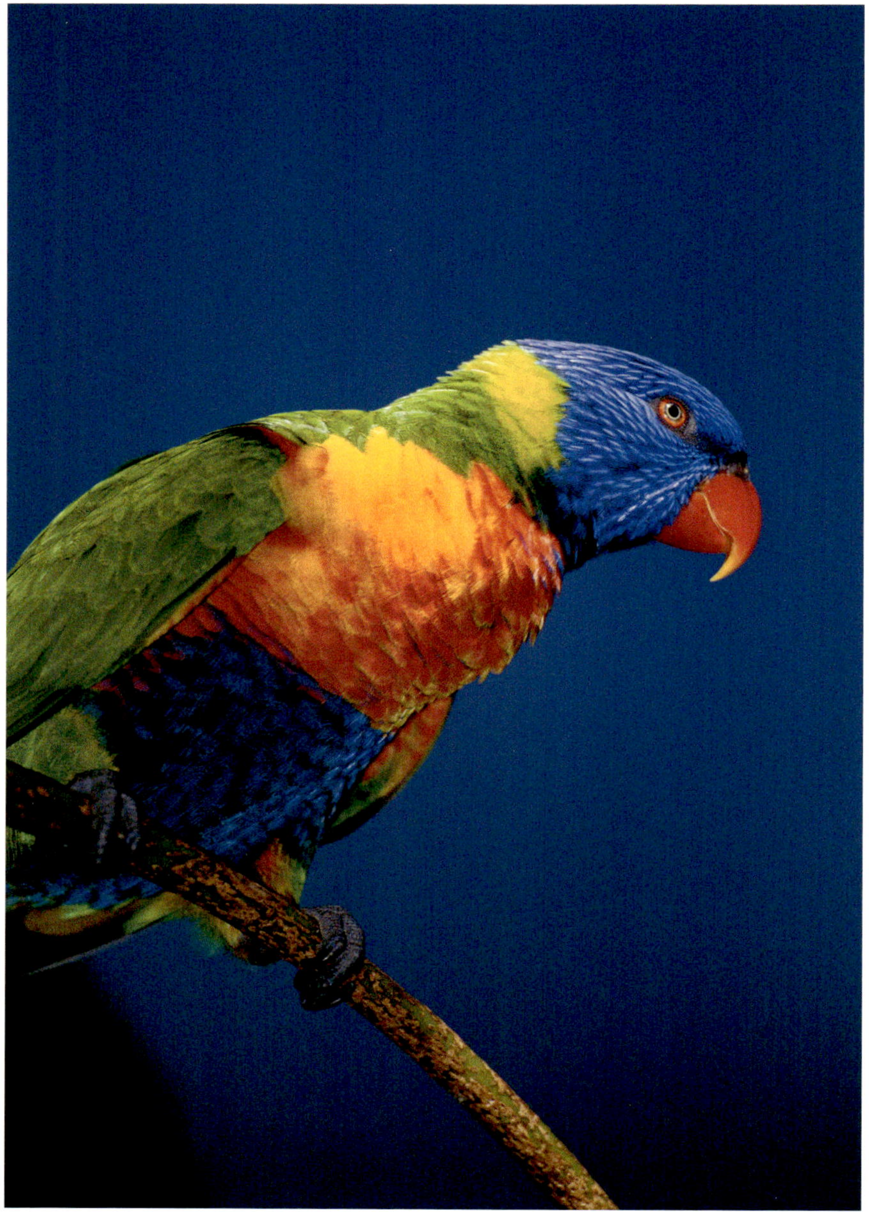

Rainbow Lorikeet, 1994, Australia

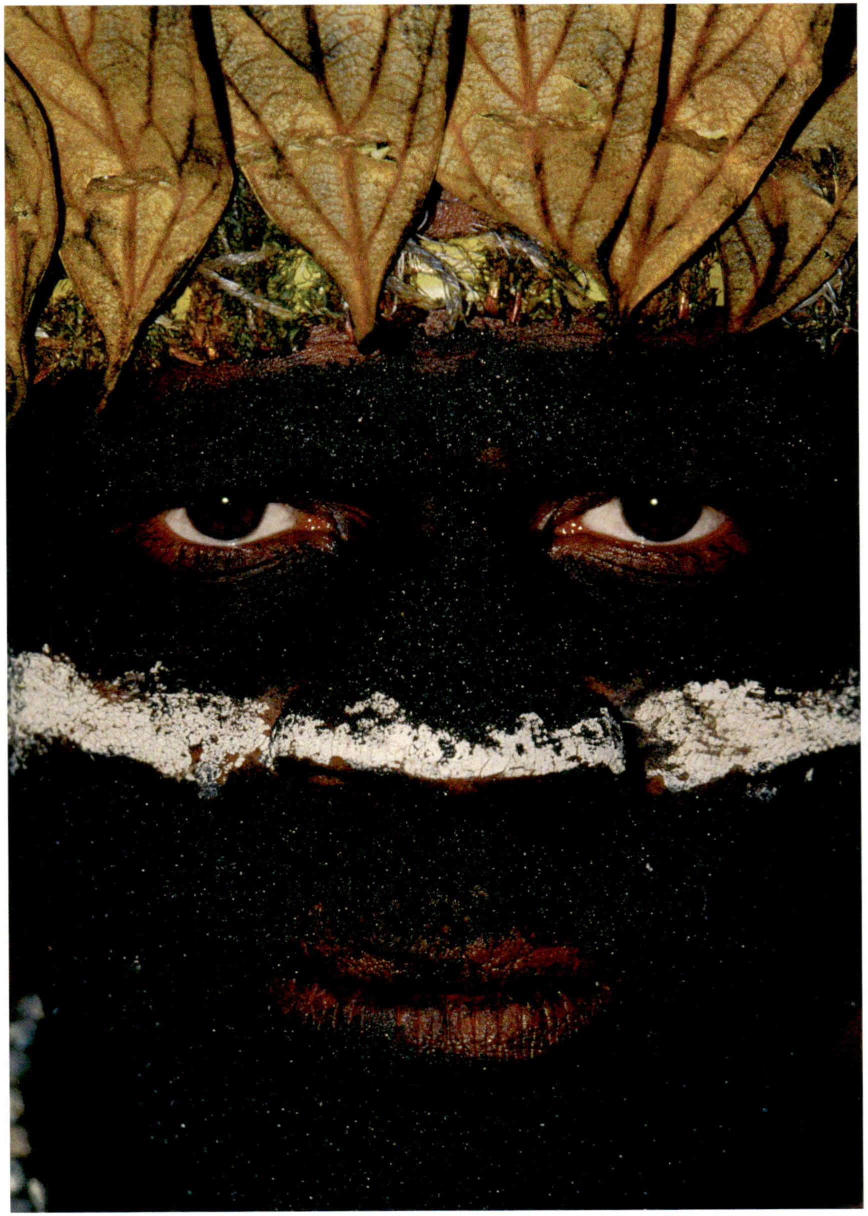

Mt. Hagen Man at Singsing, 1994, Mt. Hagen, Papua New Guinea

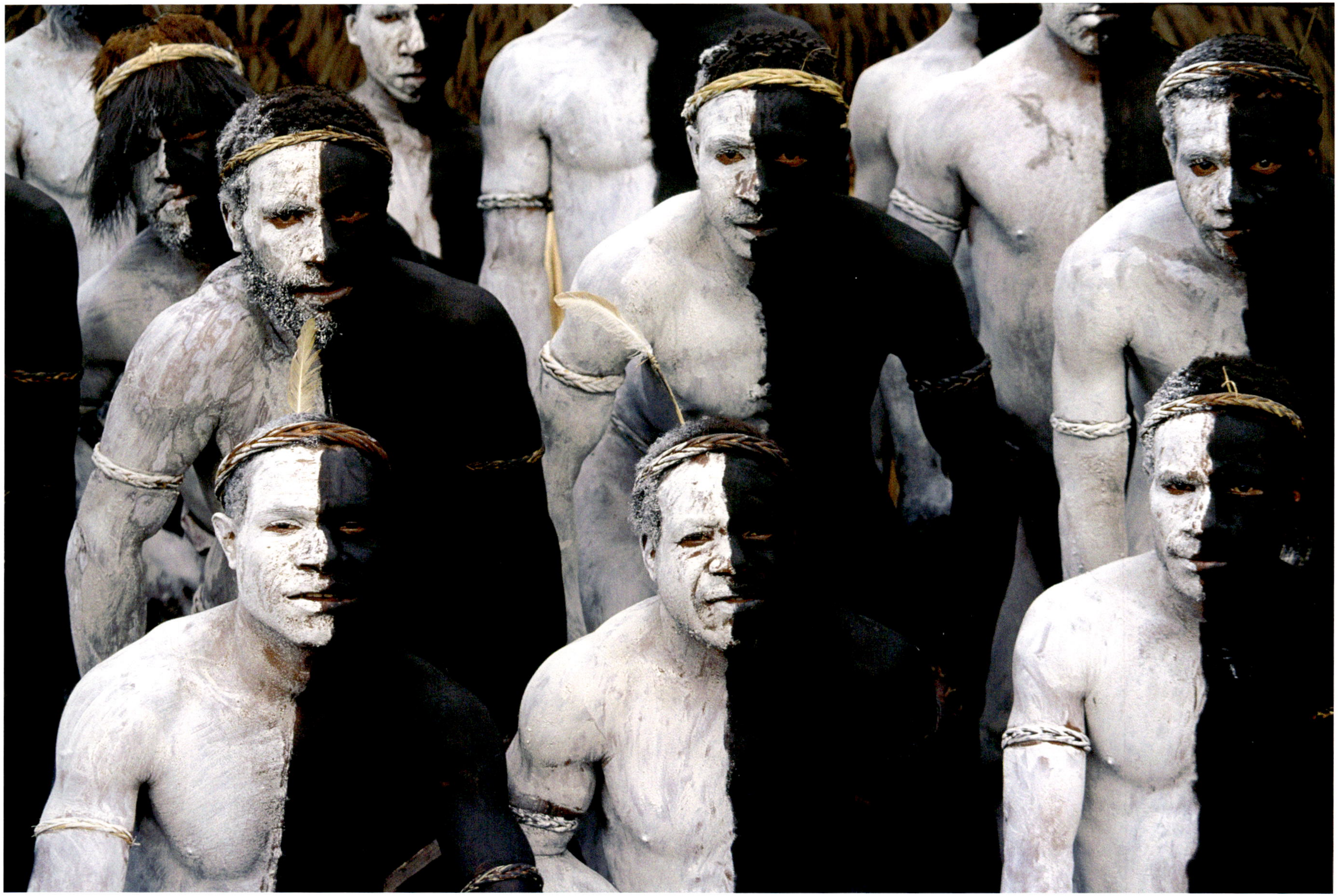

Simbu Dancers at Singsing, 1994, Mt. Hagen, Papua New Guinea

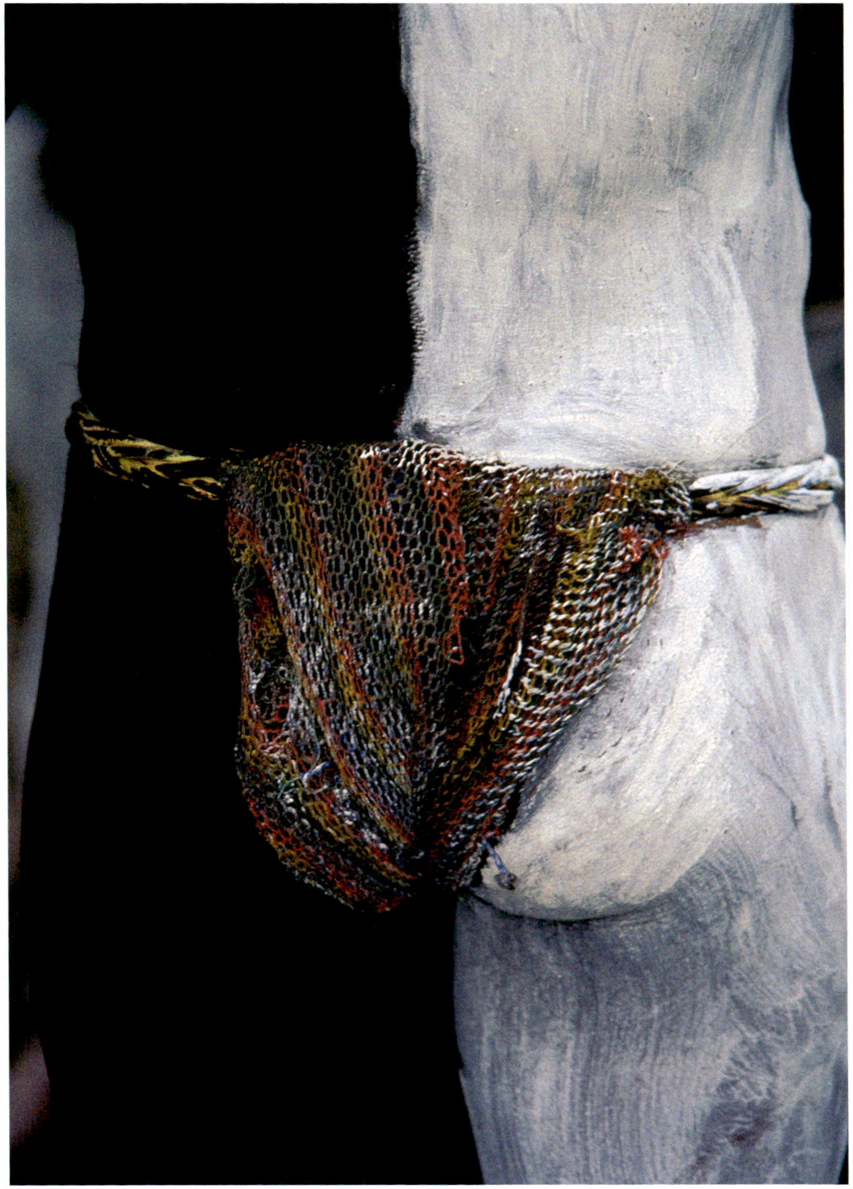

Simbu Dancer at Singsing, 1994, Mt. Hagen, Papua New Guinea

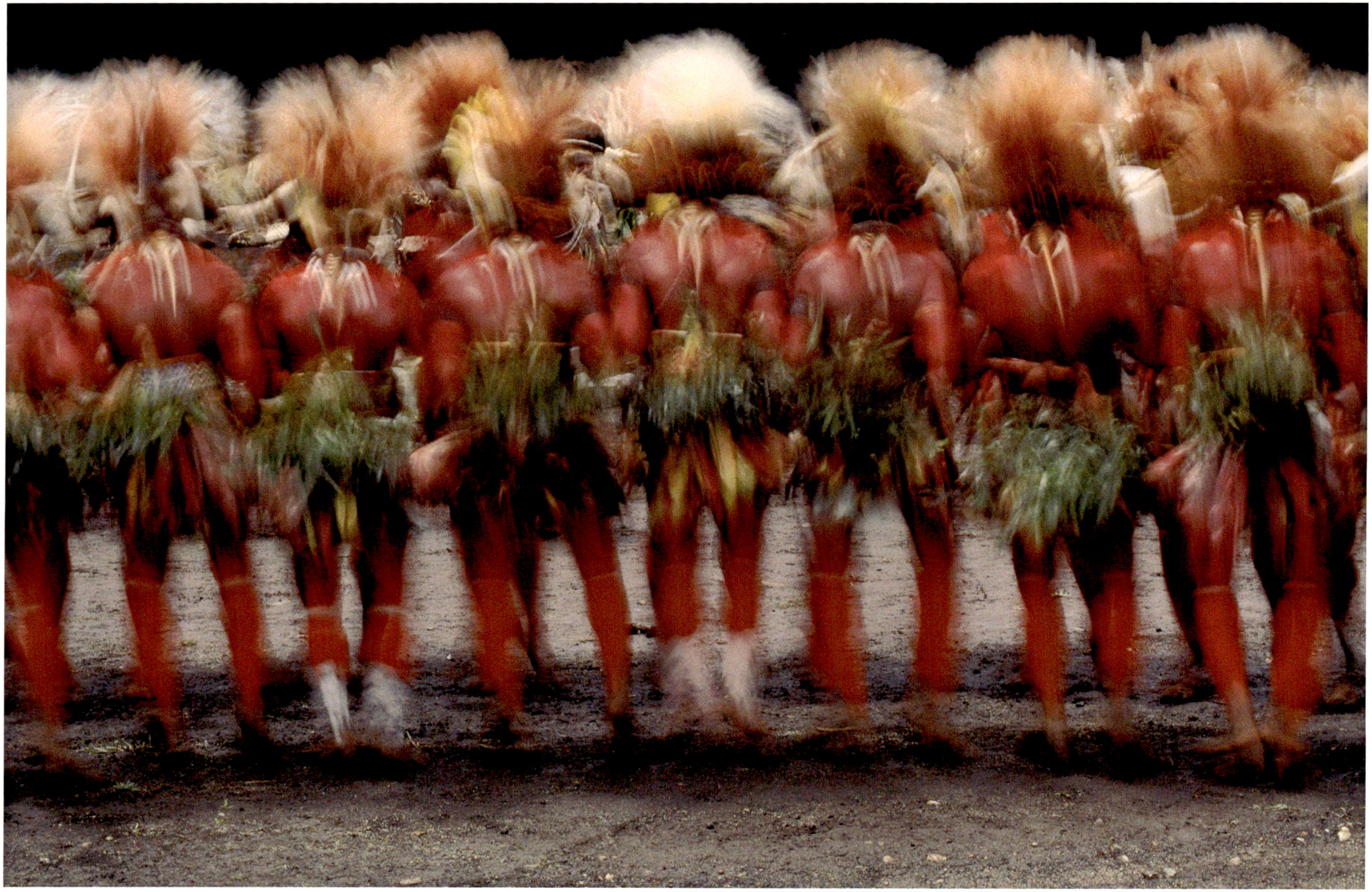

Huli Men at Singsing, 1994, Mt. Hagen, Papua New Guinea

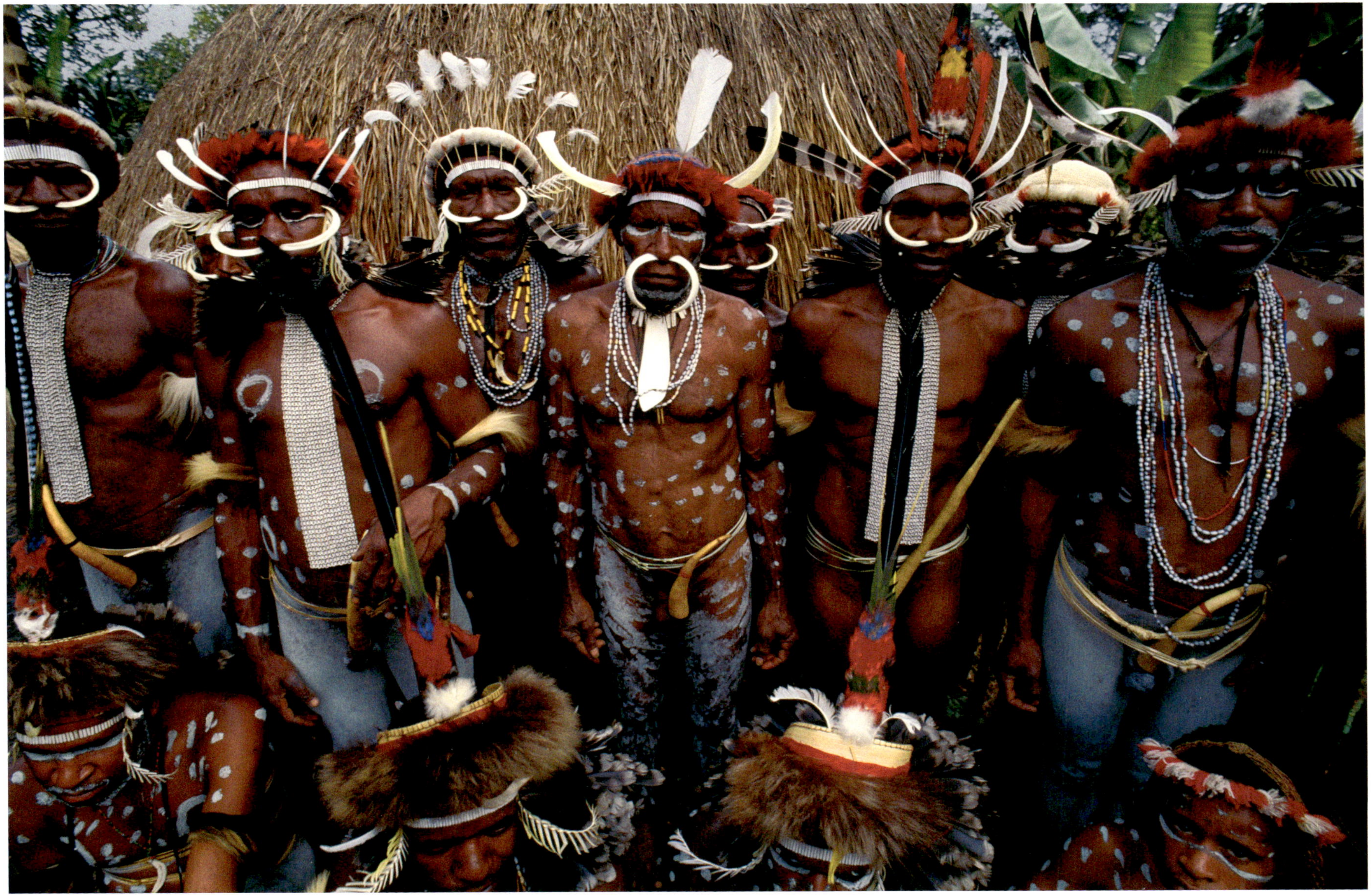

Dani Men, 1993, Grand Valley, Irian Jaya, Indonesia

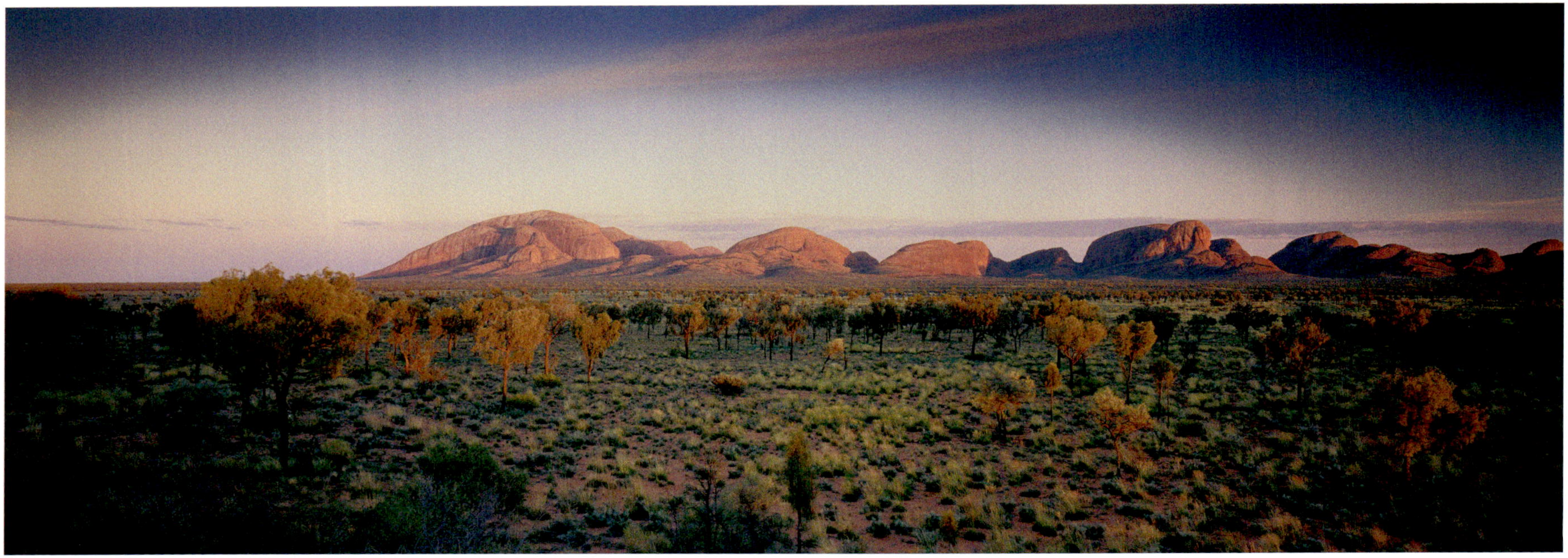

Kata Tjuta, 2000, Uluru-Kata Tjuta National Park, Northern Territory, Australia

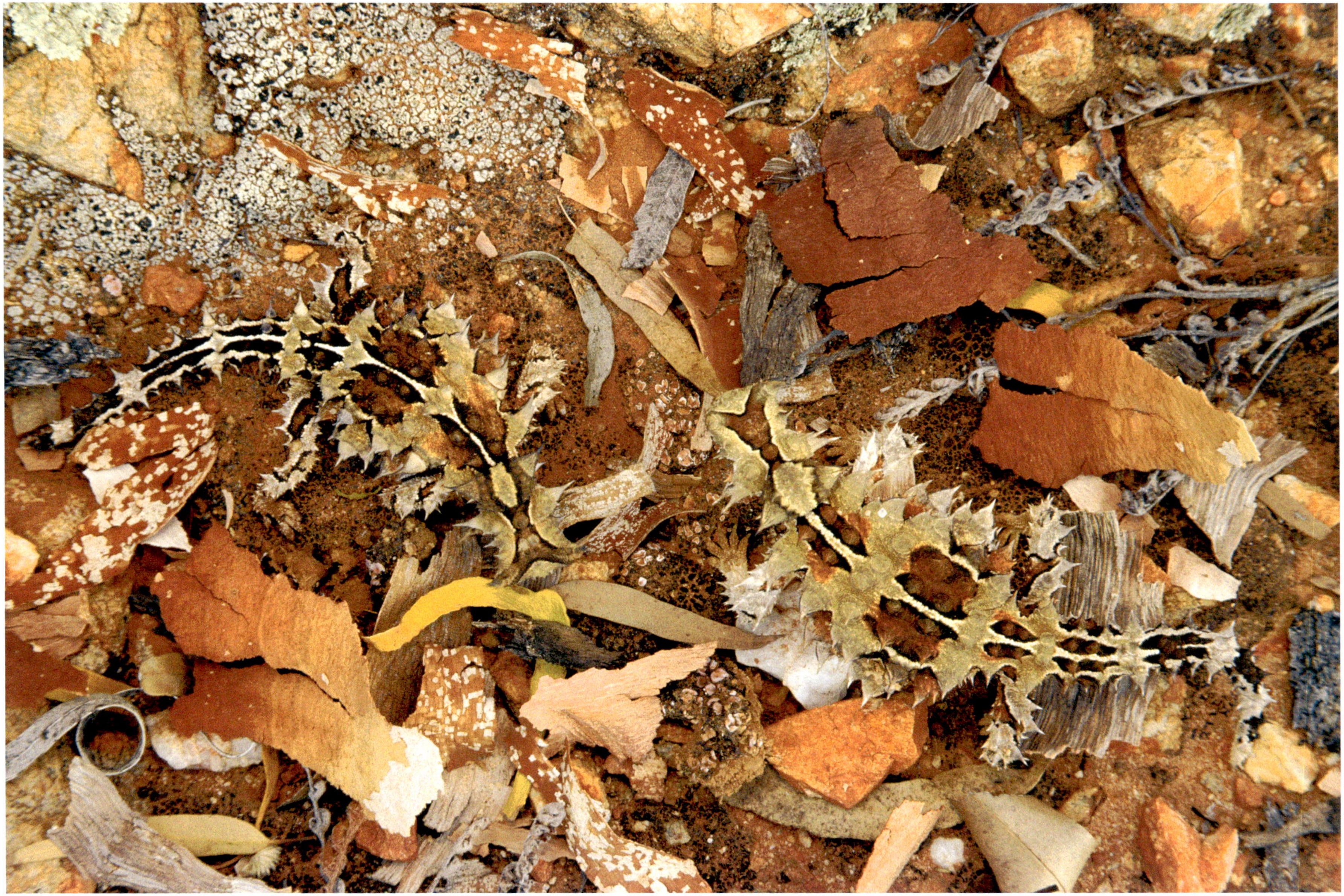

Thorny Devil, 2000, MacDonnell Ranges, Northern Territory, Australia

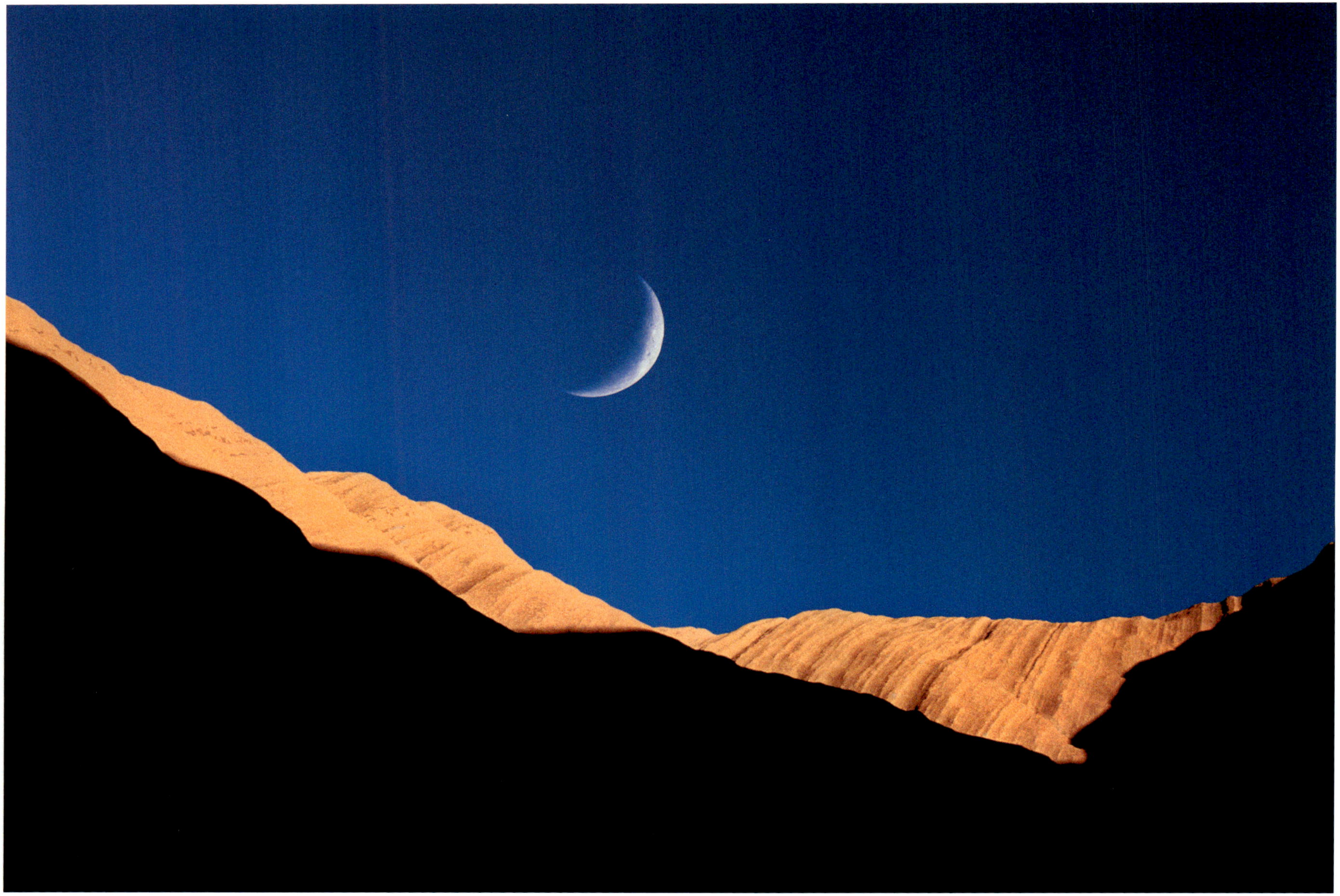

Uluru, 1990, Uluru-Kata Tjuta National Park, Northern Territory, Australia

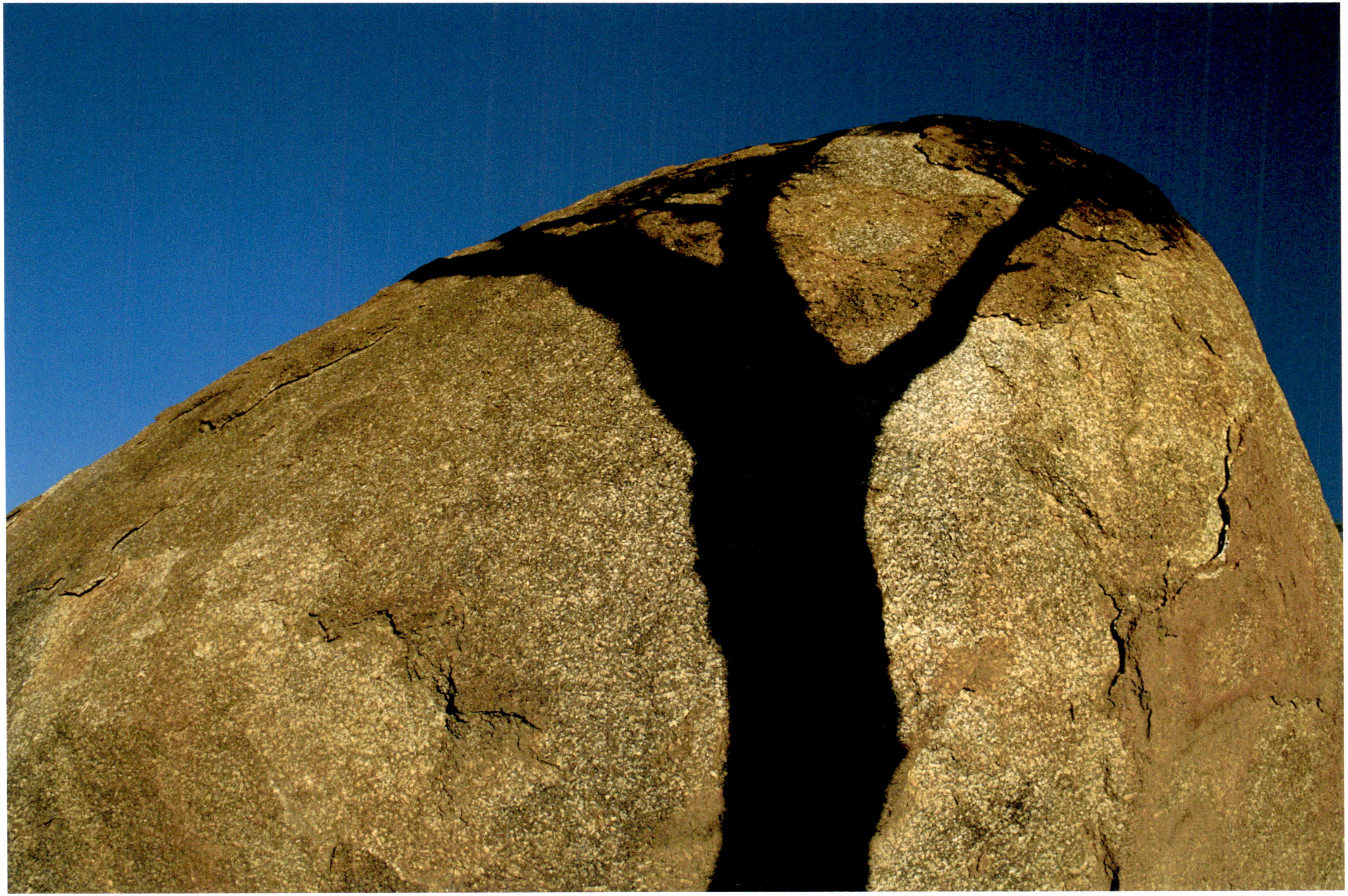

Devil's Marbles, 1990, Northern Territory, Australia

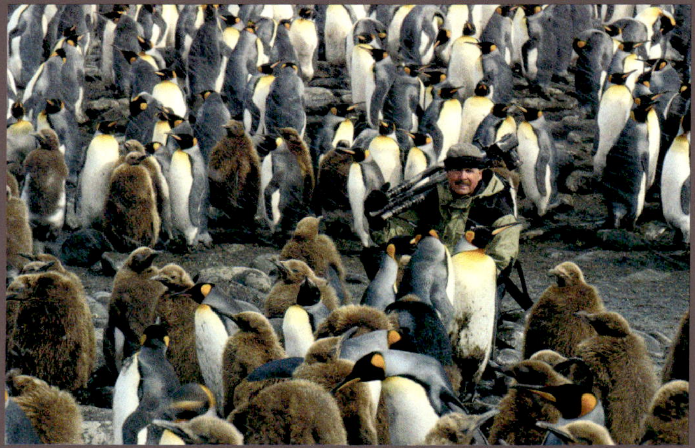

ANTARCTICA

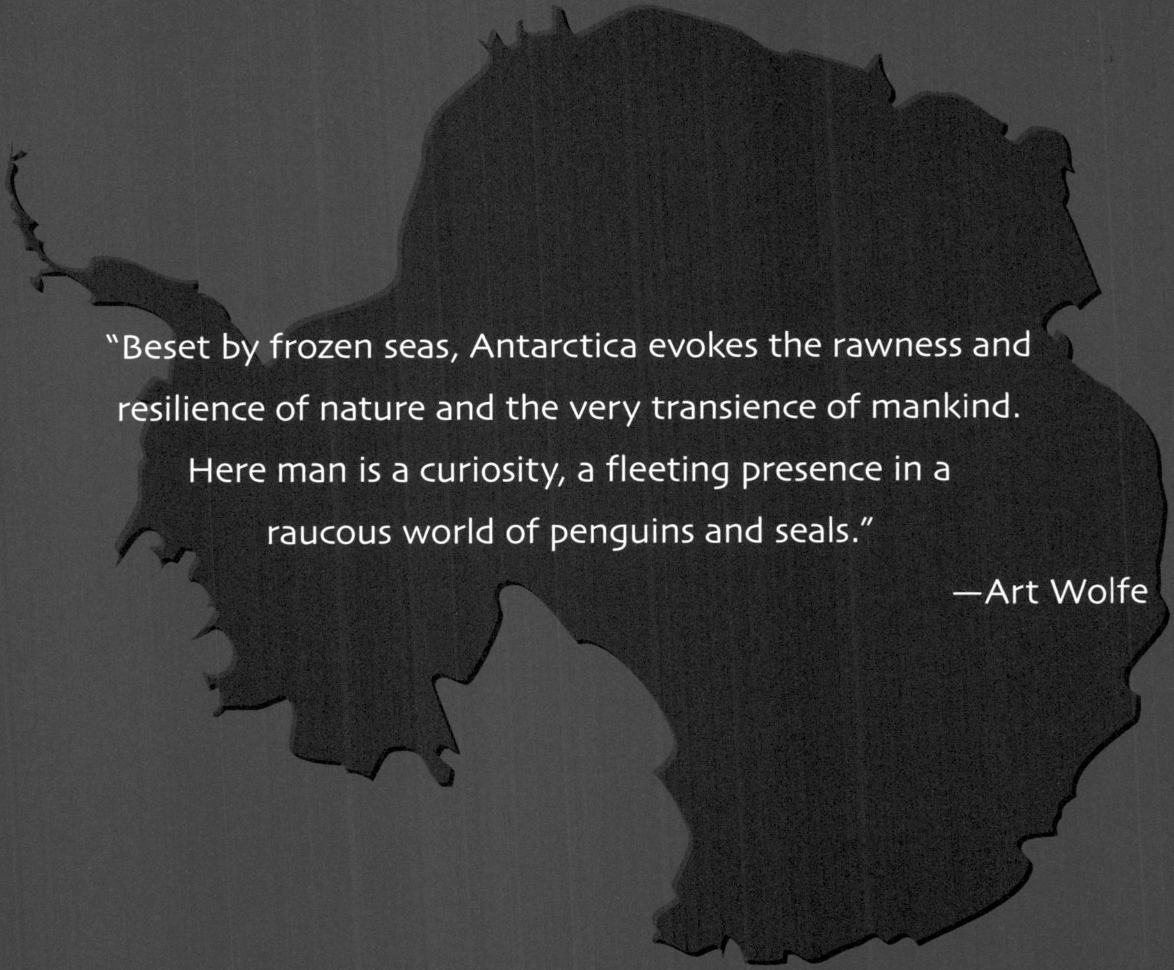

"Beset by frozen seas, Antarctica evokes the rawness and resilience of nature and the very transience of mankind. Here man is a curiosity, a fleeting presence in a raucous world of penguins and seals."

—Art Wolfe

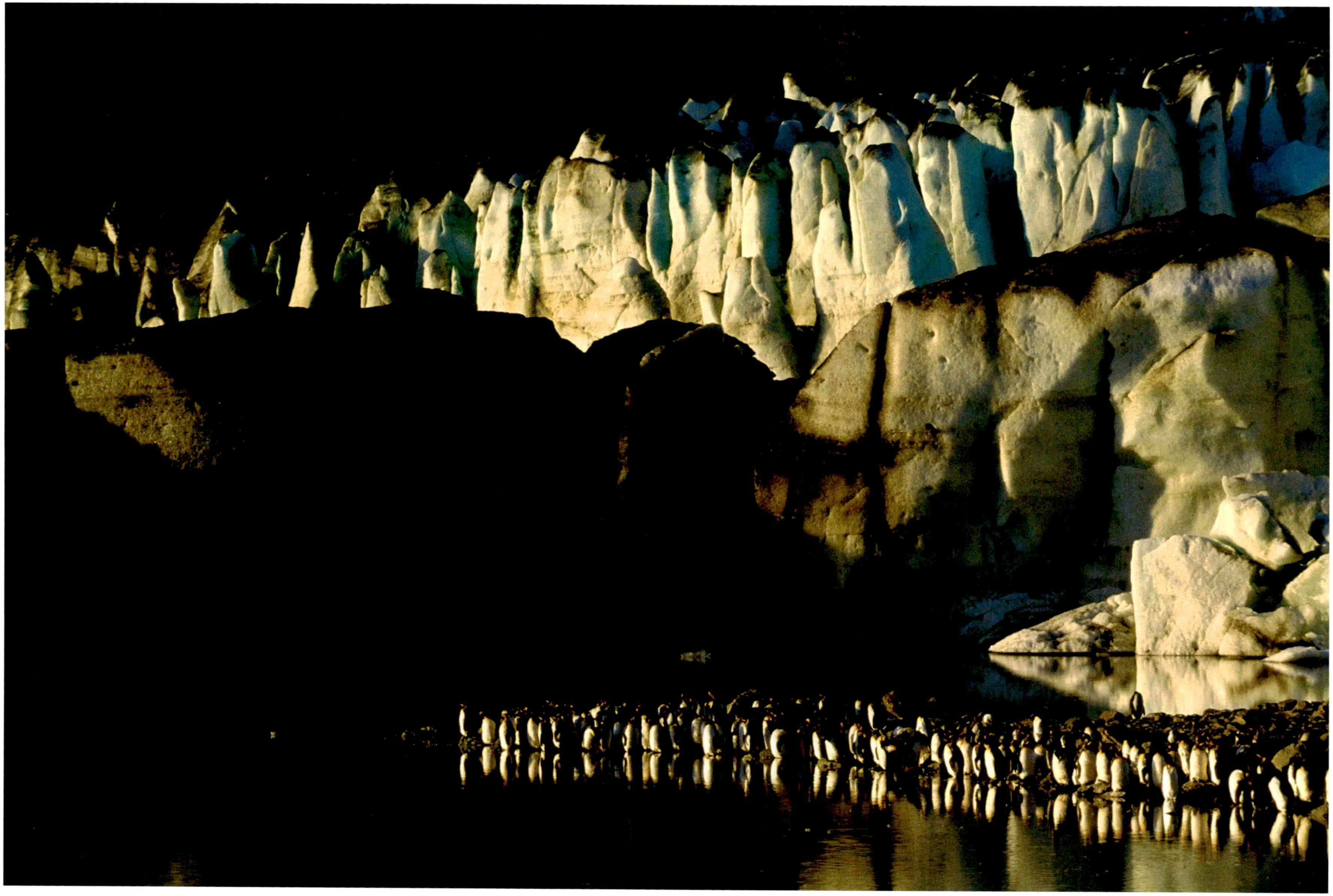

King Penguins, 1994, South Georgia Island

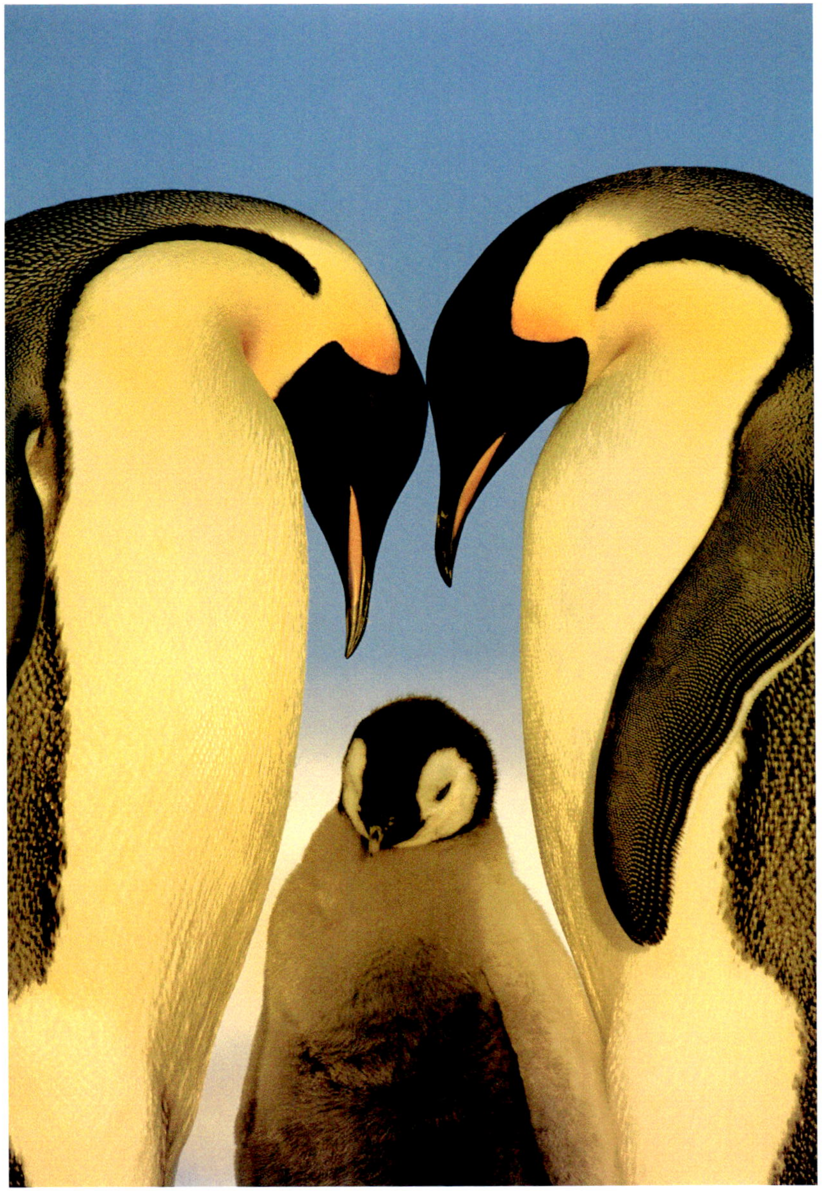

Emperor Penguins, 1993, Antarctica

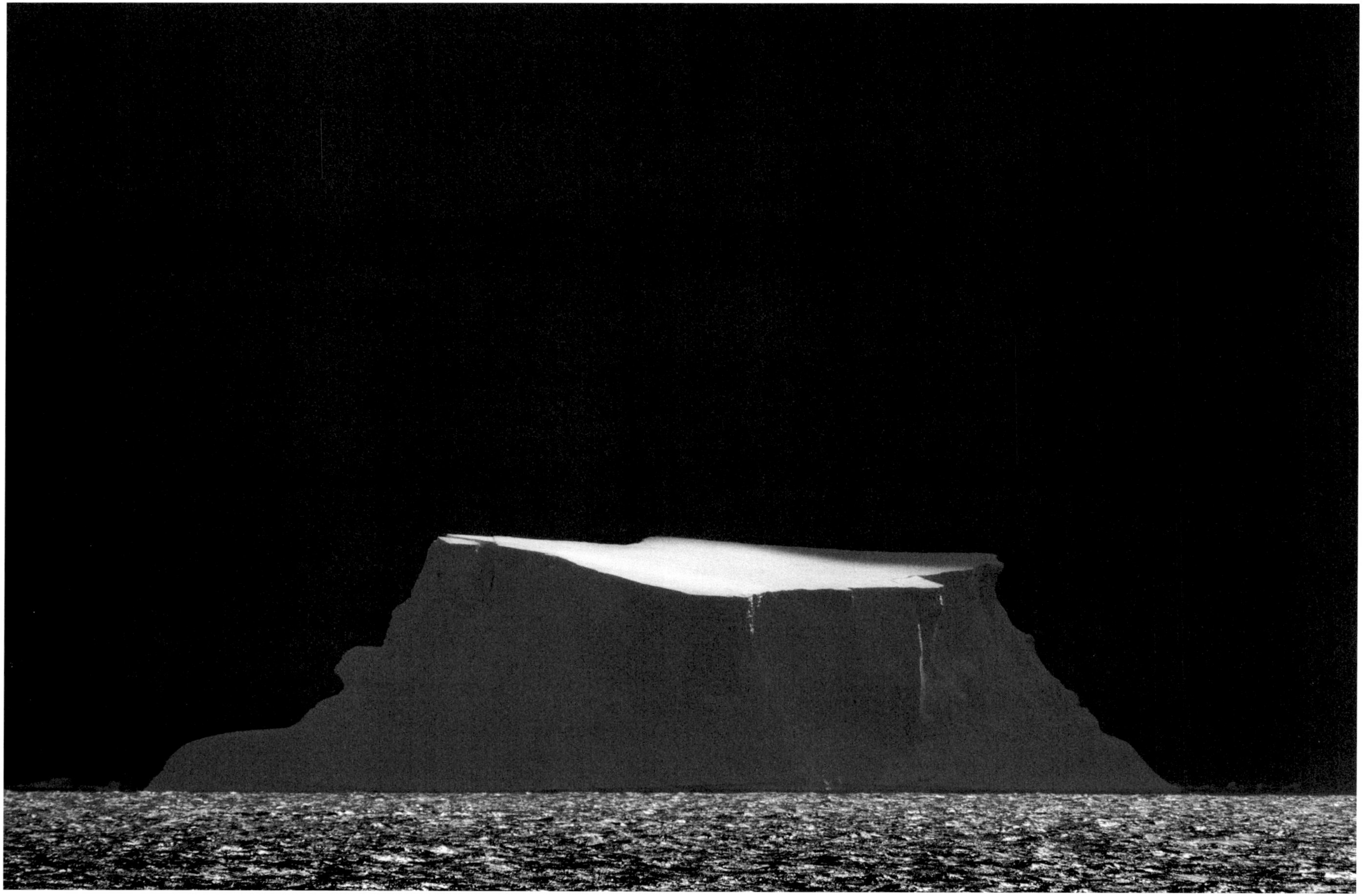

Iceberg, 1988, Antarctica

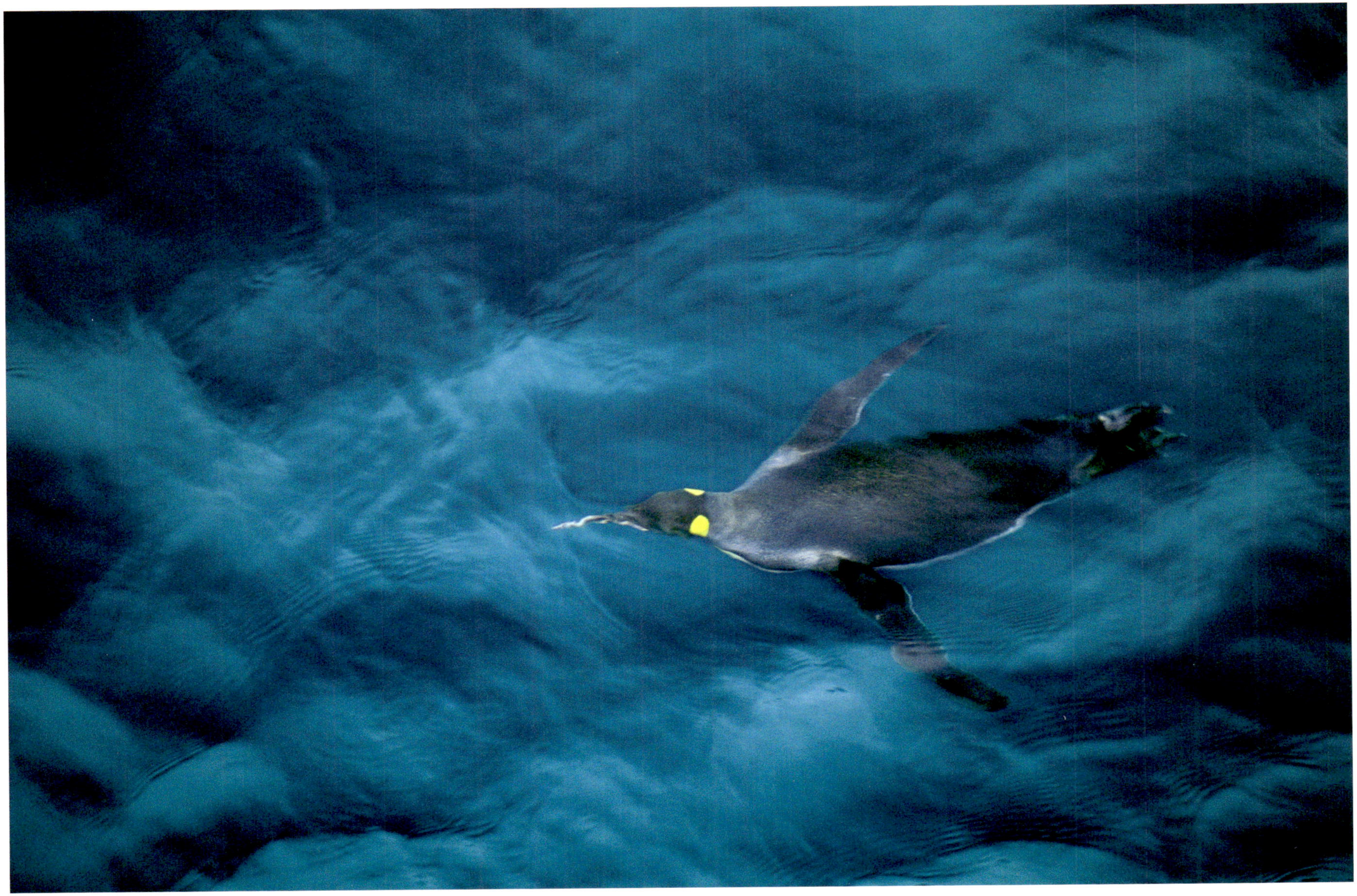

King Penguin, 1991, Macquarie Island

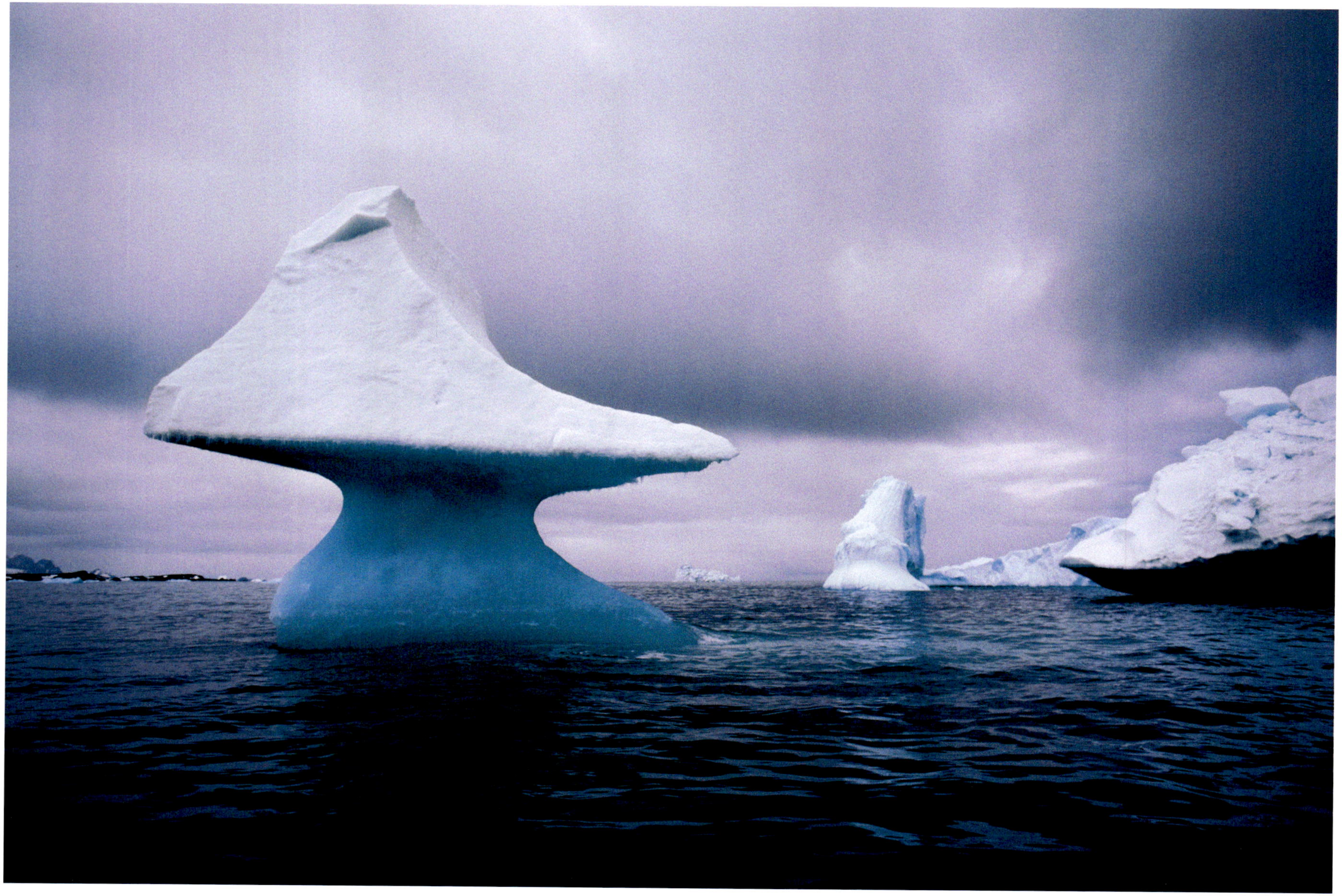

Icebergs, 1985, Weddell Sea, Antarctica

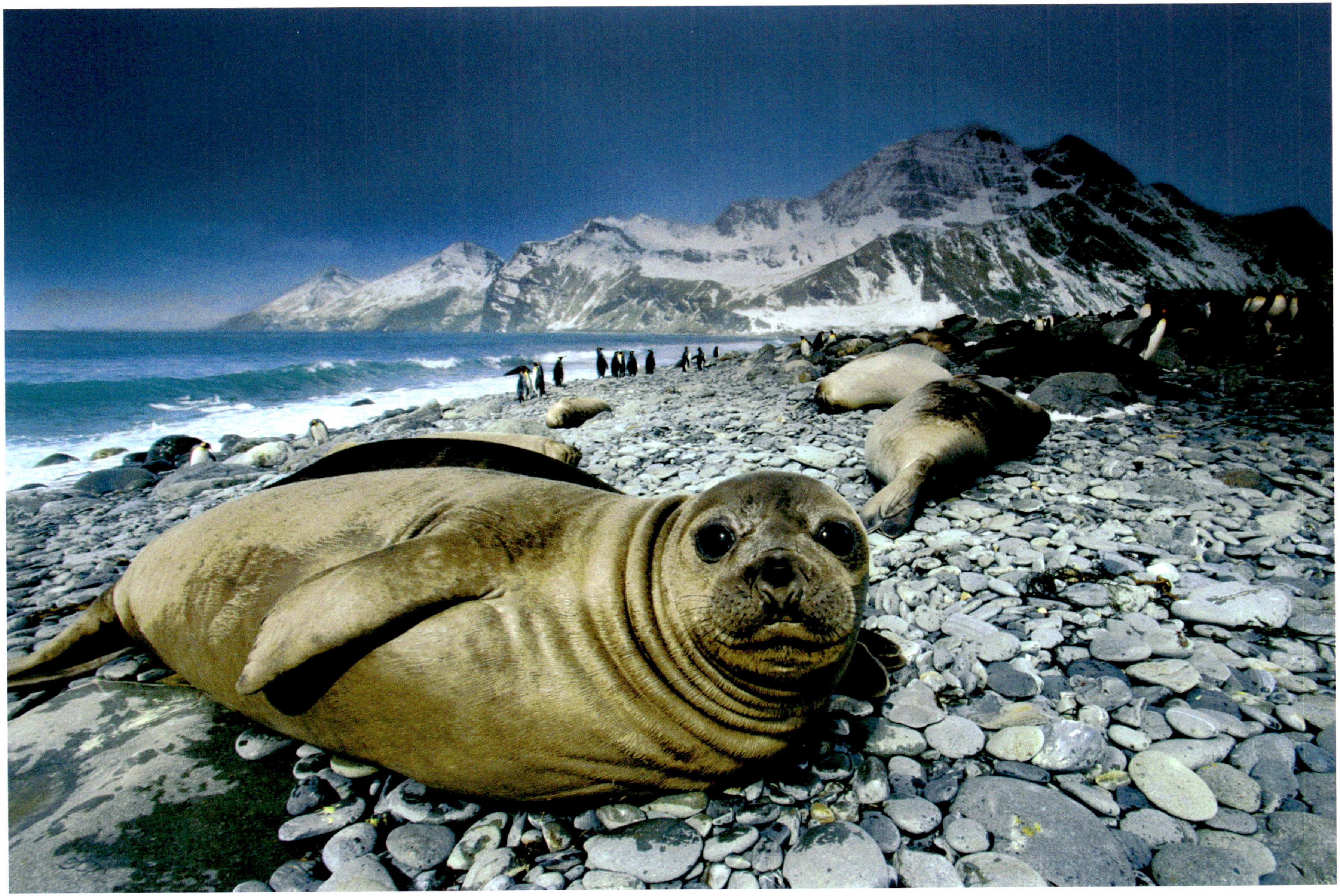

Southern Elephant Seal, 1998, South Georgia Island

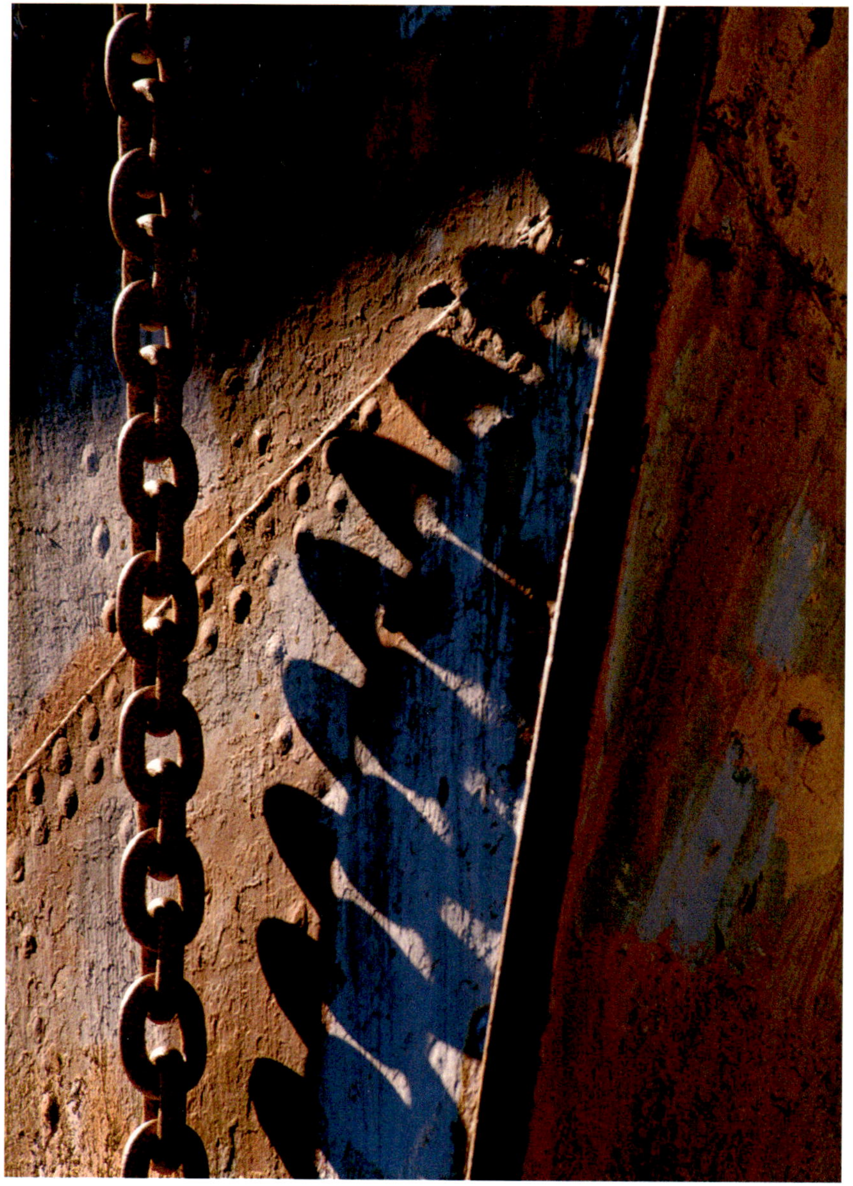

Anchor Chain, 1985, Grytviken, South Georgia Island